FRANCESCA'S VOICE

Nova Fornell

Sky Ink
PUBLISHING

Nova Fornell/Sky Ink Publishing
www.novafornell.com

Editor: Gail Bienstock

Publisher's Note: This is a work of fiction. Names, characters, places, and incidents are a product of the author's imagination. Locales and public names are sometimes used for setting purposes. Any resemblance to actual people, living or dead, or to businesses, companies, events, institutions, or locales is completely coincidental.

Francesca's Voice/ Nova Fornell -- 1st ed.
ISBN 978-82-690348-0-6 (pbk.)
ISBN 978-82-690348-1-3 (Kindle)

GET A FREE NOVELLA

Building a relationship with my readers is the very best thing about writing.

I occasionally send newsletters with details on new releases, special offers and other bits of news relating to my writing. And if you sign up to the mailing list, I'll send you my novella *Family Beginnings* for free. A story about a defining moment in Phillip and Anna's lives, and the beginning of them building their family.

This novella is exclusive to my mailing list – you can't get it anywhere else.

If interested, please use this link subscribepage.io/ENQ6JW to sign up to my newsletter & receive my novella for free.

To my family, for always loving and supporting me and my dreams

Chapter One

Francesca sat on her bed, counting down the days on the calendar of her phone.

Soon, she would be free — only 19 more days to go until the 30th of September.

She hadn't been able to afford to move out before, but now, having just started her bachelor's degree at the *Norwegian University of Business and Management*, she was entitled to a monthly student loan. It wasn't much — basically the exact amount she needed to cover rent — but through continuing to work her receptionist job at the gym a couple of evenings a week, Francesca estimated she'd be able to scrape by. She was finally moving out, and there wasn't a thing her father could do to stop her.

She'd already found an apartment, although he didn't know it yet, and neither did Jenny. Francesca had told no one.

The apartment was small, a one bedroom, yet to Francesca it might as well have been a palace, for in it she would finally be her own master for the first time in her life. She would not be around for him to tear her down with his words on a daily basis anymore. And her signing that lease agreement on the day of her 19th birthday would be the perfect birthday present to herself.

The old copper handle on her bedroom door gave off a piercing squeak.

Francesca's heart halted, and her aqua blue eyes flashed toward the door. Then there was a quick double knock on the chipping, white wooden door.

Thank god she'd remembered to lock it.

She hastily gathered the lease agreement papers together, before stuffing them into their white cardboard binder. Searching for a hiding place, she sent the binder skidding under her bed, before clearing her voice. "Who is it?"

"It's me, Jenny."

Francesca exhaled, then got to her feet and walked over to the door. Twisting the key and inching the door open, she extended her hand out into the hallway, inviting her younger sister to enter.

Jenny's lanky body came into view as she stepped across the threshold and into her sister's room.

Her lips were naturally super red, and her smile folded out into the shape of a red Jellybean, which is why Francesca had come up with the Jellybean nickname — as well as many other closely related nicknames — for her sister when Jenny was born 11 years ago. Besides, Jellybeans had always been Francesca's favorite candy, and Jenny was Francesca's favorite person in the whole world, so the association had made perfect sense to her at the age of eight when she had first begun using it.

Jenny narrowed her dark blue eyes, and let them interrogate Francesca. "How come your door was locked?"

Francesca opened her mouth, but then hesitated. She knew it was too soon to tell her. "To stop nosy sisters from busting in," she said, and ruffled Jenny's strawberry blond hair. Then she quickly broke eye contact and turned her back on her sister while shutting the door.

Jenny flung herself onto the edge of the bed, and dangled her legs back and forth. "So, whatcha doin'?"

Francesca took a couple of steps toward her sister, and noticed a corner of the binder sticking out just below Jenny's feet. "Oh, you know, just... nothin', really." She got closer, and attempted to discreetly brush the binder further back underneath the bed with her foot, but instead accidentally kicked her sister's shin.

Jenny clutched at her leg, tears welling up. "Oww, what'd you do that for?"

Francesca squatted down, placing her hands gently on her sister's leg. "Oh, Jellybean, I'm so sorry, I didn't mean to... I..."

Jenny looked down at her leg, and then at the floor below it. "Hey," she sobbed, and pointed at the piece of white cardboard visible from where she sat. "What's that?"

Francesca stepped on the binder, hiding it from Jenny's view. "What's what?"

Jenny hopped down off the bed, and let her entire weight lean up against her sister's leg, forcing Francesca's foot to lift slightly off the folder. She displayed a triumphant grin, and quickly wiggled the binder loose.

"Wait," Francesca cried out.

Jenny raised one eyebrow. "What?"

Francesca snatched the binder out of her hand, and pulled it to her chest, securing it with both hands. "That's private. Now look what you did — it's all bent."

Jenny stared at the front of her sister's precious folder, and her eyes suddenly turned into two deep wells. "Tenancy agreement for Thor Alm's road 23," she read the cover aloud. "What? You're moving?" she yelled.

Francesca held her finger up in front of her mouth. "Shhh."

"When were you gonna tell me — never? Don't you think I'd notice you were missing? I'm eleven; I'm not stupid."

Francesca's heart sank. Dropping her arms down at her sides, one hand still clutching her papers of freedom, she gestured with the other hand, "Come sit with me," she said, and sat down in the center of the bed.

Jenny hesitated for a moment, then stuck her tongue out at her sister before plopping down on the very edge of the lower end of the bed — as far away from Francesca and her binder as possible.

Francesca sighed, and moved in closer to her. Wiping a tear from her sister's cheek, she started, "Listen, Jelly, I know this looks bad. But I haven't even signed it yet — I still need my next paycheck from the gym in order to have the full amount of the deposit. Besides, the apartment won't even be available until October 1st."

Jenny wriggled herself a ways further back across the bed in the direction of the wall it was pushed up against, pulling her knees to her chest and burying her face in them.

Francesca let her hand play across her sister's back, rubbing it gently. "J-love, I'll be 19 soon. You didn't expect me to stay here forever, did you?"

"What I didn't expect was for you to sneak away and leave me here with him, all by myself. How could you? You're the worst sister ever," she snapped, before reburying her face in her knees.

Francesca swallowed hard and looked down at the tenant agreement, still in her left hand. "I can't stay here anymore. And now that I'll be able to afford to move out, he can't make me either — I'll finally be free."

"So — what — you'll just leave me behind? Why d'you think I deserve to stay here anymore than you do?" Her little body trembled like a Chihuahua. "Mom wouldn't have wanted it this way," she whispered to her knees.

Pain shot through Francesca's body, zapping her voice. In her head she counted to ten, resisting the urge to cry. She would be strong; not weak. She had to be strong for her younger sister.

"Mom..." she paused, clearing away the gravel her emotions had casually strewn into her throat. "Mom left us. There's nothing—"

"Left us?" Jenny shrieked, throwing her sister's hand off her back and getting to her feet. "Don't you mean died? D'ya think she wanted to die? D'ya think she planned on being in that car accident, thinking; *Yeah, this is just great — this just really made my day!*" she panted.

Francesca pressed her lips together tightly, afraid that if she didn't she might throw up. Her moist blue eyes made contact with her sister's. "J-love, I'm sorry. That's not what I meant."

Jenny clenched her fists. "Mom had no choice. But you do. And yet, you've decided to leave me behind. You're all I've got — have you ever thought of that?" she sobbed. "And at least you'll always have the memories of what Mom was like. I was too young — I'll never know her." Her chest popped like popcorn in a hot pot.

Francesca's eyes burned. She blinked desperately. She couldn't let Jenny see her tears. Scooting back across the bed and demanding support from the wall, she held her arms out toward her sister.

Jenny dragged the back of her hand across both eyes and then under her nose, before curling up into a ball in front of her sister.

As she draped her arms around Jenny, Francesca attempted to calm her own ping-pong heart causing breakage inside her. Placing her cheek against her sister's, she felt the dampness left from the tears that had run down it. And as she held Jenny in silence, she began rocking them slightly from side to side.

"Mom — *our* mom — was the best," Francesca started. "She was the most amazing woman that ever lived — I can guarantee it. I remember watching her rocking you in your cradle, kinda like I'm doing now. And in an attempt to make you fall asleep, she would sing to you ...only, she had a terrible voice. So bad I'd have to cover my ears." Francesca laughed. "But at least she gave it her all. A+ for effort."

Jenny ran her fingers over her eyes again, wiping away some more of her tears.

"And," Francesca continued, "she always used to take us out to this gorgeous meadow — no matter what time of the year it was — as long as enough snow and ice had melted for us to safely climb the hill leading up to it without skidding right back down like accidental alpine skiers." Francesca laughed. "I kid you not — that hill is the absolute steepest I've ever seen. And she'd push you all the way to the top in your pram that was always loaded down with way too much picnic stuff and random crap we never ended up using anyway." Francesca smiled weakly. "I still remember her face when we'd get to the top — all red and blotchy — and she'd always be panting like a workhorse."

Jenny giggled softly.

"And then, as soon as she was able to catch her breath, she'd always say — and I remember her exact words; *Don't let anybody stop you from doing what you want. All you've gotta do is push forward up the hill, and you'll get there eventually."* She paused for a moment. "Wow... I haven't thought about that in a very long time."

Jenny relaxed, and let the weight of her entire torso rest up against her sister. "Tell me more," she whispered.

"Well, during spring, the entire hill was covered in beautiful blue Scilla — the most amazingly pure shade of blue — like the color of your eyes." She craned her neck, poking her head forward to look at Jenny's eyes.

Jenny smiled, and shrugged her shoulders bashfully.

"And later," Francesca continued, "as soon as summer hit, then Lily of the Valley replaced the Scilla. And from the top of the meadow you could see everything — or, at least most of Oslo, and all the way down to the North Sea. It was Mom's favorite place; and my favorite as well. I'll take you there sometime."

Jenny turned toward Francesca, eyes still moist, but her face now filled with the potential of a smile. "Then it'll be my favorite place, too."

Francesca put her hands on her hips. "But of course."

Jenny smirked, and crossed her arms in front of her chest determinedly. "And you know what else?" she began, her eyes sparkling. "When you leave, I'm not staying here, either. I'm coming with you."

"Uh... J-love, I can't really... I mean, unfortunately that's not for me to decide."

"I know — it's my decision. And I've made it already. Right when you told me what Mom used to say; that we can do anything we want — all we gotta do is push together up the hill."

"Well... really it's up to Dad to decide, so—" Francesca paused, and turned her attention toward her bedroom door.

The sound of heavy footsteps echoed out in the hallway, then the door burst open.

Jenny jumped, her smile plummeting from her face.

"So you're both home, are ya — why the hell isn't dinner started yet, huh?" Phillip barked, while aiming his pointy nose at the girls like an old schoolmistress with a cane. His face was all screwed up, making his bushy eyebrows stick out like tiny awnings over his eyes. "What's wrong with you two? When I get home from work this late, I expect dinner to be ready. Worthless kids — I guess I have to do everything around here." He stared them down, then headed back out the door, slamming it shut behind him.

Francesca closed her eyes, and took a deep breath. She got up and locked the door.

He'd been like this for as long as she could remember. Some days were worse than others, although one specific incident had always stuck out in her mind. A moment when his verbal abuse had crippled her. Rendered her speechless.

Francesca had been six years old at the time. Or, more precisely, it had been on the actual day of her sixth birthday. All she'd wanted for her birthday was to go see the pretty ballerinas at the Norwegian Opera House, and her mom had finally agreed that she was old enough to go.

But her dad had said no. She could still hear his voice paralyzing her.

"There's no way you're going to that stupid ballet," Phillip had roared.

Anna looked at him, steadily, and her voice calm as a cat, she'd said. "Yes, Phillip, we are. This is the only thing our daughter has asked for these past few months and, since it's her birthday, we are going to let her have it."

Phillip's eyes were on fire, staring first at Anna, and then letting his gaze fall down onto Francesca. "Your mom and I — or should I say *I*, considering your mom has chosen to first be a student and then a stay-at-home mom, rather than contributing to the economy of this household — just bought this new row house. We can't afford ridiculously expensive tickets to the ballet. Now Francesca, you don't want us getting kicked out onto the street because of you, do you? You want that to be all your fault?"

Francesca blinked away a tear. She remembered having walked past a man living in a box on the street one time, and immediately felt scared. She shook her head vigorously. "No," she sobbed.

"That's enough," Anna said, furiously. "First thing Monday morning I will go out and look for a part-time job. And if you ever talk to our daughter like that again, then I will leave you."

"You see, Francesca," Phillip continued. "Now you're responsible for potentially breaking up your parents. Is that what you want? And over what — some stupid people dancing around on a stage? You're only six years old. You don't even know what ballet is, nor will you ever remember having seen a performance at this age," he snarled.

But her dad had been wrong; she did remember the ballet. And she still remembered how he'd made her feel on that day, as well as how he continued to make her feel on a regular basis.

He always told her she was way too sensitive. Too weak.

Maybe she was. Maybe she wasn't. But what she did know was that she was worth more than that.

It suddenly dawned on Francesca that her dad had been stripping away her voice and confidence her entire life. And in a way, she had let him do it, too. But back then she had only been a little kid, how was she supposed be strong enough to fight off his words?

Even though she was an adult now, she realized she was still giving away her voice for free; like it was worth nothing. In almost every situation she found herself in, she would pretty much always back down to others and their opinions; never standing up for herself and what she believed in. It occurred to her that if she didn't start using her voice soon, then it would be lost forever. She would have to choose to claim what was rightfully hers. She would have to choose to honor herself for once in her life. No one else would do it for her.

So maybe the time had come to finally do what her dad had told her all her life — to be stronger, and to stand up for herself? *Yes*, she thought. *That was exactly what she was going to do. And she was going to begin with standing up to him.*

Francesca returned to her sister, still sitting on her bed. "You're right, you can't stay here. I have no idea how it'll all work out — but one way or another, I'm taking you with me."

Jenny held her pinky out. "You promise?"

Francesca hesitated for a moment. Then she wrapped her finger around Jenny's, her gaze unwavering. "I promise."

*

Phillip slung pans around in the kitchen; like bolts of lightning crashing down into the sink and on countertops.

As the girls travelled down the staircase leading into the kitchen, Francesca attempted to make herself wider than her slender torso really was, keeping her arms out behind her, and Jenny within their perimeter.

He looked up, noticed the girls, and grunted.

"What's for dinner?" Francesca started. "And can we help you with anything?"

He stabbed the cold butter with a knife. "Don't ya think it's too late for that?"

Her eyes fell to the butter, thinking she knew exactly how it felt. "Sorry, but we—"

"Whatever. Just sit down, pasta's ready."

Francesca pulled out a chair, and glanced over at her sister.

Jenny seemed to be sitting up a little straighter than usual, and wearing the tiniest smirk on her face.

Francesca instantly felt the pressure of her promise weighing heavily on her shoulders. She pursed her lips, took a deep breath, and then turned toward her dad. "Um, so how was work?"

"Crap, of course. Like always. That damn boss of mine thinks he's God — I swear, sometimes I just wanna wring his neck," he spat, before shoving a forkful of pasta into his mouth. The tagliatelle ribbons flapped around his mouth, the bolognese sauce streaking his face.

Francesca stirred her pasta in circles with her fork. "Well... maybe you should think about changing jobs?" She tried sounding casual. "Or... you know... maybe even moving to a different city? That way you could work for a different taxi company — meaning you'd finally get a new boss. Doesn't that sound like a good idea?"

He tossed his fork down onto his plate. "Move? To where? And what the hell would I do with the two of you? I couldn't take you with me — you're a student, and Jenny's still in school, for Christ's sake. What's the matter with you?" He lowered his head and continued eating, while still fixing his glare on her.

"Oh yes," Francesca laughed eerily. "Of course — how stupid of me."

"Move?" he grunted. "Hah. I sure did raise a couple 'a dim kids."

Could she tell him the truth, she wondered? Maybe he wouldn't even mind getting rid of them? He'd never wanted them anyway. And it wasn't like he didn't run away on a frequent basis himself, leaving her and Jenny alone for several days at a time.

"Well, actually..." Francesca started, then closed her mouth again.

"Yes...?"

Francesca took a deep breath, and reminded herself that his snarl was usually worse than his bite.

"As I've just started my degree at the university, I'll be wanting to move out soon; and Jenny could always come live with me. I mean... you know, it's just a thought..." She tried to make it sound like the idea had just randomly occurred to her. Out of the corner of her eye she noticed her sister darting nervous looks at her, but managed to dodge them skillfully.

"Jenny's not going anywhere," he hissed. "If you wanna go, then you're an abandoner, and we're better off without ya anyway. It's like I've always told ya," he said, pointing his fork at them. "Never trust anyone — not even family — 'cause all they'll ever end up doing is hurtin' ya and leaving ya behind."

"But Daddy," Jenny said, her voice high-pitched. "I think it'd be fun living with Francesca for a while. And we'd come back home to visit you all the time."

Phillip shot up from his chair, knocking it to the floor. "No one," he started, his eyes burning red-hot, "will ever leave me while I'm in charge. You hear? No one! I'm the boss; and until Jenny turns 18 — she will be living with me." He stormed off, kicking the up-ended chair out of his way.

Chapter Two

The blue tram Francesca was on pulled up to the stop located at the opposite end of the street from her university. The double doors folded open, revealing a group of 20 or so soon-to-be passengers huddled underneath umbrellas on the sidewalk, impatient to board.

As Francesca waited for the people in front of her to shuffle off, she craned her neck to peer up at the dark-gray, leaking sky above.

The sky was pissed for some reason. Either that; or it just liked to cry. A lot. And growl, and throw glowing stakes at the world down below.

She stepped off the tram and onto the paved sidewalk, before making a dash for cover under the nearest tree.

Francesca shot dirty looks at the sky. What with her dad having gone completely ballistic last night, she felt like she'd already taken enough blows for one week. But at least by unleashing her accumulated fury on the weather instead of him, she ran no risk of getting punished for it later on.

"I hate you!" she hissed up at the sky. "Why aren't you sunny, huh? Why aren't you just happy — like the normal sunny, late summer skies in southern Europe? Why do I have to live in cold, rainy Norway?"

The sky ignored her.

"You know, someday I'll just move. I'll just run away — far away — to someplace warm, where September is actually considered to be a semi-warm month, and then you can just hover around by yourself and mope."

The sky rumbled its loudest roar yet.

"Don't you take that attitude with me, you..." Francesca shut her mouth; having just realized she was yelling at the sky.

She sighed, and opened her broken, black umbrella. The one half had already caved in so that it hung straight down, parallel to the right side of her face.

She left the tree she'd been standing under, and started making her way down the street.

A navy-blue Volvo skidded past her, splashing the nearest puddle all over her legs.

"Hey, come back here," she shouted, and squinted at the license plate in an attempt to memorize it.

The rain was coming down so heavily that it completely camouflaged every number on the plate; and then the car was gone, without a trace.

"Goddamn," she muttered. "Lucky for that car — and whoever's in it — that I won't be able to get my hands on them because—" she stopped mid-sentence. "Wait a sec," she let her right hand, and with it the umbrella, descend toward the asphalt. "That's it — we'll just have to run away from him. Disappear without a trace, to someplace where he'll never find us."

She strode along the sidewalk for no more than a couple of seconds, before realizing that; of course, her plan — like her umbrella — was broken. Because she and Jenny — unlike that car and its driver — were traceable.

He would find them. Then he would punish them, before making sure to keep them apart so they couldn't run away again. Francesca could escape his anger. Jenny could not.

She reached her university building, and stopped out front, just staring at it for a moment; a large, gray, block of concrete, waiting to be filled with students.

Margaret snuck up from behind her, "Hey, Francesca," she said and dished out a hug.

Francesca jumped, and turned around. "Ah, hey."

Margaret's always rosy cheeks had turned even rosier in the damp September air, like two clouds of pink cotton candy contrasting with her otherwise tan, freckled face. "Wow, your umbrella is the saddest thing I've ever seen. Maybe that's what I'll get you for your birthday." She winked. "Anyway, it's drier inside; what're you hanging around out here for? Come on." She gestured and headed toward the main entrance.

Francesca followed her friend.

Once inside, Margaret unbuttoned her red raincoat and shook a couple drops of water out of her golden curls.

Francesca glanced at her friend's hair and felt a shot of melancholy hit her. Her mother's curls had looked just like those.

Margaret turned around, her hazel eyes smiling.

Francesca studied her best friend for a second. In a way, hanging out with Margaret made her feel closer to her mother; yet, from time to time it also painfully reminded her that her mother would never again be a part of Francesca's life.

She sighed, and started folding up her umbrella. Then a bizarre idea popped into her head. *True – she would never again have a mother. But, what if...* she found herself thinking. *Could she maybe... was it possible that she could... somehow... be some kind of mother figure herself?*

"What's up with you?" Margaret waved her hand back and forth in front of Francesca's face. "You look like you just saw a unicorn or something."

Francesca gazed absentmindedly up at her tall friend. "Huh? Nah, it's nothing... I was just thinking about... adoption and stuff..." her voice trailed away.

Margaret frowned. "Excuse me?"

"Ah — you know — I'm — um — not really feeling too well..."

"What's wrong?"

"Uh, I think I might have a fever or something," she lied, and looked away. "So, yeah... anyway — see ya later." Francesca pushed her way through the crowd and bolted out the door.

"Francesca...?" Margaret called after her.

She ignored her friend, and continued running toward the tram stop.

After about a minute Francesca rounded the final corner.

The tram caught up and screeched past her, winning the race hands down.

Francesca sprinted as fast as she could, with no time to zigzag around the many puddles.

At the stop ahead, the tram sat waiting — teasing her.

Panting, she finally reached the rear entrance.

The doors snapped shut right in front of her.

Her finger attacked the button next to the door, forcing them to reopen and let her in.

Slowly, the doors crawled back open.

She slipped in and plopped down on the nearest available seat.

"Hey, Francesca!" The guy sitting across the aisle on the right hand side of the car slid in toward the window, making room for her next to him on the double seat. His tall stature and broad-shouldered build didn't leave a whole lot of space for another person on the narrow seat; but then again, Francesca's frame was a size small.

She looked over at him, and felt her heart smile. "Adrian. Hi. How are ya?" she said, slightly out of breath, and sat down next to him.

"Can't complain, just moved out of that apartment I was sharing with four other guys, and into an apartment of my own last night." He ran his hand over his stubbly face, and smiled so wide that his dimples peaked.

"Nice — congrats."

"Yeah, thanks." He nodded. "So, now all I've gotta do is make it semi-livable-ish — meaning I need to go furniture shopping for the bare essentials ASAP. But anyways, what's new with you?"

"Actually," she started, unable to contain her excitement. "I'll be moving out in a couple of weeks, too — on October 1st."

"Exciting stuff."

"For sure."

"So, where are ya off to now? Shouldn't you be in class?"

"Umm, yeah, kinda... But I just really need to get some important research done without being disturbed."

"What kind of research?"

Francesca looked around, scanning the tram for familiar faces. "Uh... well, it's kinda private... and, a secret, so..." She gazed deep into his moss green eyes. "But, can I trust you to not tell anyone?"

"Yeah, 'course."

"OK, so, I know this sounds kinda crazy and all... and at the moment I have no clue how I'd be able to pull it off, but I need to look into whether there is any chance at all that I could adopt Jenny," she whispered.

"Adopt her?" he burst out.

She held her finger up to her lips. "Shh."

"Francesca..." he lowered his voice. "I seriously doubt you'll be able to do that."

"It's just..." She sighed. "When I move out, she needs to come with me. And our dad won't let her go until she's 18."

"Alright, well, adoption seems a bit drastic, don't you think?"

Francesca turned her entire body to face him, getting so close she could smell the spearmint gum on his breath. "Adrian, you grew up right next door, that's the only reason I'm telling you this. You're basically the only one of my friends who knows how he treats us; my only friend who's heard some of the things he's said. Remember that one time on the swings, shortly after my mom died?" she whispered, her voice trailing away.

Francesca took a deep breath, and thought about the first time she'd truly realized just how much she liked and respected Adrian; just how great she thought he was. Francesca had been nine at the time. Adrian was twelve. And Phillip... well, he'd acted the way that he usually did.

Francesca was out in their front yard, sitting on one of the two swings; Adrian was on the other swing, right next to her.

Phillip marched across the lawn, heading straight toward them. "Francesca, get inside the house, right now. I've already told you once, I'm not telling you again," he yelled.

Francesca's body immediately went rigid, and her breathing halted; she wasn't able to completely stop her tears that had never been far away since her mother had died.

"OK... I'm coming..." she said slowly, in an attempt to muffle her gasping, though quite clearly failing in her attempt.

"Now means now, Francesca," Phillip continued. "Jenny won't stop crying, and I just can't take it anymore," he spat. Then he took a couple of steps closer to Francesca, and studied her face. "Oh Christ, you're crying, too?" he groaned. "What's the matter?"

Francesca looked back at him, her eyes starting to tear up even more. "Mom..."

Phillip sighed. "Still — really? Oh, come on, it's been a couple of months now; you need to start pulling yourself back together. You still have one parent left, remember?" he huffed, annoyance and jealousy competing to be the star in the tone of his voice. "That's more than what some kids have."

"But—" she started.

"No buts," he interrupted her. "It seems that even your own dad isn't good enough to put your sister to bed, so I give up. It's your turn." He looked at her face again, furrowing his brow. "And wipe those tears," he added. "Stop being so weak. Life's always going to disappoint you; let ya down. You better start getting used to it."

Francesca's gaze dropped to her feet dangling just above the ground, and she nodded slowly.

Adrian looked over at Francesca, noticing how hunched over her body was, seeing what her father was doing to her. Then he turned to Phillip. "You can't talk to her like that."

Phillip clenched his fists. "Who do you think you are, neighbor boy?" he growled. "She's my daughter, and I'll talk to her however I think is right."

Adrian got to his feet. "Her mom just died."

Phillip pointed his finger at Adrian, warningly. "You better stay out of this."

"Well—" Adrian started.

"Adrian," Francesca whispered. "Please, don't..."

He looked at her for a moment, before dropping back down onto his swing.

"Francesca, inside — now," Phillip repeated, before stomping back off toward the house.

They watched him trample across the lawn, until he'd slammed the front door shut behind him.

"Francesca," Adrian said.

Slowly, she twisted her body to face him. "Yeah," she whispered.

He looked her in the eye, his gaze upon her gentle, yet serious at the same time. "You know..." he hesitated, weighing his words. "You know, you don't have to let him talk to you like that."

She looked down at the ground, and blinked away half of the tears that had pooled in her eyes. "Yeah, well... that's easy for you to say."

He slid off his swing and took a step closer to her. He draped his arm around her, placing his hand on her shoulder. Then he just stood there, silently, for a minute or two.

She took a deep breath, and realized that she didn't want his hand to let go. She continued to sit on her swing for a few more seconds, memorizing what it felt like to have a guy on her side. But... she also knew she had to get back inside, so she pinched her eyes shut, and reluctantly peeled herself away from him. "I've gotta go," she whispered.

Francesca put her baby sister to bed, only leaving her room when she'd felt Jenny's entire body immersed in sleep as she sat on her lap. Her breathing as well as her weight had grown heavier as she allowed herself to completely relax up against Francesca's torso.

She pulled her sister's door nearly shut, leaving only a small crack so she would hear Jenny if she started crying. Letting go of the door handle, she curled her fingers up into the palms of her hands. Her fingers felt clammy as they rubbed up against each other. She let her eyelids slide shut, and noticed her throat was starting to get sore, threatening to close up.

Maybe Adrian was right? Maybe she could actually talk to her dad about how he was making her feel; possibly getting him to change, or at least making him think more carefully about the way he spoke to her?

What would happen, she wondered? Would he soften a bit, perhaps? If she told him that she loved him, would he then maybe treat her differently? Would he tell her that he loved her back? Would they ever be able to have the kind of relationship that she wanted and needed them to have — the kind that she had once had with her other parent, before it was all ripped away from her?

If she whispered to him; "Dear Dad, please change a little." Would it make a difference?

She sighed, placed her hand on the pinewood banister and started heading down the stairs.

Phillip emerged from the front door, smacking it shut behind him.

Francesca, who was now on the bottom step of the stairs, jumped and looked up at him.

He frowned, directing his gaze up through the staircase to the second floor. "So she's finally asleep now, is she?"

Francesca nodded once.

"How the hell is it that you're able to do it when I'm not," he grunted as he stomped past her headed for the kitchen table and plopped down onto a chair.

"Well..." her voice, like her body, shook. "Maybe... maybe you could try being more gentle next time?"

He narrowed his eyes at her. "Gentle? You mean being soft, like *she* was?"

Francesca shrugged.

"Let me tell you one thing: that will never ever happen. The day I start being weak is the day I know I have failed," he snarled.

Her body suddenly started swaying on the inside, to the music that wasn't really there ...at least not for others to hear. It was just for Francesca, playing deep inside her, keeping her alive; allowing her to cope.

Her mother had taught her the only defense mechanism she knew, and lately she found herself needing to turn to it on most days. "Being nice does not mean you have failed," she whispered, and imagined herself dancing freely across the beautiful meadow that her mother had taken her to so many times.

"In my book it sure as hell does. To me, the word *nice* is just another way of saying you're weak; letting people walk all over you," he scoffed.

She mustered the strength to look him in the eye, and steadied her insides for long enough to finally tell him. "You asked me how I was able to put Jenny to bed, and I told you the truth."

He rose from his chair, and started making his way over to the hallway, his gaze remaining upon her.

She held her breath, but was no longer able to keep her body from moving. Her arms started breathing for her, gently, out to either side.

"You know who's weak?" he asked her.

Her legs tightened into a fifth position ballet pose, one leg crossed in front of the other.

Phillip raised a pointed finger at her. "You're weak, that's who."

Francesca brought her arms down, curving them so that her hands ended up in front of her thighs.

"And you know who else?" Phillip continued

She pliéed, letting her knees fold out to the sides.

"Jenny's weak, too." He grabbed his leather jacket and flung it on, before leaving the house.

Outside, she heard him starting up his car. The old engine crackled, counting out the beat for her. Then he pulled away, the gravel underneath his tires continuing to carry out the rhythm. And when Francesca could no longer hear the sound of him leaving her, then she let her tears begin to flow down her cheeks in a thin, steady stream, letting them keep playing the soft melody; fueling her dancing quietly. She knew from experience that once she was done, she would start to feel better. Her ballet was the only thing that would make her feel better.

Phillip did not return to the house until two days later. And while he was away, Francesca remembered feeling terrified, mostly for Jenny, but also about the amount of responsibility he'd placed on her.

When he finally walked back into the house later that week, pretending like nothing had happened, she had no clue where he had been. He didn't say a single word about it, nor did he utter an apology.

The shock of suddenly seeing him again had silenced her. Although she opened her mouth with the intention of asking him where he had been, the words physically would not come out.

While he had been away, she remembered worrying that something bad must have happened to him — worrying to the point that she had started convincing herself that he was gone forever — that she and Jenny would be orphans from then on. That was the only possible explanation for why he had not come back home to take care of them.

So, when she saw that he was alive and well, she could hardly believe her eyes. During the next few hours, she lurked around him, waiting for her courage to come back and find her. Finally, she managed to pull herself together, and asked him what had happened; where he had gone?

Phillip had looked her in the eye; shrugged lightly; and turned and walked away.

Francesca swallowed once, and then again. Over and over she swallowed, trying to force the stinging sensation inside her down far enough so that it would never resurface.

Although he disappeared on them several more times throughout the years, she never bothered asking him about it again. By then she had learned that there would be no point in doing so.

The tram turned a corner, and let off a screeching sound against the steel tracks.

Francesca jumped slightly, and realized Adrian was sitting right next to her, contemplating her again.

He bit his lower lip, and looked away. "I guess he's no father of the year."

In Francesca's opinion, Phillip had already walked away from what he could've had with his two daughters. He had chosen to not make their family bond special, chosen to make the girls feel like they didn't really matter that much.

To begin with, for a while after her mom died, Francesca had tried really hard to make him see that Jenny, her dad and she really could become a real family. She had desperately tried to make him happy, to do whatever it took to get him to show them the love they so craved from their father.

But he had not changed, nor had he been able to provide them with the feelings of confidence and encouragement that a father should have.

And so, after a couple of years, Francesca had given up on her dad, too. She couldn't bear to feel the constant rejection anymore. She had realized it was easier on the heart to just accept the fact that he would never be there for Jenny and her in the way that they wanted and needed him to be.

"Hah," she snorted. "More like among the top ten worst fathers of the decade."

"Still," Adrian said, "adoption is no straightforward process. It could drag on for several years, causing everyone involved a lot of pain. And I can almost guarantee you wouldn't likely end up winning."

Francesca let her face drop into her hands. "Then, what am I supposed to do?"

"Hey," he said, putting his hand on her shoulder. "It's going to be OK."

She lifted her head, blinking away the tears blurring her vision of him. These past few years she'd tried keeping her distance from Adrian. The more time she spent with him, the more she seemed to like him. And that — or more specifically relationships, or even getting too close to anyone — was something she'd stopped believing in several years ago.

But, on the other hand, helping Jenny move away from their dad's house was something she did believe in. And if Adrian would in any way be able to help her get closer to reaching her goal, then she'd just have to risk spending some time with him; experiencing a stray emotion every now and again. All she'd need to do when her unwanted feelings passed through her was to promptly show them out once she was fed up with hosting them. She knew she could do it; she knew she could be strong. Blocking out her feelings was something she'd become quite good at over the years.

She took a deep breath. "There must be a way," she started. "You're a law student — can't you help me figure out a way?"

"I don't know... it'd be really hard creating a strong enough case."

"Please...?"

He shrugged. "I mean, I guess you could attempt guardianship, although—"

"Really?" she interrupted him, sitting up straight. "What do I need to do?"

"Well, I'm not clear on the specifics, but I still don't think you'd have a very good chance of succeeding, unfortunately."

"Please, just help me look into it, would you? I'll do whatever it takes — I promised Jenny I'd take her with me."

Adrian rubbed his eyes before letting his hands slide back through his wavy, dark blond hair. "I'm not promising anything, but I'll see what I can find out."

"Thank you, thank you, thank you. You're the best!" She squeezed him so hard she felt his hair gel caking into the pores of her cheek. "I'll come over tomorrow; then we'll talk strategy."

Chapter Three

All the traffic lights kept turning red.

"Fuck," Phillip yelled, slamming the heels of his hands into the steering wheel. He wanted to get home from work before the girls left to hang out with their friends in order to escape him — he wanted to make up for the way he'd acted last night. Yet again, he'd let his temper get the best of him. And deep down, he knew better, but that still usually didn't mean that he was patient for long enough to actually do better.

Of course, he still believed in tough love, though, and he would never deny it. Tough love was the only way to build strength and character. That was how he, himself, had been brought up at the orphanage, and he took pride in the fact that he raised his own daughters in the same way.

Anna, however, hadn't approved of his parenting methods. Instead, she had babied the girls, and that, in his opinion, had been her biggest flaw.

But, this morning he'd also come to realize that he might have overreacted last night. Even though it was important for him to show his daughters who was boss, he still didn't want them hating him.

A colleague had agreed to switch shifts with him so Phillip could finish earlier for a change. Although he desperately needed the extra money those late hours paid, tonight he just had to prioritize differently.

A red car pulled up on his left hand side, and begun sticking its nose out in front of him.

"Yeah, I don't think so, Mr. Sedan," he warned the driver, barely audible over the New-York-City-style honking skills he'd acquired through his 22 years as a cab driver. Phillip hit the gas, cutting the car off.

The guy driving the red Audi slammed on his breaks.

Phillip rolled the passenger side window down. "That's right, that oughta teach ya not to sneak in front of others. Everybody's gotta wait their turn."

The traffic light teasingly added yellow below the red to its color palette, before turning full on green.

Phillip shot off, ignoring the steady stream of swear words flowing melodiously from the other car, now coughing in his fumes.

His dashboard clock showed 6:35 p.m.

He knew Jenny was leaving at 7 for a Friday night sleepover. And Francesca — well, she'd use any excuse to get out of the house. He sped up some more, pushing the speed limit to a level where he knew he was risking losing his job. But at this point in his career he'd developed an intuitive eye for cops; he was usually able to guess which corners they were hiding behind, which streets they were lurking in.

*

The girls sat huddled together over the kitchen table.

"Hey, I'm home," Phillip called out.

Jenny jumped, immediately repelling herself from Francesca as though they were identically charged magnets. "Oh, hi Daddy."

He felt his chest tighten. He narrowed his eyes at them. "What's going on?"

"Nothing," Francesca said, folding up a piece of paper and putting it in her pocket. "How come you're home so early?"

"I wanted to talk to you guys before you took off to hang out with your friends; see if maybe the three of us could do something together tomorrow?"

"Yeah, well, we've got plans. Sorry." Francesca tucked her ash blond hair behind her ears.

"Both of you? The entire day?"

"Yeah," Francesca shrugged. She got to her feet and pushed the seat of her chair back underneath the table.

Phillip took a deep breath. "Listen, I took the day off from work in order to spend time with you guys. We could go watch a movie or something?"

"Well, Adrian's moving, and we already promised we'd go with him to help pick out some stuff for the apartment," she said, and started making her way up the stairs.

He felt his rage begin to bubble up to the surface. "Francesca, I'm talking to you. Don't you walk away from me when I'm talking to you."

Francesca kept climbing the stairs. "I'm already running late for meeting my friends."

He turned toward his youngest. "Jenny, surely you'll spend a minute with your old man."

"Sorry, I'm late, too." She looked down at the floor and made an unnecessarily large semicircle as she sped past him.

"Hey." He yanked at her arm with more force than he had intended to, causing her to flip toward him like a Raggedy Ann doll, her strawberry-blond hair flailing around her head.

"Stop it, you're hurting me."

"I just want a hug before you go. Is that too much to ask?"

Jenny writhed wildly. "Let me go. Francesca, help me!" she yelled, her voice reaching an all-time high pitch.

In an attempt to stop her from screaming, Phillip grabbed either side of Jenny's mouth with his fingers, and squeezed so that her lips pushed forwards like those of a fish.

Francesca bolted down the stairs, and saw his grasp on Jenny's tearstained face. "What are you doing to her?"

Phillip slowly let go of Jenny, and took a step back. "Relax; I'm not doing anything to your sister. I was going to give her a hug goodbye, and she over-reacted. That's all."

Jenny pulled away from him.

Francesca swept her arms around her sister, her eyes burning like fire. "Don't you dare touch her."

*

Francesca walked Jenny over to her friend's house for their sleepover; holding her hand; rambling endlessly about anything and everything, attempting to distract her sister from thinking about what had just happened.

After a couple of minutes, she glanced over at Jenny. Realizing her sister wasn't saying a word, Francesca immediately stopped talking as well.

Jenny didn't even seem to have noticed. Instead, she appeared to have closed herself off, not having heard a single word Francesca had said

As Francesca continued trudging down the sidewalk, it occurred to her that that was the same strategy she usually turned to as well; closing herself off from the world when things got too painful. But she didn't want Jenny to do the same — she wanted her sister to be able to tell her anything. She stopped walking, and turned around to face her. "Hey, Jellybean, you OK?"

Jenny shrugged.

"You know you can talk to me, right?"

She nodded slowly.

Francesca wasn't convinced. She gave her sister a hug before trying again. "So is there anything I could say or do to make you feel better?"

Jenny closed her eyes for a moment, frowning slightly as she considered her sister's question. "Maybe... maybe you could tell me a story about Mom?"

Francesca smiled. "Of course I can. Anything in particular you'd like to know?"

"What about how she chose my name — do you know anything about that?" she asked, her eyes hopeful.

"As a matter of fact, I do know." Francesca winked. "so at first, she was having the hardest time deciding. She must've considered about thirty different names—"

"Like what kind of names?" Jenny interrupted her.

"Hmm, let's see... I don't remember them all, I mean, I was only eight years old at the time myself. But I do know that one of the names she considered was Sarah."

"Sarah..." Jenny muttered to herself. "Nah, I already know of three Sarahs at my school — that wouldn't have worked."

Francesca laughed. "Indeed, that would've been a serious problem. But I think another name she thought of was May, because, obviously, you were born in the month of May."

Jenny shook her head. "I don't like that. A month is a month, and a name is a name. They're not the same thing, so they shouldn't be called the same."

"Alright, the verdict is in on that one! And like I said, Mom had a bunch of other names in mind, but she just didn't think any of them sounded quite right. I remember she was having the hardest time. But you were such a happy baby, pretty much from the moment you were born. You even smiled when you were only a couple of days old — although, apparently, babies aren't supposed to smile properly until they reach a certain age — but even Mom's midwife agreed that the expression on your face had definitely been an actual smile."

"Really?" Jenny giggled.

"Yeah, Mom was obsessed with telling everyone that story. Kind of annoying at the time, actually, from a big sister's point-of-view. But anyway, she couldn't have been more proud of you. And so the midwife, who was from England, kept saying what a joy you were, and started calling you *Jolly Joy*, in English. So then Mom realized that a perfect name for you would be Jenny — she always called you *Jenny Joy*, actually."

Jenny grinned. "Wow, that's a good story! And I like that she was so proud of me, even though I don't remember it myself."

"Oh, yes, Mom was *extremely* proud of you."

Jenny seemed to be contemplating something for a moment, then said, "Jenny's a good name. I've always liked it."

"It's the greatest name ever, if you ask me. Of course, as you know, being eight years old at the time I preferred the candy version of the name, myself — Jellybean."

"I think that's even better," Jenny said, and squeezed her sister's hand.

They reached Jenny's friend's house, and rang the doorbell. The girl greeted the two sisters and gave Jenny a hug.

"OK, bye girls, have fun." Francesca said, and stood there watching until the door shut behind the two eleven-year-olds.

As Jenny kept to herself most of the time, she didn't really have very many close friends. But Francesca was at least grateful that she had a few friends she could visit when things got too crazy over at their house.

She sighed, and started heading over toward Margaret's house to hang out with some of her own friends.

As she sauntered down the sidewalk, she realized she hadn't taken ballet class in a little while. She was starting to notice the lack of it; her defense against her dad was beginning to weaken. It might not be visible from the outside, but she was definitely feeling it on the inside.

Tomorrow she was meeting up with Adrian to discuss their plan moving forward, and then the following day was a Sunday. But she really needed to try to get a class in on Monday.

Francesca quickly turned her head to check whether anyone else was around. When she saw that the coast was clear, she immediately changed her gait; rising up onto the balls of her feet, and rolling gently through her feet for each step she took while continuing down the sidewalk. She held her arms slightly lifted out to either side. Glancing around quickly one more time, she extended her right leg and did three pique pirouettes in a row, her sneaker leaving slight swirling marks in the thin layer of dust on the asphalt.

She still remembered the first time she'd ever seen a real ballet performance. The exact moment she'd truly fallen in love with ballet. She remembered what it had meant to her at that time — as well as what it still meant to her to this very day.

That night at the *Norwegian Opera House*, Francesca had been inconsolable. She didn't want her dad to hate her because she'd wanted to go to the ballet with her mom. She didn't want her parents fighting like that because of her — she had no idea ballet tickets were too expensive for them to afford.

"Francesca," her mother had whispered as they sat in their seats, waiting for the performance to begin. "It's OK. It's not your fault." She put her arm around her daughter, rubbing her shoulder gently. "Your dad is just..." Anna paused, and sighed. "He's just a bit..." She paused again, searching for the right words. "Well, let's just say that he's got some issues, unfortunately." She kissed Francesca on the cheek. "But you know what?" Anna continued.

Francesca sobbed, and turned her head to look at her mother. "What?" she whispered.

"Tonight is all about you. And it's all about us, here together at the ballet. This is no time to be sad," Anna said, her eyes twinkling as she reached her index finger out and gently tapped the end of Francesca's button nose.

Francesca smiled weakly.

"So, soon, when those curtains open," she continued, gesturing at the thick, red velvet curtains, "we'll be whisked away to our very own special place. And when we're in that magical place, we can decide exactly *what* we want it to be like, and just exactly *who* we want to be. Nobody but you gets to have a say in the matter — you're the boss."

Francesca's eyes grew wide. "Really?"

Her mother nodded. "Oh, absolutely. And you know what else?"

Francesca shook her head. "No."

"If you really concentrate on imaging what you want it to be like — and I mean *really* focus on it with all your heart — then you can bring that feeling back out with you, even when you're not watching ballet."

Francesca wiped her eyes with the back of her hand. "Are you sure?"

"Oh, yes, I'm positive," Anna said matter-of-factly. Then she contemplated her daughter for a moment, before leaning in a little closer, whispering, "I know for sure that this works, because I've done it myself."

Francesca looked up at her mother for a couple of seconds, her mouth hanging slightly open. Then she let out a soft giggle.

The lights in the audience dimmed, and the orchestra began to play.

"Just you wait and see, sweetie," Anna whispered in Francesca's ear. "I think you're going to like it."

The curtains rose slowly, and majestically, the red velvet rippling in slow motion.

Francesca studied the curtains, and thought they looked like the waves of the sea. Because these waves rippled so slowly, she imagined that the waves had been put to bed; had their bedtime story; and would be falling asleep any second now.

Francesca pinched her eyes shut, excitedly. Then her eyes flared back open, not wanting to miss a single step.

The music kept playing. So much music. So pretty in Francesca's ears.

She got to her feet, leaned forward a bit, and looked down at the people playing.

The music people's hands were moving fast. Some of them held onto the ends of sticks, pulling them back and forth across the front of their music machines.

She watched them for a few more seconds, mesmerized.

Then a ballerina stepped onto the stage, her tutu dress as pink as a marshmallow.

"Mamma, look!" she exclaimed, and plopped back down into her seat. "Mamma, a ballerina — look!" She pointed.

The elderly woman in front of her rose slightly up in her seat, turning abruptly toward Francesca. She looked mad, and held her finger up in front of her mouth. "Shh."

Francesca turned to look at her mother.

"Sorry," Anna mouthed to the lady, then whispered into Francesca's ear; "I know it's exciting, sweetie, but you have to be as quiet as a mouse during the performance, OK? "

She nodded slowly, disappointedly. It seemed that all she was ever told to do was to be quiet, to just sit there and be invisible; to stay out of everyone's way. But the scariest person who told her to be quiet was her dad. He would get so mad at her sometimes. She didn't like it when he frightened her.

She sighed, and watched the ballerina, looking at the ballerina very closely for a long time. As she sat there she started squinting her eyes a bit. That was when she noticed something cool. The ballerina wasn't talking either. Her mouth did not move up and down, either. But still, it seemed like she was saying something. She was saying something with her body, instead of her mouth. Somehow, Francesca could hear it; she could feel it; and she really, really liked it. As she squinted her eyes just a little bit more, she could see the dancer's moves and words becoming clearer, reaching out even farther, like the ballerina was bigger than she really was; like her arms and legs were longer than they really were.

Soon, many more ballet dancers ran in and out across the stage, taking turns talking with their bodies.

Francesca pulled her knees to her chest, and wrapped her arms tightly around them staring at the ballerinas, transfixed for the rest of the performance, listening to what the ballet dancers were telling her.

Then, after a while, the dancers stopped. And the music stopped. And the clapping began.

Francesca banged her hands together, over and over, so many times. She clapped louder than anyone else, until her hands were red and prickly.

Eventually, the curtains came back down, and the lights were gradually turned back on.

"Mamma," Francesca whispered, bouncing excitedly in her seat. "Mamma, I wanna dance, too. Can I, please?"

Anna's eyes followed her daughter, bopping up and down. She smiled, and said, "OK, when we get home, I'll let you dance around the living room for a few minutes before you go to bed."

"No, I wanna learn how to dance like the ballerinas."

"OK, so you mean you want to take ballet class?"

"Yeah, yeah, yeah," she sang in a whisper.

Anna laughed. "Alright, I'll see if I can find a class for you to take."

Francesca put her arms in the air, and exclaimed, "Yeay!" Then she giggled.

She could dance ballet. That way, she would still be quiet; she would stay out of her father's way; she wouldn't bother him. Yet, when she danced, she could still speak, without words, using her entire body, as loud as she wanted to. And no one could stop her from being herself; no one could stop her from saying exactly what she wanted to say.

Chapter Four

Phillip stood leaning over his kitchen counter, breathing heavily, slowly, attempting to calm himself back down.

The girls had blown what had happened way out of proportion. They always did. Especially Francesca. He couldn't *believe* how ungrateful they had both been about the fact that he'd taken tomorrow off from work in order to spend time with them. Then they had absolutely refused to even attempt to make the smallest amount of time for him in their schedule. It was as if they didn't even like him; as if they didn't even love their own father.

He took another deep breath. "Well, I'll teach them how to respect me," he said out loud, for no one but the walls of his empty house to hear.

He felt as if the girls always ganged up on him; always made him out to be the bad guy.

Anna had been the exact same way, constantly taking the girls' side over his. Always putting the girls and their needs above his.

Although, of course, it hadn't always been that way. Back when it had only been Anna and him, things had been different. Things had been better, in a way.

Not that he didn't love his daughters. Of course he did. But probably, most likely, Anna had loved him a bit more before Francesca was born. Anna had needed Phillip more back then. That was a time when she had needed him in the same way that he had — and, in a way, how he still — needed her.

But as soon as Francesca had been born, it was like Anna's love was spread out more thinly; like she divided the total amount between her husband and their daughter, and Phillip usually ended up drawing the shortest straw.

For Phillip, however, gaining a daughter didn't mean he had any less love left over for his wife. If anything, it had made him love Anna even more. But not having felt needed anymore had only resulted in him becoming even more needy, bringing out the worst in him. It had taken him right back to the inferior feeling he had felt every day growing up at the orphanage.

He couldn't stand it. It infuriated him.

And now, 19 years later, Francesca was acting the same way about Jenny as Anna had acted about Francesca. She really was the spitting image of her mother.

He sighed. He just didn't know what to do.

Now, he could always force the girls to stay at home with him tomorrow — couldn't he? He contemplated that idea for a moment, absentmindedly swiping the palm of his hand back and forth across the wooden kitchen countertop.

He shrugged. Of course, that was always one way to go, although he would have preferred for them to actually *want* to spend a couple of hours with him. So... he thought, maybe that meant changing his tactic a bit? At least, maybe he would need to reconsider his initial approach. Maybe make it a bit... milder? ...perhaps try using a calmer voice?

He shook his head, resignedly. What, so now he was actually turning into the kind of parent Anna had been, then? Was that it? A mushy kind of parent?

He dropped down into one of the chairs at the kitchen table. In any case, he figured he'd blown his chances of getting any quality time with the girls tomorrow. But what really bothered him — and what he suspected had made him lose his temper with the girls in the first place tonight — was the fact that they would be spending the entire day tomorrow with Adrian.

Phillip had never liked that neighbor boy. He was always meddling in their family matters, getting in the middle of stuff that had nothing to do with him and always making Phillip out to be the bad guy.

Although, he'd been surprised to notice that Francesca had actually seemed to avoid Adrian on a couple of occasions. Maybe she, too, had finally realized just how nosy and annoying that boy was? One could always hope...

Yes, he nodded tiredly, and rubbed his eyes. He'd definitely already lost any time he might have spent with them tomorrow, and him taking the day off from work had all been for naught.

But, he realized, considering Anna had been gone for 10 years now, maybe it was time to put in a bit more love into his two daughters, or at least make it a bit clearer to them that he actually did love them. Sometimes, he wondered whether they even believed that he loved them at all. After all, Anna wasn't ever coming back, and the two girls were the only family he had. So, yes, he would need to at least try again to get them to spend a bit of time with him at some point, even if that only meant a couple of hours every now and then.

*

It was close to 2 a.m. when Francesca slipped quietly in through the front door.

"Where've you been?" Phillip said, the squareness of his face becoming extra prominent around his jaw line as he frowned.

She jumped slightly at the sound of his voice, though pretended that she hadn't. "Out," she mumbled, shutting the door and started heading for her room.

"Francesca, please come sit with me." He took a deep breath and, in his head, started choosing his words carefully. Though he hated admitting he'd made a mistake; hated to expose himself like that; making himself seem weak... he still knew that that was what his daughter wanted to hear. "Listen... I know I messed up."

She stared at him. "Yeah, you sure did."

"Please," he repeated. "Just hear me out."

She hesitated at first. But then reluctantly made her way over, and sat down next to him at the kitchen table.

"I'm sorry."

She sighed, and shook her head.

"I really am, you know."

She closed her eyes for a moment, and appeared to be focusing deeply on something. She straightened her back up, while her torso seemed to grow a tiny bit wider and sturdier. Then she opened her eyes again. "You're always sorry," she said. "Yet you still keep saying and doing hurtful stuff to us."

He combed through his thinning blond, pin-straight hair with both hands. "What can I do to make it up to you?"

She looked him dead in the eye. "You could've just not done it in the first place."

He sighed, and realized that this time it might not be quite as easy as it usually was to get his daughter's forgiveness. "I'll do better — I will"

"Jenny's afraid of you. You know that, right?"

"Well, I promise to never grab hold of her like that again."

Francesca looked away, and shrugged.

He could tell she didn't believe him. He took her hands, and held them in his. "Come on now; don't be so hard on me. I know I'm not perfect, but we've had some good times, too. Remember that weekend the three of us went camping in the woods?" His eyes grew wide with hope.

"I remember." She nodded. "We all got into the lake, and together we taught Jenny how to swim. The water was absolutely freezing, but still, all three of us refused to give up until she could do the breaststroke, and successfully stay afloat by herself."

"And then we roasted hot-dogs and marshmallows on the fire, and stayed up all night talking and laughing."

She smiled weakly. "That was a good weekend."

"It really was. And we could do it again sometime if you want?"

"I don't know... maybe..."

"So, does that mean you forgive me for earlier today, then?"

She traced the graining on the oak kitchen table with her index finger for a minute or two.

Then she opened her mouth for a second, before closing it again. She furrowed her brow and allowed another minute to pass.

"Alright," she finally said. "I forgive you — this one, last time. But it's not me you need to apologize to, anyway — it's Jenny."

Chapter Five

Phillip drove off in his private car — a run-down, gray Ford station wagon — his tires digging into the dry road and ripping open the surface.

Francesca watched from her bedroom window on the second floor, holding her breath until he was no longer in sight.

She had no idea where he was going on his day off. And it didn't really matter, either. Maybe he'd be back soon. Maybe he wouldn't.

For a moment she thought about how sorry he'd seemed last night. Maybe he was really trying to change? She continued to stare at the road.

The little puffs of dust his tires had raked up settled back down haphazardly, the particles arranged in a slightly different way than before.

It reminded her that, through the years, he'd left them so many times; and he'd hurt them with his words so many times. And although they looked the same to others on the outside, something had clearly shifted on the inside. Each time he'd stirred them up, the pieces never fell back down in quite the same place as they'd been before; each time they'd become a little bit weaker.

And now he suddenly seemed to be regretting the way he had acted their whole lives, like he was trying to fix the broken pieces. But it was too late for that. He was the grownup, he should have known better.

"Yes," she said out loud. "I'm doing the right thing."

*

Francesca rang the doorbell of Adrian's parents' house next door.

A couple seconds later, Adrian opened the front door, "Hey," he said and gestured with his arm, welcoming her in.

"Hey," Francesca said, and searched his face in an attempt to see what he'd found out. But she wasn't able to read him today in the way that she usually could. She entered the hallway; then pulled him with her into his old childhood bedroom; and sealed the door shut with the weight of her body up against it. "So... good news? Bad news? Tell me what you know."

His eyes fell to the floor. "Well..."

Her heart started racing. "Please, Adrian — I'm dying over here."

"I'm afraid," he started, slowly shaking his head, "there's not much hope."

"Fuck." She let her back slide down against the pinewood door until she'd dropped into a squatting position.

"Your dad's got the parental responsibility," he continued, "and according to Norwegian law, children are always better off living with their parents. Your only chance is—" he paused to listen.

There were footsteps out in the hallway. Then the door burst open.

Francesca was knocked forwards onto her kneecaps. "Ah, what the hell?" she yelped, and turned around.

Jenny stood in the doorway in front of her.

Francesca exhaled, and gently rubbed her throbbing knees. "Jenny, what're you doing here?"

She raised one eyebrow. "What kind of a question is that — what do you think I'm doing here?" she shook her head. "You think you're so clever, always outsmarting me. Well, guess what? I knew you'd sneak over here without me; so I watched you; and I followed. Now who's the brilliant one?" she smirked and crossed her arms in front of her chest.

Francesca got to her feet, towering over her little sister. "Alright, you're smarter than me — absolutely amazing. Happy? Now, bye-bye, I'll see ya later." She placed one hand on either of Jenny's shoulders, and turned her torso around so she was facing the door.

"Oh, I'm not leaving."

"Ah — yeah, ya are." She pushed her sister toward the door.

"Hey!" Jenny yelled.

Francesca jumped and covered her ears.

"Good, I've got your attention. Now, this is *my* future we're talking about here, and if you think for a second that I intend to miss out on your plotting of it, then you're wrong. And if you do leave me out of it, then who knows... I might just accidently end up revealing to a certain someone what you're up to."

"Hah," Francesca snorted. "What's wrong with you — you do realize that I'm actually trying to help you out here, right?"

"Of course, that's why I'm here — to help you help me." She shut the door, and turned toward Adrian. "So, Adrian; I believe you were saying something about what our best option is?"

Francesca rolled her eyes. "Child — you're nuts." But then again, she knew Jenny would never tell their dad — she desperately wanted to be free of him. And Francesca also knew Jenny was right; she deserved to know what was going on. "OK," she sighed. "But not one word to anyone — not even your closest friends. We can't afford to risk anything, you hear me?"

"'Course," Jenny shrugged. "What am I, stupid?"

"Alright, then," Adrian exhaled. "So, the only chance you've got is to somehow prove that Jenny is neglected. They'd only take her away from your dad if you could provide solid evidence that it's not in her best interest to continue living with him."

"That's it?" Francesca scoffed. "Done."

"Ah, yeah, it's definitely not as easy as it sounds. I'm not talking about telling stories of occasional yelling or verbal abuse. I'm talking about serious stuff — like violence or severe abuse — things that are directly damaging to Jenny's physical or emotional health."

Her heart sank.

"The only real help would be if you could apply in order to be considered as Jenny's second parent."

"OK, so let's just do that, then."

"But even if you were somehow miraculously able to make a case for that, you still wouldn't necessarily gain permanent guardianship due to the fact that you're young and still a student. And besides, in the unlikely event there'd be a change at all, Jenny would probably get appointed some substitute guardian other than you. And the substitute guardian would only be temporary until your dad could prove he'd cleaned up his act, at which point she'd be given back to him."

"Geez..." Francesca closed her eyes and took a deep breath. "Well, I'll just have to do whatever it takes."

"Francesca, I don't know about this," Jenny weighed in. Her eyes were pink and concerned.

"Jenny's right. It's a gamble, and any such process could end up taking forever — probably even a year or more."

Francesca looked from one to the other. What was wrong with them? "Have you guys all of a sudden forgotten what he's like? What he's done; the things he's said?"

Jenny wiped her eyes. "No, I'm just saying we need to be careful. I don't want to get separated from you for good — you're my only family."

Adrian cleared his throat. "Actually," he turned toward Francesca, "it would've been really helpful if you were Jenny's only blood-related relative."

Francesca's hand abruptly stopped stroking her sister's back. "What do you mean?"

"Nah, I'm just saying if he hadn't been Jenny's real father then you'd have a way better chance of becoming her guardian."

"Aha..." Her eyes glazed over.

"Well, it's a shame we can't take that approach."

Francesca stood up a bit straighter. "What's a shame..." she covered Jenny's ears, and whispered into Adrian's ear. "...and something that might even work to our advantage — is that he's probably never had a DNA test."

Adrian looked at her, concerned, and muttered. "What are you talking about?"

"My parents were actually separated when Jenny was born, and as a matter of fact," she continued, her aqua blue eyes gleaming. "Mom had a new boyfriend at that time."

"What, I didn't know about that?"

Francesca nodded her head in the direction of her little sister. "I'll tell you later."

Chapter Six

Francesca snuck outside, and crept down the road to a spot where she couldn't be seen from the house; her head jerking steadily back over her shoulder like a twitchy metronome. She dialed Adrian' number.

It only rang twice before he picked up. "Hello."

"So, about this DNA test..."

"You're definitely going through with that, then, are you?"

"'Course. Now how does it work? Can I just use a strand of his hair or something?"

"There are home-testing kits you can get, where you ship a swab off to a lab after he's—"

"Great, where do I get one?"

"Well, that doesn't really matter, because it's illegal to take a test on his behalf without him consenting to it first. According to law, only the mother, the father, or the child can raise a question of paternity — and you, big sis, are unfortunately none of those things."

She stomped her foot forcefully on the ground. "Crap."

"Well, what about that old boyfriend of your mom's you mentioned? Do you still have any contact with him? If he believed he might actually be Jenny's biological father, then he'd be allowed to raise the issue as well."

"No, he died along with my mom in the car accident."

"Oh... I'm sorry."

Francesca blew air out of her mouth, while curving her lower lip in such a way as to direct the air up toward her eyes. "It's fine. I mean, I didn't even know him. Mom didn't really want to advertise the fact that she'd met someone new until the divorce was finalized. I just found out by accident, and demanded to meet him. And I only met him once or twice."

"OK, so... I guess you're dropping the whole DNA test, then? That is, unless Jenny would like to raise the issue herself, of course."

Francesca traced the number 14 on their mailbox with her index finger and waited; hoping the answer would come to her. "I don't want to hurt her any more than necessary..." she started. "But... I'll get one of those at home tests, and then I'll figure out a way to get my hands on some test material

— I just need to know if we can use this to our advantage."

"Well, how do you suppose this is going to help you? Having taken the test illegally without his knowledge, you still won't be able to use the results for anything — no matter what the outcome is."

She fidgeted uncomfortably in her stiff denim jacket. "If the results do end up showing that he's not actually her dad, then I could involve Jenny — I could get her to raise the issue and have another test done legally."

Chapter Seven

"Alright, Google: enlighten me about DNA tests," Francesca said, and started typing away at her keyboard. 90 million search results appeared, and she started clicking and scrolling. "Now; prices, prices... Come out, come out, wherever you are — I fear ya, but I still need to know ya."

The different sites all confirmed that it was going to cost her at least 2000 kroner.

Her heart sank. She'd finally managed to save up enough for the deposit on her future apartment. However... this was an unforeseen cost that would just have to be dealt with.

There were different tests. The test where you used one swab on the inside of the father's cheek; and then another swab for the child; was the most reliable, and also the least expensive one.

But, of course, Francesca would never be able to get the sample from her dad.

Or, she could use strands of his hair for an 80 percent success rate. However, she would need at least seven strands — with the roots attached.

Another possibility was to steal his toothbrush and ship it off to the lab, leaving her with a 75 percent chance of success.

She went into Phillip's bathroom, and started searching for suitable strands.

His comb was cleaner than a newly shaven head.

Then she noticed his toothbrush there in the cupboard above the sink, up for grabs.

But then again, taking it would only feed his suspicion that she was up to something.

Francesca returned to her oracle. "Come on, there's got to be something here that I can use." Her eyes wandered, sweeping across every tab on the website she'd been looking at on her computer, and then landing like a couple of flies on an interesting piece of information she hadn't noticed before.

There was also a sibling test to determine whether two people were half-siblings.

She kept on reading, excitedly.

...and DNA material from the mother would significantly increase the chance of success for the sibling test.

She sighed. Well, in this case, the two girls would just have to do.

"Swab away, swab away, swab away with me," she sang as she got her credit card out. Although, how she would convince Jenny that she needed to swab the inside of her cheek without her getting suspicious, she had no idea. She would just need to come up with some brilliant explanation.

But then she was hit with a pang of guilt. Did she really want to worry Jenny about whether or not Phillip was her biological father?

Francesca got to her feet and shuffled around in the shape of figure eights across her bedroom floor.

If Phillip turned out to not be Jenny's biological dad after all, she'd have to break it to her sister that both her parents were dead, meaning she had never really — nor would she ever — get to know either one of them.

"Francesca, are you home yet?" Jenny called from the kitchen.

"Ah, yeah, hang on. I'll be down in a sec," she hollered, before shutting down her laptop, and hurrying down the stairs. "Hey, how was school?"

"Boring, as always."

"Cool," Francesca said, not really listening to Jenny, and giving her the thumbs up. "Anyway, I'm heading over to the store; gonna pick up a few things. Wanna come along?"

"Sure, what're you getting?"

"Oh, I need a new toothbrush, among other things," she mumbled. "And hey," she turned and smiled at Jenny. "You know what, you should get one too — we could get matching ones."

"Yeah, awesome!" She grinned.

"And you know what else?" Francesca continued. "Let's get lots of candy, too."

"Yeah, and then we'll really break in our new toothbrushes good tonight."

"It's a plan, Jenny-man." Francesca held her hand out toward her sister. Jenny slapped it five.

Chapter Eight

Jenny hopped up into her sister's bed, nudging Francesca's shoulder. "Wake up, wake up, wake up," she sang.

Francesca rolled a smidgen in the direction of her sister, and groaned. "Go away, munchkin. I'm sleeping."

"Happy 19th Birthday, old lady," Jenny giggled. "I've got a cupcake here for you — and don't forget to make a wish when you blow out the candle."

Francesca gave a huge yawn and heaved herself into an upright position, her eyelids heavy like the dumbbells at the gym where she worked part-time. Prying her eyes open slightly, all she could see was the hot pink frosted cupcake sitting on the little plate Jenny was holding out right in front of her face. Then she eyed the thin white candle. She didn't need any time to think — her wish had been the same for as long as she could re-member. She drew her breath, aimed, and killed that candle with one short and sweet blow.

"Yeay!" Jenny clapped her hands together. "And also," she turned and grabbed another plate from on top of the nightstand. "I made one for me, too." She blew out her own candle, and started digging in.

Francesca watched her sister and smirked. "I thought only birthday girls got candles? Your birthday isn't until May."

Jenny looked up, frosting all around her mouth. "Yeah, well, I figure a girl's gotta sneak an extra wish whenever she can, so, you know..."

Francesca laughed, and wondered when Jenny had all of a sudden be-come so grown up. "Alright, fair enough." She sampled the frosting with her index finger. "So, what was your wish?"

She frowned at her sister. "For me to come live with you, of course. Was that not obvious?" she mumbled through a mouthful of chocolate cake. She wiped her mouth with the back of her hand. "And we're gonna do it, too, I just know we are. We're like the three musketeers."

"Three? Who's the third one?"

"Adrian, of course."

"Adrian?" Francesca laughed. "J-love, I think he'd prefer to be left out of this mess from now on. I don't want to bother him anymore after he's been nice enough to help me do all this research."

"I think you're wrong. I think he likes you." Jenny winked.

Francesca instantly felt her body temperature rise a tiny bit. "Likes me?" She laughed eerily. "Nah, you're wrong — we're just friends."

"We'll see."

Francesca rolled her eyes. "Whatever." But it was too late; annoying thoughts had already started creeping into her mind. Was Jenny just imagining things? Or did Adrian maybe like her in that way... at least a little bit? Why else would he bother spending so much time helping them?

She shook her head vigorously. This was dangerous territory, and she immediately needed to change the subject up for discussion inside her head.

She lifted the duvet off her legs, and got to her feet. "Anyway, I've gotta start getting ready. I'm meeting my new landlord before class to sign the contract for my apartment."

Jenny licked some frosting off her fingers. "*Our* apartment."

Francesca thought about the DNA test. The results were due to return from the lab any day now. "Right — our apartment."

*

"Happy Birthday, lovely lady!" Francesca's three best friends chorused as they greeted her in front of their university building; all three girls handing her a single yellow rose.

"Aww, thanks my lovelies." She smiled, and joined them in a group hug.

"My God, I can't believe you have your own apartment now," Margaret squealed, revealing her super white teeth that were surprisingly small considering she was the tallest girl Francesca knew.

"I know." Francesca pulled the keys out of her brown leather bag and dangled them in the air. "Check it out. This bundle right here is officially my most precious possession."

"Ah, sweet," Tina said, grabbing the keys and holding them up. "Now all you need is an awesome keychain." Tina's brown hair that was so long it reached down to her bellybutton, had been ruffled by the wind, but was now quickly settling back down — the strands as straight as the ruler-drawn line she put under her results of the mathematical calculations she was always the first one in their class to solve.

"Dayum, you know what this means, dontcha?" Emily grinned, her green eyes gleaming behind her oversized, square, black signature glasses. The glasses were without strength, she only wore them to make her-self look more sophisticated "It means," she continued, "that you'll be throwing lots of parties in our near future — starting with this weekend for a combined birthday and housewarming party." She snapped her fingers triumphantly. Emily was infamous for all the parties she liked to attend, and the many guys that were constantly swooning around her. The last of them in all like-lihood had something to do with her free-flowing red hair, and the fact that her body was shaped to so closely resemble an hourglass that Francesca sometimes wondered whether one of Emily's ancestors had actually been the model way back when the hourglass had been constructed. Francesca had then started suspecting that maybe the shape of one of her own ances-tor's torso had at some point been the inspiration for the chopping board.

"You got it." Francesca nodded, her eyes widening. "I'm in desperate need of a break from all the troubles of life."

"What troubles?" Margaret tried to catch her evasive glance. "Seems to me you should be in a pretty great place right now."

Francesca hesitated. As far as her three best friends were concerned, she and Jenny had always had a decent relationship with their father, and there was no reason to let them believe otherwise now. In their company she'd always been able to escape the issues at home, and that was the way she wanted things to remain. "Uh — yeah — well — ya know, just a fun break from our classes, and the infinite hours of studying and all." She turned and led the way into the school building. "Anyway," she said, chang-ing the subject, "about this party; let's start planning it already."

"Awesome," Tina pretended to kiss the keys before handing them back to Francesca. "So, who's invited?"

"Well, the apartment isn't exactly huge, so let's just start with our group of close friends, and then see how we go from there."

"Great, let's send out a Facebook invite during our lunch break." Emily jotted down a digital reminder on her Smartphone.

*

Francesca felt her cell phone vibrate in her jeans pocket.

She reached into her pocket and pulled the phone out, making sure to hide it from their professor in her lap underneath her desk. Discreetly, she pushed her chair back just enough so she could peek down at the screen of her phone.

It was a text message from Adrian.

Her heart pounded so hard she was afraid her friends sitting next to her would hear it. With trembling fingers she opened it.

It just arrived in the mail.

She texted him back: *OK, meet me at our place at 3 o'clock.*

*

Like they had agreed, Francesca went straight from class to their usual, secluded meeting place; a dead-end located three streets over, and around the corner from their houses.

She didn't want to take any chances, and had therefore asked Adrian if he'd be willing to let her put his name and address on the forms for the return of the DNA test.

And because Adrian was such a nice guy, he'd agreed to her request.

While waiting for him, she busied herself with tracing the edge of the cul-de-sac sidewalk with her feet, putting one foot directly in front of the other all the way around the dead-end.

A minute later, Adrian appeared from around the corner. "Hey." He nodded once.

"Hey," she nodded back.

"So, um... Happy Birthday there, old neighbor." He hesitated for a second, and then moved in closer to give her a hug. But for some reason he seemed nervous, and came at her with way too much force, almost knocking her over.

Her face was squished up against his shoulder, and all she could see was his blue and green plaid shirt, while a whiff of his cologne pleasantly filled her nose. She tilted her head back a bit, freeing up her mouth so she'd be able to answer him. "Yeah, thanks."

He let go of her and took a step back. "So... unfortunately I haven't bought you a present or anything... but, um... I was thinking we could always go out for a bite tonight, if you want? It'll be my treat."

"Oh, Adrian... that would've been nice... but I really couldn't let you do that — you've already done way too much. Besides, I kinda have dinner plans with Jenny and the girls tonight, so..."

"Of course, yeah." He shrugged. "Some other time, maybe."

"Yeah... maybe some other time." She smiled awkwardly, and looked down at the ground. "Although," she changed the subject and pointed at his hand. "I do believe you actually did bring me a present of sorts."

"Right." He handed her the package. "Happy birthday — hopefully."

The results were delivered anonymously, as promised; in a white envelope with no telltale name, address or logo on the outside.

She took a deep breath, and started cracking her knuckles, slowly; one finger at a time. When she had finished, she just stood there, staring at the envelope in her hand.

"You know," Adrian said. "That envelope won't open itself."

She sighed. "I don't know if I can do it — I don't think I can open it."

"Well, then that will have been a complete waste of money," he teased, and ruffled her hair in a quick, circular motion, making it look like a tornado had passed through on the top of her head.

Francesca gave him a stern look.

He smiled. "Sorry," he said, not looking very sorry, and patted the top of her head which only reached up to the middle of his chest.

She rolled her eyes at him, and flattened her hair back down.

Adrian lost his grin, but a touch of amusement remained in the corners of his mouth.

She pinched her eyes shut, and drew a deep breath. "Alright, here goes." She pulled the documents out, and opened one eye a sliver.

There were the results, right in front of her — black on white.

Her whole body felt like it was instantly paralyzed, and then nausea started to roll through her. She just stood there for a good 30 seconds. So that was it, then. Now she knew the results.

"And...?" Adrian urged her. "What does it say?"

"It says," she gulped, digesting the news — both the good and the bad. "He's her dad, of course. I knew he would be — she's inherited his square face as well as his stubbornness."

He sighed, and put his hand on her back. "Alright. So... now what?"

Her eyes moistened, and she blinked repeatedly. Then she turned toward him. "I don't know."

Chapter Nine

Francesca put her finishing touches on the place: a happy birthday banner in the one corner next to the window, the 12 plastic folding chairs around the folding table — all of which she'd borrowed from Margaret's parents. And, of course — walking the five steps it took her to reach the kitchen counter in her tiny combined kitchen and living room area — she pulled the copious amounts of alcohol she'd bought out of their bags and completely filled her half-size refrigerator.

Apart from the appliances that came with the apartment, the only furniture she currently had in there was a bed. But for now, it didn't matter. It was *her* home — her very own, very first home.

"Ring; ring; ring." Her phone sounded, its vibrating causing it to wriggle slightly along the surface of the oak kitchen counter where it lay.

She reached over and picked it up.

It was Adrian.

"Adrian, hey. What's up?"

"Hey, just wanted to see how you were doing? I hadn't heard from you since the other day with the DNA test results and all."

"Yeah, I've been kinda busy moving ...and also, trying to come up with a brilliant solution to this mess — which, unfortunately, I haven't succeeded with just yet..." she sighed. "But, I'm throwing a party tonight to celebrate my birthday, and also to drown my sorrows, if you wanna come over for that?"

"Yeah, sure. Sounds good."

"Great. People are coming over at around eight-ish."

"That works."

"OK, cool. See ya then."

*

"No more alcohol for you," Francesca giggled, waving her finger in Adrian's general direction.

"Hah, yeah I'm pretty sure you're the one who's had too much." He took her outstretched finger and turned it around, pointing it toward Francesca instead, while removing the wineglass from her other hand.

"Hey," she protested, and drunkenly grasped at his hand.

"Trust me, you'll thank me tomorrow."

"Mr. Adrian, you're no fun," she pouted, crossing her arms in front of her chest. Then she stuck her tongue out at him, and skipped over toward a group of her friends. "Now, who's ready to hit the town?"

"Absolutely, let's go!" Emily slapped her hand in a high five.

"You only turn 19 once — better do it right." Tina winked.

"Well, let's round up the troops, then." Francesca spun around a few times, making swooping motions with her arms.

"You got it." Margaret started blowing out the candles and clearing away the cans. She was always helpful like that.

Francesca paused for a moment. Her multiple twirls had shaken things up, and out of her control, allowing a soreness to trespass across the indifference barriers she had set up around her heart. She missed being able to channel the majority of her time and energy into ballet — she really did. But more than anything; Francesca really missed her mom. And through her drunken haze she felt the truth that she had buried deep inside her begin to seep out.

Despite having worked so hard these past ten years to convince herself that she didn't ever want to be in a relationship — that she didn't need it — she was now surprised to catch herself thinking that maybe, someday, she could again be a part of a strong, loving family, just like when her mom had still been alive . . .to once again feel complete. Maybe, one day. If she were lucky enough to find the right someone, and if she could manage to trust him in the way that she needed to in order to let go of her own insecurities.
. .

She spun around again. And again. And then she prepared for a proper pirouette.

She made it, kind of; a single, off-balance, drunken pirouette.

Her confidence mounted, and she started preparing again; this time she would go for a double. Through the blur, she felt her heart beating; heard it counting out the rhythm. She closed her eyes and extended her right leg to the side, her big toe at the end of her pointed foot drawing a quarter of a circle on the floor as she directed the foot behind her. Slowly, she lowered her foot down flat onto the floor, bent both knees slightly, and then took off for the double pirouette.

But as she was spinning, something tightened inside of her, and she suddenly realized she was heading toward the floor.

Adrian caught her flailing arms. "Whoa, girlie — you OK?"

Francesca gulped. Laying her head back to look up at his face, she saw a tiny mole right on the edge of his upper lip that she hadn't noticed before. She stared at it, and as she did so it suddenly seemed to be multiplying. She blinked violently a couple of times. "Mhm... yeah, I'm fiiiiine."

Emily had just finished ushering their friends out into the hallway, and called over to Francesca. "Everyone's ready."

"OK, I'm coming." Francesca staggered to her feet, allowing her hand to linger in Adrian's. Then she turned toward him, and lowered her voice. "Um, maybe I should just stay here... I, I don't really feel so good, after all."

"You sure? It's your party and all... But, I mean, I'll definitely stay here with you if you want, though."

She concentrated on breathing, inhaling deeply in order to let the air help counteract her urge to vomit. "Um... yeah... you're right. I'll go get my purse."

*

Francesca slapped her elbows onto the bar. "I'll have a beer, please." She grinned at the bartender.

A handsome brown-hair-blue-eyed guy swooped up on her right hand side. "That's on me," he said, handing the bartender a 100 kroner bill.

"What?" She put her hands on her hips and tilted her head. "But, I don't even know you."

"It's fine," Emily waved her hand casually through the air, and winked at Francesca. "I know him."

"Well in that case; thank youuuuu," she slurred, and curtsied.

"No problem, baby," he said, caressing her cheek.

Francesca waltzed back over toward the table Adrian was holding for them.

Adrian eyed her.

She threw herself into the chair next to him.

"Careful," he said, his voice sober.

She raised both eyebrows and gazed at him. "'Bout what?"

"That guy you were talking to — just be careful."

"I'm always careful," she spat. "I'm always a good girl; I always do as I'm told in order to make everyone else happy. Maybe just this one time I wanna be bad. Maybe I should be allowed to do what I want for once —

damn it, I'm nineteen, I'm a grownup now, and no one but me gets to decide what I should or shouldn't do." Her chest heaved.

He looked her in the eye, and took a deep breath. "You're right. I'm leaving. Enjoy your night."

"Yeah, that's right, just leave whenever you feel like it — that's all everyone around me seems to be doing anyway," she yelled after him, gripping the armrests of her barstool to keep herself from falling over, her knuckles whitening.

Margaret rushed over from the bar. "You OK?"

She took a swig of beer. "I'm fine."

"Hey, birthday girl," her friends shouted from the dance floor. "Come dance with us!"

Francesca slammed her glass down onto the table. "Come on, Margaret; let's have some fun," she said, and started skipping over to join her friends.

Tina knocked her left hip toward Francesca's right hip to the rhythm of the music. "Yeah, shake it!"

"Let's do this!" Francesca pulled out her best salsa moves, walking forwards with an exaggerated sway of her hips; her short, royal blue dress outlining her every move. She put her left foot forward, and bent her knees slightly, before pulling her foot back in for a swivel. Then she started striding backwards.

"So, Emily tells me it's your birthday — Happy Birthday," a male voice whispered into Francesca's right ear.

She spun around.

The handsome guy from the bar was standing right in front of her.

"Oh, hey." She stumbled a couple steps backwards. "Thanks."

"I'm Eric, by the way." He held out his hand.

Her hand reciprocated. "Francesca."

"Wow, what a beautiful name. Not all that common either; don't think I've heard it before."

"Thanks." She giggled slightly. "Yeah, my mom wasn't the most traditional woman, I guess."

"Wasn't?"

"She passed when I was nine."

"Oh, I'm so sorry."

"Well." She shrugged, "there's nothing anyone can do about it now, so..."

"Yeah..." he rubbed his hand across his newly shaven face. "But anyway, I just came over here to let you know that I think you're very beautiful."

She blushed and looked down at the floor. "Gee... thanks."

"Wanna dance?"

"Um, yeah... sure."

As he started moving, his captivating blue eyes lit up — contrasting with his tan face like the aurora borealis playing across the dark winter sky in the northern part of Norway. He placed his hand firmly on her waist.

She felt his fingers caress her body. Francesca's breathing became shallow, and she realized how lightheaded she was becoming. She needed to make sure she didn't drink anymore tonight. Except water; water was good.

He was an amazing dancer, taking charge and leading her confidently through every move, making her feel so desirable.

Francesca was sure she wasn't the first woman he'd ever charmed, nor would she be the last. But she didn't care. He was hot, free and right there — everything she wanted for tonight.

After another 15 minutes or so of dancing he pulled her in closer to his body, his lips inches from hers.

She knew what was about to happen, and had no intention of stopping it.

His lips made contact with hers. So soft, and so moist, like marshmallows.

Her entire body started tingling as though she had filled it with Pop Rocks. She closed her eyes and kept them closed for almost the entire duration of their kiss, only briefly opening them once, noticing a couple of her friends giving her a thumbs-up.

She suddenly felt nauseous, and pulled away. "Uh... I think I need to sit down for a moment."

"Yeah, 'course. I'll get you some water."

"Great, thanks." She sat down in the nearest chair, focusing on breathing in and out as slowly as she possibly could.

"Here," he said, handing her a glass.

"Thanks." She took a couple of sips. "I should probably be leaving soon; I mean it's almost two o'clock and all..."

"Alright... well we could share a cab if you want?"

"Um, OK. Just let me go say bye to my friends first."

"Yeah, sure. I'll be over here stealing some of your water in the meantime."

"Go for it," she said, before turning and making her way through the crowd on the dance floor.

"Bye, my lovelies. Thanks for a great celebration!"

Her friends joined her for a group hug.

"Text me when you get home, OK?" Margaret shouted over the music.

"I will."

*

"Ding dong."

Francesca opened one eye. "Gah... what's that sound?" she mumbled, and lifted her head slightly up off her pillow. "Ahhh..." she groaned, before dropping back down onto the pillow. Her head felt like a well-utilized punching bag. She instinctively rolled over onto her right side to check her phone lying on the floor.

The battery was dead.

Then she rolled onto her back again, and turned her head to the left.

Eric lay on his stomach next to her, his dark brown, almost black, hair visible above her duvet.

"Aw, crap," she uttered, before immediately covering her mouth, hoping she hadn't woken him.

He didn't stir.

She sighed, and rubbed her temples as she started mentally reliving the night before.

"Ding dong."

She slipped out from underneath the duvet and shut the bedroom door gently behind her. Pussyfooting across the living room to the entrance door, she braced herself before looking through the peephole.

It was Adrian and Jenny.

She immediately ducked, as if they were able to see her as well. "Shit."

"Ding dong."

"Alright, alright already," she whispered, and started searching for something to cover up her half-naked body with. She sprinted into the bathroom, and threw her silky black bathrobe with pink flowers on it over her underwear. Stealing a quick look in the mirror, she stuck her tongue out at it for being so honest.

She opened the door a sliver. "Hey, guys. What's up?"

Jenny pushed the door open further and wrapped her arms around her sister. "Francesca, he's gone again. He never came back after leaving that night before you moved out. I've tried calling him, but he won't pick up. And now that you're gone, too..." tears welled up in her dark blue eyes. "I just don't wanna stay in that house all by myself."

"Hey, J-love," she hugged Jenny tightly and kissed the top of her head.

"You can stay here with me tonight, and then we'll figure something out, OK?"

Jenny nodded. "OK."

Adrian stepped inside as well, and closed the door behind him. He buried his hands in his pockets, and just stood there watching the two sisters for a few seconds, looking awkward. "Jenny tried calling you, but your phone was off," he started, "so she came to see me; asking if I knew where you were. She was really worried, so I said I'd bring her over here; show her where your apartment was."

Francesca felt the guilt take over, rendering her unable to look him in the eye. "Thanks, Adrian. That's just... Thanks."

A dull thud came from the bedroom.

Adrian moved in closer. "What was that?"

Francesca froze. "What was what?"

"That noise."

"Oh, that — that was nothing," Francesca raised her voice. "My cell phone must've slipped off the bed and onto the floor, that's all." She interlaced her fingers tightly.

Adrian studied her, narrowing his eyes slightly. "Just like that — all by itself?"

She nodded. "Mhm."

Adrian didn't seem to be buying her feeble explanation. He glanced around the room, before his eyes landed on something down on the floor to his right.

Francesca followed his gaze, straight to Eric's shoes. She blushed and tried to catch Adrian' eye — she didn't want Jenny realizing what was going on.

He turned his back on Francesca and opened the door. "Hey, Jenny, why don't I take you back home so you can pack a bag; give your sister a chance to get ready in the meantime, alright?"

"OK. See ya later." Jenny waved casually before turning and heading out the door.

"See ya," Francesca said, and then mouthed a *Thank you* to Adrian.

His face was drained of all color; his eyes glazed over.

She shut the door, and sank down into a squatting position. She sighed. The look on Adrian's face haunted her... like he was looking at someone he didn't know. He was so disappointed in her... And she was disappointed in herself, too.

She barely knew this guy's name, and they'd... she rubbed her eyes, hoping to erase the pictures that were steadily flashing back in front of her.

She didn't yet know to what degree this would end up affecting her relationship with Adrian. But, at least, she really hoped he wasn't disgusted by her, that he would still want to be her friend, and maybe... Oh, who was she kidding, she didn't know what the hell she was hoping for, or wanted from Adrian. She was so confused... But that didn't matter right now. She didn't have time to obsess over her confusing relationship with him.

One thing she did know for sure, though — she got to her feet and marched into her bedroom — that was enough sleeping in; she was kicking Eric out immediately. Then she'd hurry up and get dressed before heading over to her dad's house to pick up Jenny.

*

Adrian felt like hell. His whole body was burning up. Almost like Francesca — through her actions — had strangely trapped him into something resembling a sauna, before pouring an entire jug of water onto the coal oven; the steam rising rapidly and making everything obscure. He couldn't breathe, and imagined the humidity forcing itself deep into his lungs. The more he tried to gasp for air, the worse he felt.

Although he desperately attempted to block them out, flashes from last night of that sleazy guy making a move on Francesca — *his* Francesca — managed to get past his mental guards. Like deer jumping out on the road in front of you when driving late at night, there was no way to swerve around them, and usually no way of even seeing them coming. Suddenly, they were just there, and it was impossible to escape. All you had to do was keep on driving straight through them, and hope you'd make it out OK.

Then, there were those shoes, just sitting there right by her door. Like they belonged. Like they had been invited in, in a way that his shoes had not. God, how he hated the sight of those shoes. Brown leather loafers, the really expensive kind that only snooty kids with rich parents wore. That was not the right kind of guy for Francesca. His Francesca.

He meandered on down the street for a little while. That was the real problem... Unfortunately, she had never been *his* Francesca. A couple of times over the years they had gotten close to looking like there might be something more between them, but then she'd always end up pulling away from him. *Why*, he didn't know for sure. Maybe he would never know.

Of course, he'd always liked her, but actually, it wasn't until they'd started spending all this time together lately that Adrian truly realized just *how* much he liked her. Her compassion for Jenny; her refusing to give up and admit defeat once she knew exactly what she wanted, had made him see that he definitely wanted to be with her.

In a way, it was like she was a lawyer, up there in a courtroom, arguing her case. A case she wholeheartedly believed in. And in that, she kind of reminded him of some of the lawyers he looked up to and respected, not to mention, the reason for why he himself had wanted to become a lawyer in the first place.

Like him, Francesca was passionate about fighting for those who were treated unfairly — defending those who, for whatever reason, weren't always able to defend themselves. It had made him see how much he really wanted her to be *his* Francesca. So... he thought ...now he knew.

Though, last night she had shown him quite clearly that she really wasn't into him. "Whatever," he muttered, and kicked a small rock so that it skidded along the sidewalk. He could take a hint. Maybe he should just give up and let her go. What was the point anyway? By now she'd basically gotten the help she'd needed from him; there was no reason for them to keep hanging out.

*

Francesca made her way up the stairs to the second floor, and called out, "Hey, J-love, you ready to go?" she continued walking down the hall and into her sister's room.

Jenny sat on her bed, twisting a purple headband in her hands. "But Francesca, I'm a little scared... He said I couldn't live with you — I don't know what he'll do when he comes home and I'm not here," she sighed. "Maybe I shouldn't go... It's OK, I'm sure he'll be back soon.

Francesca watched her sister — afraid when he was away; afraid when he was at home. Jenny had a point... But then again; was she just supposed to leave her here, all by herself? What kind of sister would she be if she did?

She bent down and placed her hand underneath Jenny's chin, gently lifting it up. "Hey, Jellybean," she kissed her forehead. "Grab anything you think you'll need right now, and then we can always come back and do more rounds. From now on you'll be living with me, OK? I'll deal with Dad when he gets back."

Chapter Ten

Phillip zipped his sleeping bag shut and laid it out across the back seats of his run-down, gray Ford station wagon. He rolled it up tightly, before stuffing it into its dark green, cylinder-shaped, polyester drawstring bag.

He opened the trunk, and threw the sleeping bag as well as his toiletry bag into the spare tire compartment.

Just the thought of having to watch Francesca pack up her things last Thursday had been more than he could bear, so he'd taken off. But he'd been sleeping in his car for the past five nights now; his back ached for a proper mattress, and he was running out of clean socks and underwear. And by now, he figured, she'd probably be completely moved out. Besides, it was time to go back and check on Jenny. He had left some money for food in the jar on top of the fridge, but still, it was time. After he finished his shift tonight he would go back to the house.

The small clearing in the woods in which he had parked his car was the perfect hiding place, and had been for years; secluded enough that no one had ever stumbled upon him, yet usually not muddy enough to dirty his car to any great extent.

He pulled out from the clearing, and drove down the narrow dirt path. Upon reaching the end of the path, he sped up as he turned onto the main road. Twenty minutes later he returned to the suburbs of Oslo. Kids on their way to school filled the sidewalks, parents holding hands with the younger ones.

He felt guilt hit him like an arrow. Was he a bad parent? Maybe the girls had been a bit young the first few times he'd left them alone, but Jenny was eleven now, she was able to handle a few days by herself. Besides, it was good for her, she was always so weak and emotional, she needed to toughen up, learn that life was no cakewalk.

It wasn't like he, himself, hadn't been on his own practically since birth. Sure, there were adults at the orphanage, but he had never had any real parent figures to speak of.

He took the E18 straight through the city to the taxi hub, where he parked his own car and switched to his cab.

His first passenger of the shift was scheduled to be picked up outside her house just north of the city center at 8:15.

A voluptuous blond woman in her mid-thirties walked over to his window. "Hi, are you here for Fredriksen?

"Yes," he mumbled, and got out of the car to heave her huge navy-blue suitcase into the trunk. Then he settled back behind the wheel. "Where to?"

"The Airport Express Train platform at Oslo Central Station, please," she enunciated slowly. Then she fiddled with the seatbelt for a good 15 seconds, leading it through the maze of her fluffy silky scarf; the oversized carry-on duffle bag on her lap; as well as her small additional purse. "You know, I just hate flying," she said, her voice high-pitched. "It really makes me nervous being up in the air like that."

Phillip glanced at her in his rearview mirror.

"But it's my younger sister's birthday, and I've never missed any of her birthdays," she continued. "And she just moved to Bergen six months ago, so now I guess a sister's gotta do what a sister's gotta do — even if it means flying, am I right?"

"Hmm," he grunted.

"And I got her the most amazing gift — can you guess what it is? I'm sure you'll never be able to guess, it's just so unique. Do you wanna guess? I'll let you have one go." She resurfaced for air. "Never mind, you'll never get it, I'm just going to tell you: It's a fishbowl." Her smile made it look like the hinges of her mouth were being pushed to their max.

Phillip frowned.

"Well, the thing is," she laughed. "When we were growing up my sister was so jealous of the two little goldfish I had gotten for my birthday, and I'd never let her go into my room by herself to look at them. So now I'm getting her some of her own. Of course, I'll get the actual fish in Bergen," she said, laughing some more. "Isn't that great?"

"The real genius thing would be to just buy the actual bowl over there as well, rather than risk handing over a suitcase full of shards," he muttered, stating the obvious.

"Yeah, well..." she paused to consider the logic of his comment. "I've already bought it, though, so you know..." She waved her hand through the air. "Anyway, how about you — any siblings?"

Phillip preferred complete silence when driving, and through trial and error, he had discovered that direct insult was usually the way to go. But either this lady hadn't realized he had just insulted her stupidity, or else she didn't care.

One way or another, though, he intended to block her voice out — whether literally or just inside his head, and so he turned around to face her while answering her question, and gave it his best shot.

"I was abandoned at an orphanage when I was only a couple weeks old, never knew my parents, and if I have any siblings then I'll never know them either. And before you start asking — growing up in an orphanage sucks; and no, people do not randomly break out into song in order to soothe their sorrows like in *Annie, the Musical*. Although Annie was right about one thing — it's a 'Hard Knock Life'. But if anyone's ever told you the rumor about how 'The Sun Will Come Out Tomorrow', then they're clearly lying," he said coolly, while looking her dead in the eye in order to achieve the maximum effect.

"Oh, I'm... I'm so sorry," she said, and then just sat there for a while, opening and closing her mouth several times.

He could see she'd been spending way too much time studying those precious little fish of hers.

Then she closed her mouth permanently, and instead pretended to study something intently right outside her window.

He smirked, and made a mental note to add another person he'd managed to silence onto his list.

A moment later, while driving along, he suddenly found himself thinking about what she'd said. He sighed. What was so special about birthdays anyway? It had always just been like any other day to him — it would have to, wouldn't it, when clearly he'd never known anyone who'd been excited about his whole coming into existence.

A couple of minutes later they arrived at the Central Station.

Phillip lugged the monstrosity of her suitcase out of the trunk, this time knowing all too well what the bulging round thing in the middle was.

"Well, thank you," she said softly, her face still apologetic. "Here, take an extra 100 kroner."

Ah, yes, he thought; the pity-tip. He would have to remember that; whenever possible, to always pull the sympathy card rather than offending his passengers too gravely — the pity strategy always yielded more money. Besides, he'd already had enough complaints, and his boss had made it quite clear that with the next strike he'd be out. He held his head low, still in character. "Thank you," he said. "Have a safe flight now."

"Thanks," she nodded, and dragged her suitcase behind her across the parking lot and into the ocher yellow train station building.

With no more passengers scheduled for pick-up at the moment, it was the taxi stand for him the next few hours — and the fact that it was a Tuesday morning meant time would be passing by slowly. But then again, that also meant it would feel like he had more time before he'd have to go home and find Francesca's room completely empty.

She was gone now, for good, and he didn't suppose there was any way he could persuade her to come back. He took a deep breath. "Damn fishbowl lady," he spat, "I guess I'll have to go find Francesca a belated birthday present now." But on the plus side, he realized, at least that would give him a valid reason to go over and see her in her new apartment.

He got back into the car and let his hands play across the steering wheel. He still remembered the very first time he'd gotten behind the wheel; the sense of freedom that had rushed through him was like nothing he'd ever felt before.

The day he got his license was one of the proudest days of his life — he'd worked hard, refused to give up, and finally, he'd achieved it. At the time, he'd gotten his license for the sake of his dear Anna. Now, it had come to mean something completely different — now it meant he would always be able to drive away; he could leave before anyone else left him first; he would forever be in control of the situation.

...Well, mostly in control... Francesca had still been able to move out of his house while he was away. And, unfortunately, there was nothing he could do to stop her. But at least he would be in control of Jenny for the next seven years. She couldn't go anywhere.

Then it suddenly dawned on him. "That's it," he told the empty car. "That's what I'll give Francesca for her birthday — driving lessons with me. She's nineteen now, she's definitely old enough to get her license, and I can be the one to help her get it." That would even mean them getting to spend a little quality time together. Maybe then their relationship would improve, at least a little bit. Maybe he could make her see things from his perspective; maybe allow her to understand why he was the way that he was.

But then he had a conflicting thought... in a way, teaching her how to drive would mean he'd be giving Francesca a means of getting away from him whenever she wanted to, as well — just like he did. He started biting his nails, reconsidering this genius birthday present idea of his. At least, it wasn't as stupid as a fishbowl, he thought.

But... he then realized that Francesca didn't have anything close to the average sum of thirty thousand Norwegian kroner that she'd need to pay in order to go through the whole process of officially getting her license, let alone a car. Yes — he would stick with offering to give her at least a few lessons with him. *That*, he thought, was a great present.

*

Phillip stepped in through his front door and crossed the living room, reaching the kitchen. He checked the jar on top of the fridge to see whether Jenny had run out of money while he'd been gone.

There was still some money left.

Then he looked back down and noticed a yellow sticky note on the fridge with Francesca's new address on it.

He stuck the note in his pocket. "Jenny," he called out. "I'm going over to see your sister. Do you wanna come along for the ride?"

There was complete silence.

"Jenny?"

Still nothing.

He grabbed hold of the banister and stomped up the stairs. Tired from work, as well as not having had the best quality of sleep these past five nights while sleeping in his car, he could feel his patience running danger-ously low.

Her door was closed; the multicolored wooden letters spelling out her name hanging innocently on the outside.

He clutched the handle, ready to burst in.

His flaring nostrils were reflected in the metallic purple color painted on the letter *J* hanging right in front of his face on her door.

He released the handle; inhaled deeply, making sure his nostrils settled back down; before knocking softly. "Jenny, are you in here?"

There was no answer.

He gently pushed the door open.

She wasn't there.

Phillip got back into his car and started heading over toward Frances-ca's apartment. He knew that was where he would find Jenny.

*

Phillip had managed to slip into Francesca's apartment building when an-other resident had entered through the front door, and was now standing right outside the door of her new apartment. He knocked three times.

Francesca opened the door a crack.

Jenny popped her head out from behind her sister, peering at him.

"Hi girls."

"Hey," Francesca said, her face neutral.

"Can I come in?"

She hesitated for a moment, and looked down at Jenny. Then she opened the door further, allowing him to enter.

"So..." he said, stepping over the threshold. "It's a nice place you've got here."

"Yeah, thanks."

His eyes scanned the apartment.

Most of her belongings were still in bags and boxes on the floor.

"It's small, though," he commented. "Do you really have enough room for all your stuff? I mean, if not, you can always come back home, you know."

"I am home — this is my home now."

He stared her down.

She didn't blink.

"So I guess Jenny and I are just never gonna see you anymore, then?"

"Oh, Jenny will see me whenever she wants — she's always welcome to stay over here."

"And what about me?"

"This won't be much of a change — you've never been around a whole lot anyways."

His chest tightened. "The reason I came over here was to tell you what I wanted to give you for your birthday."

"Well, a text or a phone call on the actual day would've been nice."

He clenched his fists. "Don't you dare talk to me like that. Who the hell do you think you are?" he said through gritted teeth.

She looked like she was trying to make him feel bad; like she was trying to make him see how Jenny would be better off living with her. She remained completely calm. "I think I'm your daughter — your daughter; who wanted nothing more on her birthday than a hug and to be wished a *Happy Birthday* from her father."

He looked down, and then over at Jenny.

Jenny was biting her nails and studying a book in her lap, pretending to be unaware of the conversation that was going on.

He took a deep breath, and reminded himself how important it was that he didn't raise his voice. "I'd like to give you driving lessons with me for your birthday — however many you'll need until you're able to drive well."

She crossed her arms and contemplated his offer for a few seconds. "No thanks."

"You ungrateful little piece of..."

"Piece of what?"

He panted, and realized the vein in his forehead must be bulging out more than his overstuffed sleeping bag cover. "You piece of..." he paused. "Shit."Francesca clapped her hands together. "Bravo — father of the year award goes to you. Mom — or any other normal parent for that matter — never would've talked to their child like that."

"You think I wanted your mom to die and leave you guys with me? You think I asked for that, huh? I never wanted you guys in the first place — it was all her. All she did was use me to get pregnant, and the moment she'd become pregnant with Jenny, she left me. Once she had you to love, she didn't need me around anymore. There was no more love left..." his voice burst. He paused for a moment, not really knowing how to recover from his unexpected display of emotion. Then he cleared his throat, and snarled, "She was a horrible person — good riddance is all I can say."

Tears started overflowing Francesca's eyes. She pointed her finger at him. "You take that back. Mom was the most amazing person who ever lived, and you know it."

"I can't take back something that's the honest truth. I may be many things, but I am not a liar."

"You loved her once, I know you did."

"That's not true, I never loved anyone. And you know what? You're just as terrible a person as she was — all you've ever cared about is yourself." He grabbed Jenny by the arm. "Jenny, we're leaving. What kind of a parent would I be if I left you here with your selfish sister, stuck in a tiny apartment with no furniture and lots of bags and crap floating around like she was a bag-lady?"

Jenny's eyes were horrorstruck, pleading with Francesca.

Francesca grabbed her sister's other arm. "Jenny's staying with me."

"No, she's not. In fact," he poked Francesca on the shoulder with his index finger. "I forbid her to stay here ever again."

"And if she does so anyway?"

"Then I'll take you to court for kidnapping my child. Until she's 18, I have custody over her."

"Yes, you do that. And I'll tell them how you left an 11 year old all by herself for five days. And how you've just up and left us both many times through the years. Not to mention the verbal abuse. I think they'll see what I did wasn't so bad."

"Don't you understand? You can't support her — you're still a student, you can barely scrape together enough for rent. Do you know how much raising a child costs? Well, I do. Instead of attacking me, telling me I'm such a bad parent, you should really be thanking me for taking you in, putting a roof over your head and feeding you."

Francesca wiped her tears. "This isn't over."

Phillip grabbed Jenny's bag. He opened the door and shoved her out in front of him.

"I love you, Francesca," Jenny cried.

"Love you, J-love — I'll see you soon, OK." Francesca's voice shattered.

Chapter Eleven

Jenny sat in the back seat of Phillip's car, her face buried in her hands. Her entire body shook as she wept inaudibly.

"Jenny, it's OK;" he said, attempting to comfort her. "We'll have fun living together just the two of us."

She lifted her head for a second, as though she were about to say something, then dropped it back down into her hands.

"Come on, talk to me — what was I supposed to do? I had to be a responsible parent."

Her nose was all gunked up from crying, forcing her to breathe entirely through her mouth. She took a deep breath. "I hate you," she whispered.

He slammed the palms of his hands into the steering wheel. "Damn it."

She jumped, causing her hands to plummet from in front of her face down into her lap.

"I'm sick of not being shown any respect. Now, you will apologize, and you'll stop that crying — you're not a baby anymore, so quit acting like one," he barked, and peered at her in his rearview mirror.

She seemed to be trying her hardest to calm down, but her body continued to pop like she was having a hiccup attack played out in fast motion. "I'm... I'm sorry."

As he watched her, he realized just how frightened he was making his daughter feel, and felt a stab of regret. He'd crossed the line again. He sighed, and counted to 10 in his head. "Jenny, I'm sorry for yelling at you." He reached his hand back and patted her on the arm. "Please don't cry."

She pulled away from him.

"It's OK, we'll have Francesca back home again before you know it."

"She's not coming back."

"I know everything looks real bad right now, but we'll manage to prevail over her — just you wait and see."

"No, she'll win," Jenny started, having found a bit of courage. "She and I will be the winners in the end. As soon as she manages to..." her voice faded away.

He tightened his grip on the steering wheel, and pricked up his ears. "As soon as she manages to do what?"

Jenny fidgeted underneath her seatbelt. "Nothing."

They came up to an intersection with a red light.

Phillip quickly started slowing down, and when he'd reached a complete stop he turned around in his seat to face her. "Jenny, what is your sister up to?"

"Nothing, she's not up to anything — really, she's just down, down with everything." She avoided his gaze.

He turned back to face the windshield and placed his hands on the wheel. Mentally, he started going over their argument in Francesca's apartment, searching for clues. He remembered that she'd said something about what she would use against him in a court of law.

The traffic light turned green.

He hit the gas and accelerated steadily.

They drove in silence for a while, but Phillip kept checking on Jenny in his rearview mirror. He knew it was important that he give her a chance to calm down at her own pace.

Finally, after a few minutes, her breathing rate returned to normal, and her body had let go of most of its tension.

"I'm sorry Jenny," he repeated. "I really am just trying to do the right thing here — you know that, right?"

She nodded so slightly that it could have been mistaken for just a passing glance.

"I'll tell you what; how about we go get some ice cream, doesn't that sound good? I know that place down the corner from us always has pistachio — that's your favorite flavor, isn't it?"

Her nod was a bit more evident this time.

"OK, then that's what we'll do," he said, and turned his head to smile at her. "So does this mean we're friends again, then?"

"Yeah," she whispered.

"Good."

He allowed for even more time to pass, while still continuing to secretly watch her in his mirror.

"So," he started, after a few more minutes. "How's Adrian doing these days? I understand you and your sister have been spending quite a bit of time with him lately."

Jenny seemed surprised at the mention of Adrian, yet relieved to talk about something else. "He's good," she said, her voice considerably lighter.

"He's still studying, right? What is it that he's studying again?"

"Yeah, he's a law student," she said absentmindedly.

He felt like he'd just been pricked by a thorn. His hunch must've been right; she must be trying to find a way to somehow take Jenny away from him legally. Who did she think she was — did she really think she could take him to court; to take his child away from him without him putting up a fight? He wasn't like his own crappy parents — just gladly giving their child away without a second thought. Hah; Francesca didn't stand a chance against him.

He glanced back at Jenny again.

Her face seemed to wear a secretive look; like she knew something he didn't.

His throat tightened. Was he imagining that look on her face, or had Francesca indeed already found a way to beat him?

He accelerated unintentionally, speeding down the highway at a potential-for-losing-his-license speed.

If he let Francesca win; if he let Jenny move in with her — would they ever come visit him? Would they ever want to spend any time with him again?

True, in a way, he did resent the girls because once they were born, Anna had seemed to love them so much more than him.

He knew it was wrong. He knew it made him a terrible father. And even though he'd tried to ignore these feelings, he had never been able to shake them off completely.

But more than that, his biggest fear — and what had always been his biggest fear, for as long as he could remember — was to be completely alone again. To leave this world exactly as he had come into it, when his parents had handed him straight over to the orphanage pretty much the minute he was born.

He couldn't let both his children abandon him as well. After all, he really did love them, even though he knew he wasn't usually very good at showing it.

He looked down at Jenny's pink, flowery duffel bag next to him in the passenger's seat.

Whatever Francesca was playing at, he would stand in her way, and he would find a way to win. Even if it meant losing Francesca for good, at least he would still have Jenny, and having one child was better than being completely alone.

But then again, he knew that as long as he had Jenny, Francesca would never be able to stay away. He would have it his way in the end.

Chapter Twelve

Francesca wanted to talk to him — she needed to talk to him. So she'd called him up that morning, asking if he'd be free to hang out with her for a little while that afternoon.

The tone of his voice on the phone had suggested that he wasn't exactly thrilled about the idea of talking to her at the moment. But, even so, after a few minutes of convincing, he'd agreed to meet her in Frogner Park at two o'clock.

Francesca waited for him by the granite and wrought iron front gate at the park's entrance, pacing back and forth, while fiddling with the coins and lip balm in her pockets. She checked her watch; she was twelve minutes early.

After a couple of minutes had passed, she realized how stupid she must look performing her anxious pitter-patter, so she decided to walk over toward one of the two avenues of trees leading up to the sculpture park.

She stopped and gazed at the statues in the distance, as though she were a first-time tourist. Then she looked down at a small information board on her right hand side that had been stuck into the grass.

It stated, among other things, that the park contained 214 sculptures.

Geez, she thought, *If Gustav Vigeland could create all those 214 sculptures, then surely she would be able to find a victorious way out of this mess, and then — then she would finally be free. But first, she needed some help; and she needed some strength and support. He was the only one who could help her get out of her situation. She knew he'd have an answer — he always did.*

She returned to the main entrance in time to meet him.

Adrian wandered over, hands in his pockets; but his smile that was usually reserved for Francesca was absent.

She waved violently, as though he were three blocks away, despite the fact that he was now almost right in front of her. "Hey," she said.

He barely nodded.

She wanted to give him the customary hug, and started reaching out toward him.

The look on his face, though, was pretty much the same look he'd gotten the moment he'd noticed another guy's shoes in her apartment.

She felt disheartened and decided against the hug, dropping her arms back down by her sides. "So, how are ya?"

He shrugged. "I'm OK."

"OK, that's good..." she paused, and interlaced her fingers tightly, making her fingertips turn pink. "Well... I... I wanted to apologize for what happened the other day — what you saw."

He rubbed the palm of his hand over his barely-there dark blond stubble, and his jaw tightened. "It's really none of my business."

"No, I know... But, um... I didn't plan for it to happen or anything, you know — I was just really upset and all..."

He cleared his throat. "Yeah, whatever."

"And thanks for getting Jenny out of there before she realized."

"Yeah..." he mumbled, nodding impatiently. "So, was that all, or did you have something else you wanted to talk about?" His gaze pierced right through her.

She took a deep breath, then opened her mouth, before shutting it again.

Adrian kept watching her.

"It's... It's Jenny — he won't let her stay with me ever again, and I know she's just so scared living with him." She felt something inside her rupture, and covered her face in an attempt to catch the tears gushing out through the spillway of the dam she'd built.

Adrian looked around uncomfortably.

A group of Japanese tourists close by lowered their cameras and stared at Francesca, no doubt wondering what Adrian had done to make her cry.

He put one arm around her shoulder and pointed toward the closest bench with his other hand. "Come on; let's go sit down over there."

Francesca tottered along in his arms, laying her right cheek on his chest to conceal her sobbing from people passing by.

"Here you go." He sat her down and slid in right next to her, still keeping his arm around her.

Francesca felt his heart beat against her cheek; steady, calm and reassuring, and she suddenly noticed how good he smelled. Although, it wasn't a cologne kind of smell — she doubted he was even wearing any cologne at all — it was just a nice comforting kind of scent. Somehow. She couldn't really explain it.

She sat there for a moment, waiting for him to speak.

He didn't say a word.

Then she realized he was waiting for her to gather herself enough to be ready to share. She let her head continue to lie supported up against his chest, took a deep breath, and started telling him what had happened; "My dad came over last night and basically dragged Jenny out of my apartment."

Adrian continued to listen.

She caught herself thinking how nice it felt to talk to a man who, for once, actually listened — as opposed to just yelling at everything she had to say. She allowed herself to just sit there in silence for a little while, slowly breathing in and out, before she continued; "My dad threatened that if Jenny ever stayed over at my place again, then he'd take me to court for kidnapping her."

He sighed, and rubbed his hand slowly back and forth across her back.

Francesca lifted her head to look at Adrian.

Through her tears, his face appeared slightly blurry.

"Would he technically be able to take me to court for kidnapping Jenny if she stayed at my place again?"

His eyes apologized in advance for what he was about to say. "I mean, he's got the parental responsibility, and — as I've said before — that's essentially the highest card in the deck, so if he were to take you to court it would end up being a very ugly battle, and it's hard to say exactly what the outcome would be. "

She let her face fall into her hands. "Fuck."

"Hey," Adrian said, handing Francesca her brown leather purse from where she'd dropped it onto the bench. "I think your phone is ringing."

"Gah, what now?" She tore the zipper open and looked down at the screen of her Smartphone.

It was Jenny.

She wiped her eyes, as though her sister would somehow be able to see her tears through the phone. Then she cleared her throat, and put on a strong voice. "Hey J-love, how are you?"

"Francesca, I've done something bad I think?"

"What do you mean — are you OK?"

"Yeah, I'm fine, but, uh..." Jenny started sobbing.

"Just breathe, sweetie. It's OK; tell me what's going on."

"At first, I didn't understand what he was fishing for, but then I've been thinking some more about what he said, and now I'm worried I might've accidentally given him the information he needed. I think Dad's on to us — I think he realizes what we're up to."

Suddenly, there was no sun, no sound in the park, and all Francesca could hear was her sister's voice. "What do you mean?"

Jenny recounted their conversation from the previous night.

Francesca's face went white, and the phone slipped out from her hand, crashing into the ground. She knew Jenny was right. The urge to vomit rolled over her and she covered her mouth, breathing slowly through her nose in an attempt to calm herself back down. She then remembered that Jenny was on the other end of the phone she and picked it up off the ground. "Jenny, are you still there?"

"Yeah, I'm here."

"So, I'll figure something out, alright, sweetie?"

"O...OK." Jenny stammered."

"I love you, Jellybean, and I'll see you soon, OK?"

"Love you."

Francesca hung up and slowly turned toward Adrian. "Dad knows. And he also knows you're helping us."

"Damn," Adrian pinched his eyes shut. "Are you sure?"

She sighed, slumped down further on the bench, and whispered; "Yeah."

"Hey," he said, putting his hand on her shoulder. "We'll find a way — I promise."

Her bright blue eyes glazed over. "There is no way — you said so your-self. I give up. I'll just let him win. He always does anyway."

Chapter Thirteen

Adrian tossed the pans and utensils clumsily around in the kitchen of his new apartment. He started straining the spaghetti, and wound up sloshing almost half of the salted, boiling water onto the kitchen counter.

Francesca watched the water trickle from the oak kitchen countertop and down onto the parquet floor. She would've helped him clean up if it weren't for the fact that her body felt as weak as if she'd just lost a major boxing match.

Adrian grabbed a wad of paper towel and quickly mopped up the mess.

Then he returned the steaming pasta to its pot and topped it with sautéed onions and mushrooms, crunchy bacon, fresh cherry tomatoes and a sprinkling of parmesan cheese. He stirred everything roughly together with a big spoon before dividing the dish evenly onto two plates. He brought them over to the coffee table, announcing; "Dinner is served!"

She studied the plate in front of her. Despite having been absolutely sure just a moment ago that she didn't have an appetite, the smell of the crispy bacon seeped into her nostrils and convinced her that maybe... she might be able to eat a little something after all.

He handed her a sheet of paper towel, and a glass of water, all the while watching her out of the corner of his eye.

Francesca looked down, pretending not to notice him observing her.

"It's nothing fancy or anything, but it should fill an empty stomach."

"Thanks Adrian, it looks delicious." She managed a smile.

He smiled back.

Then they began eating in silence.

After a couple of minutes, Francesca looked over at him.

He noticed her gaze, and looked back at her.

She quickly stared right back down at her food.

He grinned, and returned his focus back to his plate as well.

A few seconds later, she let her eyes wander over toward him once more.

Again, he noticed. He looked amused, and wiped his mouth with his paper towel. Then he touched his fingertips to his temples and squinted. "I'm sensing that you'd like to ask me about something...?"

"Why are you so nice to me all the time?" she burst out. "You don't have to be, you know. You've got your own life, and your own problems to worry about — you don't need to spend so much time helping me."

He knew she was right. And he also knew that he'd told himself he wasn't going to spend quite so much time with her anymore, considering that their relationship didn't appear to be going anywhere.

But then again, seeing her crying like that in the park, he couldn't help himself, and it had made him realize that he still wanted more. He still wanted her to be a part of his life, and he wasn't ready to give up just yet, even though he didn't think this was quite the right time to tell her, not now when she was this vulnerable. So instead, he replaced his grin with a stern look, and said; "Yeah, you know, you're absolutely right." He nodded and checked his watch. "And it's getting pretty late, so I think it's time for you to show yourself out now." He pointed toward the door.

Her face went blank.

"I'm kidding — of course." He winked. "Now, eat your dinner and quit your bellyaching."

She stuck her tongue out at him. "Haha, very funny."

"No, but really, I mean we've been friends ever since your parents bought the house next to my parents' house. And, to be honest, I don't even remember how many years ago that was, but what I do know is that we've got quite a few years of friendship right there — of course I care about you. Whatever you need, I'm here," he said casually.

She reached out and flung her arms around him. "Thanks, Adrian. You're the best — you really are."

The corners of his mouth started twitching into a slight smile, and he patted her on the back. "Well, you know... I'm just doing what any decent friend would've done, so..."

She felt her appetite return, and it suddenly dawned on her that she hadn't eaten anything since lunch the day before. She let go of him and picked her fork back up off her plate.

Then she looked over at him again. "Guess what my dad wanted to give me for my birthday?"

"What?"

"Driving lessons with him," she snorted. "Like I'd ever voluntarily spend hours and hours in a car with him." She shoveled a forkful of pasta into her mouth and started devouring.

"Actually... that might not be such a bad idea."

She stopped chewing, and through her mouthful of food, mumbled; "What do you mean?"

"Well, as we've already established, pretty much your only shot at getting custody of Jenny is to prove it's not in her best interest to keep living with him, right."

"Yeah, so..."

"All I'm saying is maybe during these lessons you do your best to push his buttons, and then you happen to catch it on a tape recorder."

Francesca sat up straight. "You're wicked..." she paused for a moment. "and I think I like it." She swallowed the last bit of food in her mouth. "But, of course," she added. "He's bound to be on his best behavior now that he knows and all."

"Yeah, I know, but then again, his personality is what it is, and if you go at it hard enough, I'm sure you'll be able to make him show his true colors in the end."

"Yeah, I guess it's worth a shot..." She took a sip of water. "But how do I keep him from getting too suspicious about me changing my mind all of a sudden?"

"Well, you should probably come up with some kind of plan, or some kind of line to feed him that would sound credible to him."

"OK, like what...?"

Adrian shrugged. "I'm not sure. I mean, you know him way better than I do. Maybe just let it stir in your subconscious for a little while and then you'll probably figure something out pretty soon."

"Yeah, I guess you're right... But then that still leaves me with my biggest problem; what about Jenny? Now, there's definitely no way he'll let us spend any time together."

"Maybe... you might need to consider moving back home..." he mumbled, looking anywhere but at Francesca.

She got to her feet and slapped her hands on her hips. "Oh, hell no — are you out of your mind? That's a step back; a step away from the goal, remember?"

He raised both hands up in the air. "I'm just saying it might make him less suspicious; make him feel like he's got more control over the two of you; like he's won the battle. A keep-your-friends-close-but-your-enemies-closer kind of a strategy. And also, you'll get to be there for Jenny."

"What do you mean by *less suspicious*? If anything, I would've thought me moving back into his house would only make him more suspicious. He knows how badly I wanted to get out of there in the first place."

"Yes, but he also knows how much you and Jenny really want to live together, and by him denying Jenny's ever going over to your apartment again, then he's probably also banking on you realizing that your best bet of hanging out with her for any substantial amount of time is going to be over at his house."

She stared at him, considering what he'd just said. "Well, listen to you — you sound like a lawyer already."

He smirked. "Well, ya know, that is what I do."

"At least you're arguing my side of the case." She sighed, and threw herself back down onto the couch. "But moving back into his house... that's a sucky suggestion."

"It's only a suggestion, it doesn't mean you've gotta choose to go down that road."

"Well... I can't... I don't... I just won't," she huffed. She crossed her arms and shot him a dirty look.

About a minute later, she mumbled. "I can't believe you're right, though."

"Yeah, I'm smart like that sometimes."

She pushed him teasingly. "So smug, you apartment-and-freedom-taker-awayer."

"But," he started, "you know, I've got this new place now, so if you do decide to move back in with your dad, then you're welcome to crash here whenever you want — I mean, if you ever feel like it's getting to be too much over at the crazy-house and all..."

"Thanks, but I'd feel bad making you sleep on the couch in your own apartment." She winked at him.

"Well in that case, you're in luck — there's a second bedroom."

"There is?"

"Yeah, you were so out of it before that I decided to save the grand tour for later. The room is really small, though, and I'm also cramming a desk in there in addition to the one twin bed, but at least it'll give you a break if you ever need it."

"So, I guess you've just got a solution for everything, don't you?"

He grinned. "I guess I do."

She contemplated him for a moment, and noticed how his moss green shirt accentuated his green eyes. Her gaze lingered as she continued to study his face.

"What?"

"Nothing." She immediately looked away and started scrolling through the contacts on her phone, searching for her landlord. She sighed. "Oh, man, do I really have to go through with this?"

"Nope."

She looked up at him.

He smiled understandingly. "You don't have to do anything."

"Jeez..." She banged the palms of her hands lightly against her forehead a couple of times. "Damn — why couldn't I have been an only child?"

"I guess to make life more, er, what's the word... interesting, maybe?" He gathered their plates and brought them over to the sink.

Francesca's finger hesitated, dancing around and over the dial, getting dangerously close but never quite dropping down onto it. She'd waited so long to finally be free of her dad — she couldn't just surrender and walk right back into his trap. She shook her head, then pressed the home button on her phone before quickly placing it back on the coffee table in front of her.

"Alright," she huffed, crossing her arms in front of her chest. "So, I've decided that I won't come to any final conclusions about the apartment situation today. It's just too big of a decision to make this quickly. But, like you said, I'll sleep on it, and then I'm sure I'll have the right answer tomorrow. And if not... then I'll just have to make some kind of decision anyway."

"OK." Adrian nodded from where he stood over by the sink. "I think that sounds like a good plan."

*

But when Francesca woke up the following morning, she still didn't know what to do. And although she spent pretty much every minute of all her classes at the university that day trying to come up with a solution where she would still get to hang out with Jenny a lot, without having to move back in with her dad — she just couldn't seem to find a scenario that left her with her desired outcome.

After her final class of the day, she headed back home to her tiny, one bedroom apartment. She unlocked the door; stepped inside; and dropped down onto one of the folding chairs still there after she'd borrowed them from Margaret's parents for her birthday party.

She started rubbing her temples, begging for an answer — the right answer — to come to her. She glanced around the room, and suddenly remembered how she'd drunkenly started twirling and doing pirouettes at her party, right before they were about to go out.

Imagining how stupid she must've looked, standing there doing off-balance pirouettes in the middle of the floor like that, she started chuckling. And then she remembered how for that last double pirouette she was heading toward the floor, but then Adrian caught her just in time.

But before that, her dancing had loosened things up inside her, helped her see more clearly — the kind of effect that ballet often had on her. Whenever she felt particularly stressed or bogged down, she would use her ballet classes as her thinking time. As a way to escape everything and everyone else around her; a place where she could just be herself — just Francesca.

She sighed, got to her feet, and slung her ballet bag over her shoulder. It was worth a shot. Besides, she thought, she could use a little break.

Francesca found a spot at the barre — her favorite spot — on the longest barre in the studio. The one that ran parallel to the mirror clad wall, on the opposite end of the room. From this spot, she used the mirror to help her see right through herself; getting deep down, into the buried truth of what things were really like.

Just like when she'd seen her very first ballet performance at the age of six, and she had noticed the ballerinas talking with their bodies — now she, too, allowed her body to communicate with her; to say exactly what it wanted to. No words spoken, only the expressive movements to loosen up all of her tension; allowing her true energy to flow freely again.

Her ballet teacher had just finished demonstrating the first exercise of the day; the plié exercise. Then she turned toward the pianist, counting out the tempo in which she wanted him to play.

For the first four counts, Francesca extended her right arm slightly up and out to the side, like a breath of fresh air. Then she brought it back in and carried it upward in front of her torso, holding it in a curved position. Upon reaching bellybutton height, she led her arm back out to the side.

"And plié," the teacher instructed through the music. "Really bend deep down, and then stretch your legs back up again. But keep everything slow and even; make the quality of your movements look like you're standing in a large pot of honey; stretching those muscles to the max. Remember that this is a warm-up exercise, setting your muscles up for the rest of the class."

Francesca turned her head to study her body in the mirror. She let her knees glide out to either side, as far back, and as deep down as they would go without her having to lift her heels off the floor, before she started coming back up.

"So, with the plié," her ballet teacher continued, "you're laying the foundation for almost every other exercise that we do today. Especially when we get to the center, where you're really going to need that soft and con-trolled plié in order to take off properly for all your pirouettes as well as your jumps, big and small."

That was one of the things Francesca liked the most about ballet — the fact that the soft and flexible plié was exactly what enabled you to perform your best and most dynamic turns and leaps.

In her opinion, that was what her dad had never understood. You could-n't just start out harsh and mean and ruthless, and still expect to succeed. The only right way was to be soft, and understanding — only then would you be able to gain control of the situation when it really mattered.

She continued to watch herself in the mirror, and noticed how her deep breaths were helping her let go of her tension.

But then it dawned on Francesca that, in this case, she, herself, was act-ing very stubborn and firm in her unwillingness to give up her apartment — taking the same approach as her father usually did.

"And we'll move right on to the other side," the teacher called out.

"Francesca turned, and placed her right hand on the barre, holding her left arm out to the side. Again, she studied herself in the mirror on the op-posite wall. *So,* she caught herself wondering, *did this mean that she was now turning into her father; using the same ruthless strategy that he usually chose?*

She shuddered at the thought, but continued to perform the rest of the plié exercise, still observing herself in the mirror.

The ballet teacher began demonstrating the next exercise, but Fran-cesca was only half paying attention. All she could think of was: *soft in the beginning, in order to perform strong and dynamic turns and leaps; starting out in a soft and controlled manner always yielded the best results in the end.*

*

After ballet class that evening, Francesca again went over to hang out with Adrian at his apartment.

She plopped down next to him on his black three-seater couch, and they started watching TV.

"So..." Adrian said, glancing discreetly over at her. "Have you made up your mind about the apartment yet?"

Francesca pressed the home button on her phone, and the wallpaper on the screen showed Jenny and Francesca sitting side by side at the beach, linking elbows and eating fudgesicles.

She felt the guilt well up inside her, rising until it reached her throat. She'd given Jenny her word that she would get her out of there; to take her with her when she left — and a promise was a promise. She couldn't postpone her decision any longer. "Yeah." She nodded. "I think I probably have." She would have to be soft and accommodating to begin with; using her calm and controlled actions to set her up for what was yet to come. Soft and flexible in the beginning, in order to accumulate the momentum she needed, allowing her to finish up strong.

She pushed herself up out of Adrian's comfy black couch, took a deep breath, and found the strength to dial her landlord's number.

As she waited for him to pick up, she paced Adrian's combined kitchen and living room floor at an alarming speed.

"Hello, this is Christian Monrad speaking."

"Hi, Mr. Monrad; this is Francesca Hansen. I'm calling to inform you that, unfortunately, I won't be able to keep renting your apartment after all," she blurted out quickly before she was able to change her mind.

"But, you've only had it for just over a week." His voice was dark and gravelly.

"Yes, I know." Francesca was mentally kicking herself. "But something's come up. Some family stuff."

He grunted. "Well, you're in luck — I just had someone call me up a few hours ago, asking if the apartment was still available. If you can be out by the weekend I'll return your deposit in full."

"Thank you, Mr. Monrad."

"But this means you have to be absolutely sure — there's no going back after I let that other young lady know she can have the apartment after all. Do you understand?"

Francesca sighed inaudibly, and seriously considered telling him it was just an April fool's joke played out five months late.

He cleared his throat. "So, what's it going to be?"

She drifted over toward the hallway and noticed a door ajar. She pushed the door open and poked her head into the room.

It was the spare bedroom, with a narrow bed pushed up against the opposite wall with a window on it, the bed taking up almost half the floor space.

The sight of the bed suddenly made her feel stronger. "Yes, Mr. Monrad, I understand. I'll be out by the weekend." She hung up and wandered back over to the living room, tossing first her phone and then herself onto the couch. "Well, I did it," she announced, and started biting her nails.

"Hey," Adrian put his hand on her shoulder. "I think you made the right decision."

She looked up at him. "Yeah, I hope so." She sighed. "I swear, if I ever get out of this messed up situation, then... I'll get a micro-pig or something."

"A what?"

"You know, one of those tiny pet pigs that you can have inside — like a dog, kinda."

He burst out laughing. "Alright, I did not see that coming. But hey — whatever floats your boat."

She managed a weak smile. "Yeah, see, the only way I'll be able to get one of those pigs is if I have my own place again. So then this will be an extra bit of motivation, in addition to Jenny, of course — saving Jenny will entitle me to my own apartment *and* all the pigs I'll ever want. Rescue Jenny; build a home — and the micro-pigs will come."

"You're nuts," he laughed, "...and most likely just a little bit delirious." He patted the top of her head.

Chapter Fourteen

Francesca was back, marching the creaky pinewood floorboards in her old bedroom. She looked over at Jenny sitting on Francesca's bed. "OK, so the name of the game is to throw Dad off the trace of what we're up to — no matter what — you got it?"

"Got it." Jenny's eyes followed Francesca back and forth as though she were watching the ball at a tennis match.

Francesca stopped abruptly and held her hand out. "Alright, Jellybean; we can do this."

Jenny looked nervous, but hi-fived her sister nonetheless. "OK."

"Good. Now, let's go downstairs and get dinner ready. I've prepared a little act for when he gets home, and I swear it'll change his mind about what he thinks we've been trying to do — he'll think we've surrendered. Remember; he doesn't know that we know he's onto us."

*

Phillip entered through the front door of his house. "Jenny," he called out, his voice sickly sweet. He shut the door behind him. "Are you home?"

Jenny hurried out into the hallway to meet him. "Hi Daddy," she said, and forced something resembling a smile, displaying almost every single one of her teeth.

"Are you hungry? I bought us a couple of frozen pizzas."

"Actually..." Jenny started.

"Hey Dad." Francesca said, emerging from the kitchen. "Actually, dinner's almost ready."

"Francesca?" he smirked, crossing his arms. "What're you doing here?"

"Well..." She paused for effect, and put on a defeated face, just like she'd practiced in the mirror. "You know, you really were right; and I was wrong — I'm just not ready to live by myself yet." She held her hand, concealing a piece of red onion in it, up to her eyes. Her eyes quickly began to water, and she looked back at him. "Is it OK if I come back and live with you guys for a while?"

He studied her for a moment, his face remaining completely neutral. "Of course, you're always welcome here. It'll be just like before — The Three Musketeers."

Francesca put the ventriloquist skills she'd acquired through the years to good use and muttered softly near Jenny's ear. "More like the Three Blind Mice."

"What's that?" Phillip asked.

"Nothing." She pretended to clear her throat. "I just had a tickle in my throat is all. But, how about some dinner?" she asked, while keeping the apologetic look on her face. "Are you hungry?"

Phillip had discarded his previous smirk, and instead replaced it with an intense interrogation carried out through his eyes. "Yeah, sure."

"Alright then, let's eat." She turned her back on him, breaking eye contact, and started heading toward the kitchen.

He followed close behind.

She could feel his stare remain on her, piercing through her back.

"You know..." He came up next to her, and stuck his head out right in front of her face.

Francesca jumped slightly.

Still staring at her, he grabbed the oven mitts from the kitchen counter. "I've been doing some thinking, and I realize I was too hard on you guys the other day."

She didn't trust him for a second, and all she could think of was how to avoid making him even more suspicious. "Really? In what way?" Francesca's voice had gone up an octave, and she exhaled in an attempt to force it back down again, looking anywhere but directly at him.

"Oh, come on now, you know what I mean." He pulled the glass dish with baked salmon out of the oven and placed it onto one of the cork trivets on the table.

Francesca insisted on continuing to play naive. "Well, you only did what you felt was best. It's OK."

"True as that may be... it still doesn't make it OK."

Francesca glanced over at Jenny. "Jenny, can you bring the salad over to the table? Oh, and the dressing's in the fridge," she said, and busied herself with draining the water off the potatoes.

"Yeah," Jenny muttered, and snuck past her father, keeping her head down.

Phillip took a seat at the kitchen table.

Jenny pulled out the chair on his right hand side, and moved it slightly further away from him before sitting down as well.

Francesca grabbed the box of napkins from the kitchen counter and handed one to her sister. "Here, Jenny." Then she pulled out another one and held it out in front of Phillip. "Dad, a napkin for you."

He yanked hard at one side of the white tissue paper.

She jumped, but instinctively held onto the other side of the napkin even tighter.

He narrowed his eyes at her. "A napkin's all well and good, but when are you going to admit defeat and hand Jenny over?"

"What?"

"Oh, don't play dumb with me. I know you're trying to find a way to legally take her away from me."

Francesca felt her heart pick up its pace, but she knew she needed to stay calm. "I don't understand..."

"OK," he snickered, realizing she wasn't giving up quite so easily. "Well, then let me paint you a picture," he continued. "You see this napkin right here; let's say it's your sister. We can both hold onto it as hard as we want, and — let's face it — neither one of us is ever going to let go without a fight. So, sooner or later the paper is going to tear." He peered over at Jenny. "Is that what you want?"

Francesca glanced at her sister as well.

Jenny gasped. "Stop it — please stop fighting over me."

Phillip ignored Jenny. "You see, this is no good for any of us."

Francesca felt her jaw tighten, and she hissed. "What's good for Jenny — what's good for all of us — is for Jenny to come live with me."

"Live with you where? You both live with me again now, remember?"

Francesca let go of the napkin.

"Listen, I'm a reasonable man."

Francesca snorted.

He held his hand up to silence her. "Let me finish, please." He lowered his hand back down. "I'll let Jenny move in with you."

"What?" Francesca and Jenny blurted simultaneously.

"As I've been trying to tell you; I'm not as bad as the two of you may think."

Francesca was beginning to feel queasy, and started rubbing her stomach gently. "OK... So, what's the catch?"

"I'll allow Jenny to move out... that is, as long as you fulfill my requirements."

She held her breath. She didn't like where this was going. "And these requirements are...?" she urged him to continue.

"So, you wanna play parent for your sister? You think it's so easy, huh? Well, if you can prove to me that you're able to make enough money to fully support both of you, as well as find a suitable apartment with two bedrooms, then Jenny's free to choose who she'd like to live with."

"Aha, first of all, she's gonna wanna live with me. Second of all—"

"Don't be so sure." His smirk had magically reappeared.

She shook her head. "Whatever. And, as I was saying; second of all: mission accepted — all I'll do is drop out from the university and start working full time. So, are we done here?" She held her hand out for him to shake.

"You think nowadays you don't need an education in order to get you anywhere at all?" His entire body shook as he laughed. "Boy, did I ever raise a stupid child."

She retracted her hand as quickly as though she'd accidentally laid it on a hotplate, and felt her hatred for him grow even stronger. "Why not? It worked for you," she spat.

"If by *worked for me* you mean working twelve-hour shifts at any hour of the day or night, driving all kinds of ungrateful people around for minimum wage — then yeah, absolutely, I really made it big time. And, as opposed to the two of you, I was never lucky enough to have any parents around to offer me good advice." He divided a fresh batch of dirty looks evenly between the two of them.

Francesca rolled her eyes. "Yes, yes, let's skip the guilt game and get to the point, shall we? We all know you grew up in an orphanage and that it sucked, but that's rather irrelevant right now, don't you think?"

He narrowed his eyes at her, and hissed, "The point, rude child, is that you will continue studying until you've completed your Bachelor's degree—"

"Done."

"And just so we're completely clear here, there won't be any postponing of your studies in any way — you still need to graduate in just under three years from now. ...and, you'll still need to achieve good grades — let's define this more specifically by saying you need to maintain a B-average minimum."

"And how exactly do you expect me to accomplish all this whilst working full time?"

"Well, that's for you to figure out now, isn't it?" He gave her the thumbs up. "Oh, and I suggest you get on that sooner rather than later, as I'm only giving you until the end of this year to get the job as well as the apartment sorted out."

Panic started to flow through her like a leaky faucet. "The end of this year — are you out of your mind? We're already in the second week of October."

"That's my offer — take it or leave it." This time Phillip was the one holding his hand out.

Jenny grabbed hold of her sister's hands and pushed them away from their dad's hand. "Francesca, I don't think this is a good idea."

"Hush, sweetie, the grown-ups are talking."

"Sure, why should I have a say in this — it's only my future living conditions we're talking about here." Jenny raised her voice.

Francesca ignored her sister, and slipped her hands out from within Jenny's grasp. She stared Phillip dead in the eye. "OK, and if I fail?"

"Then Jenny continues to live with me until she's 18. No more questions asked; no more involving your little lawyer buddy in family matters that don't concern him — you give me your word that that will be the end of you attempting to take her away from me."

"OK, so say I do succeed in finding a suitable job and an apartment before the end of the year; then that means she gets to stay with me until she's 18, right?"

"Well, here's the thing — you still need to get that university degree completed by June in about two and a half years from now; while maintaining the B-average minimum grades; as well as a steady income. If not, she comes straight back to live with me, and then there will be no second chances. There are still seven good years left in which I'm her legal guardian. Because, you see, I'm not giving you any legal rights, and if you, at any time, are unable to meet my requirements, then you no longer serve as a fit parent. Do you understand?"

"Hmm, why do I feel like I'm making a deal with the devil here?"

"Interesting choice of words there, daughter of mine."

Francesca looked over at Jenny.

Jenny shook her head profusely. "Don't do it, Francesca — don't do it," she pleaded. "You need to talk to Adrian before you make any decisions."

"Ah, yes, that's another thing..." Phillip raised one eyebrow. "Your friend Adrian is going to be sorry if he ever tries to meddle with this matter again."

Francesca got to her feet. "What the hell is that supposed to mean? You better leave him alone."

"Don't test me, Francesca. He has always been way too nosy — this has absolutely nothing to do with the boy next door."

Jenny tugged at her sister's shirt. "Francesca, I'm begging you, don't agree to anything just yet."

Phillip slid his hand across the table closer to Francesca. "Really, though, what other options do you have?"

She thought about it for a moment, and realized he was right — how else would she possibly be able to get Jenny? *Yes,* she thought, *now was the right time to begin standing up to him. Finally standing up to him in a way that she had never dared to do before. But first, she'd need to start out carefully; to keep her cool in a way that her father didn't understand. She would need to adhere to his rules, and then, along the way, she would gain the power and control she needed in order to finish up strong.*

"My grades are already an A-average," she said. "And even when I was dancing every day after school, I still managed to do my homework and keep my good grades. I'll win; just you wait and see — I'm telling you, I can do this." Francesca reached for his hand and shook it confidently. "Done, Mr. Dadvil."

Chapter Fifteen

"So, basically, I'm screwed," Francesca recounted last night's events to Adrian as they wandered down one of Oslo's main shopping streets, *Karl Johan's street.*

He listened, tension mounting around his eyebrows and forehead as he took in what she was saying.

She waited for him to speak; to offer an opinion.

He said nothing.

Francesca felt his silence devour her patience. She looked over at him and pleaded. "So... tell me what you think, already — I'm dying over here."

"To be honest, I think he was worried you might've actually figured out some way to gain custody over Jenny; I think he was testing you to see if you'd come up with a solution. If you had, you never would've agreed to his proposal."

"Well, we don't have any other way."

"Yeah, I know. But I don't think he knew that for sure ...until now. And there's no way he thinks you're going to succeed; he's only waiting for you to fall flat on your face and give up."

"Yeah, well, I won't — I'll show him that I can do this."

"Alright, well I applaud your determination. However, unless you've got an identical twin I don't know about, you won't be able to both attend class as well as show up for work at the same time every single day."

"Ah, yeah, I kinda realized that already... So, ideally I need to find a job that'll allow me to work a few hours in the evenings, as well as during the weekends, yet still earn me the same amount of money as if I were working a full time job."

"Right," Adrian gave her an ironic thumbs up. "Well, sounds like you've got yourself a mission impossible right there."

Francesca sighed.

They continued walking in silence, and reached Oslo Central Station at the bottom of the street. They crossed the highway on the other side of the Central Station; and then the white marble bridge allowing them to step out onto the roof of the Norwegian Opera and Ballet House, rising up from the

Oslo Fjord like an iceberg.

Francesca sat down on the slanting marble roof, close to the edge where it reached right down into the sea. She stretched her legs out in front of her and pointed her feet the best she could in her sneakers. "I wonder what my life would've been like if I'd really pursued ballet," she started. "I wonder if I'd ever be good enough to become a professional."

"Yeah," Adrian sat down next to her. "But it's never too late, you know."

"Hah, when it comes to ballet it's always too late. The competition is ridiculous, and you're never good enough for your age. And, despite the fact that it has brought me more joy and self-confidence than anything else I've ever experienced — dancing ballet on a high level like I used to do, is still the most demanding thing I've ever done."

"Yeah, well, except for what you're attempting at the moment."

She chuckled ruefully. "Yeah, that's true."

"So, do you miss being able to put all your time and energy in it?"

"Sometimes," she said, and started using her finger to trace the spaces between the square marble slabs they were sitting on. "But mostly, I miss what it represented."

"What do you mean?"

"My mom used to take me to the ballet; it was our special thing that we did, just the two of us. I was only six years old the first time, and I loved it so much that I started taking classes the very next week." Francesca's eyes began tearing up. "And after she passed, the only time I could still feel her around me was when I was dancing."

"So... why did you quit?"

"When I was 15 I was all set to audition for *Oslo National Academy of the Arts*, but then my dad and I got into a huge fight the night before. He told me I couldn't go, because dancing for a living wasn't a real job. And especially, how ludicrous it was to waste three years of education on the mere hope of maybe someday being able to make it. So then I told him I knew chances were slim in Norway because we only have the one classical ballet company, but that I'd move abroad to wherever I got a job — and that just really seemed to fire him up even more than anything else." She sighed. "Of course, I was planning to sneak out and go anyway when he left for work, but then he stayed home all three audition days, holding me hostage. And he wouldn't even trust me enough to let me leave the house to go to school instead. To my knowledge, he's never taken a sick day before or after that — he doesn't believe in taking sick days; thinks of it as something only weak people do. But... to crush my only dream he was willing to do whatever it took. And after that it was too late. It took me almost a year before I was even able to take another ballet class again. It was just too painful."

"Wow..." Adrian raised both eyebrows, and looked over at her, softly, apologetically. "Francesca, I'm so sorry."

"Yeah," she started sniffling. "And even to this very day I just cannot understand why he would deny me the one thing that made me the happiest I've ever been, the one thing that defined me more than anything else; the one thing that really gave me my confidence — my true voice. Why would he choose to take something like that away from his own daughter? I mean, what kind of a parent does that?" She paused, attempting to gather herself; breathing slowly, in and out; in and out. "I just cannot understand why he would do something like that," she repeated, shaking her head. "And I've still never forgiven him for it, either."

Francesca sighed jaggedly from her crying, and wiped her eyes with the tips of her fingers. "And... I know it sounds stupid," she said, her cheeks turning light pink. "But in a way I felt like I relived my mom's death those days when I was stuck at home. Kind of like that's when I knew for sure that she was truly gone forever. She always cheered me on when I was dancing; always told me how proud she was of me; calling me her beautiful baby ballerina. Those three audition days were the longest days of my life — I just kept feeling my mom slip out of my life for good, and all I could think was: how would she know where to find me; when would we ever be together again; to see each other again. Even now, after all this time, when I'm dancing, it still doesn't feel quite the same for some reason — I just can't seem to picture my mom's face as clearly anymore. I mean, don't get me wrong, I still love ballet, and it still makes me feel more like my true self than anything else I've ever done. I still use it as my thinking time. My very own time to myself, where nothing else in the world matters. But... it's just... it's just not exactly the same anymore, you know?"

Adrian reached over and wiped away a tear running down her cheek with his index finger. "I never knew this version of the story, I just thought you quit of your own accord."

"Yeah, that's what I told everyone."

"Well... why lie about it?"

She shook her head. "To be honest, I'm not really sure, but I've always covered for him; always made up excuses. And... I think... I think a large part of it is just because... he's always made me think it was my fault. He's always made me believe that everything that was wrong; all the times that he's been so mad... he's just always made me believe that I've done something wrong — something to deserve it." She shrugged. "And I think a lot of kids with verbally abusive parents do feel guilty about it, and ashamed about it. I think that's probably why they don't tell anyone about it — they just feel too ashamed. But..." She sighed. "I'm not a kid anymore. Now I know that it's not my fault; that I don't need to feel guilty or ashamed when he gets mad. I know that I haven't done anything wrong. But Jenny is still too young to fully understand that. That's why I need to get her away from there — that's why I need to have her come live with me instead."

She turned her head and looked him in the eye. "You're the only one who knows what he's really like. I was never able to have friends over at the house growing up. Well, at least not when he was around. Of course, whenever he took off and left us I invited my friends over for sleepovers. I just felt less lonely that way; it made me forget how I was really forced to act as a parent for Jenny most of the time."

He looked down. "I never knew it was that bad."

The wind stirred up around them.

She shivered, and pulled her knees to her chest. "Yeah... well I'm not covering for him anymore. From now on I'm telling the truth."

"You know," he put his arm around her and rubbed her back to keep her warm. "The perfect revenge would be if you were able to succeed in becoming a ballet dancer."

"Yeah, sure..." she started laughing. "Or, you know, I could just gamble on winning the lottery instead." She looked at him and smiled. "Thanks for making me laugh, though."

"Of course, and don't be so pessimistic, you've got at least a one in five million chance of winning the lottery." He grinned.

They sat there laughing for a little while. And as the laughing gradually died down, their eyes on each other grew more intense.

All of a sudden she realized just how close his lips were to hers, and she felt her heart turn somersaults. "Yeah," she whispered, her breath growing heavier. "The odds are definitely on my side."

His grin gradually melted away. He leaned in even closer.

She followed his lead, and closed her eyes.

Their lips met, soft and warm.

She noticed how she felt dizzy, and excited, yet terrified of what this would do to their friendship — all these mixed emotions crashing down on her at the same time.

Adrian was nervous; his arm around her shaking slightly. He broke contact with her lips, and instead touched the very top of his forehead to hers.

"Sorry, I a... I'm not really sure what I was thinking there..."

She smiled. "Nah, it's OK," she whispered. That's all she could say, because, yes, it felt OK — it felt better than OK.

They sat in silence, Adrian still keeping his arm around her, watching the sea lap onto the edge of the Opera House, the water washing away the old; constantly surging; never stopping; never giving up.

Francesca exhaled slowly. It felt so good to just sit there; to enjoy a short worry-free moment with the greatest guy she knew.

Chapter Sixteen

Francesca sat at a table in the university cafeteria, her face buried in her laptop, scrolling through job ads posted on every online marketplace she could think of.

"What're you doing on that computer that's so important?" Emily stuck her head between Francesca and her screen.

Francesca snapped her laptop shut. "Nothing."

Emily immediately retracted her head. "Hey, watch it."

"Sorry."

Emily's green eyes narrowed as she observed her friend. "What exactly is going on? You never bring your laptop to school, but today you've done nothing except stare at that screen constantly all through class. And now you can't even break for lunch?"

"Ah, nothing..." Francesca hesitated. "I'm a... I'm just looking for a new job is all."

"Why? You already have a job." Margaret said, and bit into her ham and cheese sandwich.

"Yeah, but I need a new one — a fulltime job. It a... It turns out I couldn't afford that apartment after all," she lied. "So I just moved back in with my dad."

Tina choked on her water, and started coughing. "Wow, really? Then why did you move out in the first place if it was only for like a week? You must've looked at the financial aspect of it before you moved, right?"

"Yeah, I guess I just miscalculated the figures."

Francesca's three friends exchanged looks.

"What? It's not like everyone's the math genius that you are, Tina." Francesca barked.

"Excuse me," Tina snorted. "You always average an A in math." Francesca sighed, and looked around from one friend to another. "Alright, guys, here's the deal." She gestured for them to gather in closer around the table, lowered her voice and then finally told them the truth for once.

"What the hell! You can't let him get away with that ultimatum!" Emily cried out.

Francesca put her index finger to her lips.

"I'm so sorry," Margaret said, her eyes moistening. "I never knew about him leaving you guys alone like that." Margaret looked at Tina and Emily. "Although, to be honest, a couple of times we have actually talked about how strange it was that he was always away when we were over at the house, but we just figured he was working a late shift or something... But how come you've never told us about this before?"

"Well, it wasn't exactly something I was proud to share."

Tina reached over and touched her hand. "Francesca, this is not your or Jenny's fault — you need to report him to the child welfare authorities for neglect." Francesca shook her head. "Trust me, he's got all the rights. I've been over it again and again — it is what it is. And if I report him then it'll only result in a lengthy process where Jenny will most likely end up being placed with some foster family. This is my only shot."

"But," Emily started, "how are you possibly going to find enough time for it all?"

"I'm not really sure yet," Francesca's eyes teared up, though her voice remained steady. "I mean, it'll be really tough, but somehow I'll just have to make it work."

The other three girls looked at each other, then nodded in agreement. "We'll help you," they chorused.

Francesca looked at her friends. "You will?"

Margaret put her hand on Francesca's back. "Of course we will — we're family."

"Thanks, guys — you're amazing, you really are."

The girls continued eating their lunches, none of them speaking or looking at each other.

"So," after a few minutes Emily broke the silence. "Do you have any idea about what kind of job might work, or...?"

"Well, I've come up with lots of ideas, but none that are very likely to pan out, unfortunately."

"How about just putting in more hours working the reception at the gym?" Tina suggested. "Evenings are the busiest times anyway, right? They might need you to work extra shifts."

"Nope, I've checked, they've already got a long list of people in line for any available shifts. However, they do need more personal trainers, but I'd have to pay just over 40.000 kroner to take the needed course, and I can't be doing that — I need to save as much money as possible. Besides, it could take many months to build up the client base I need in order to earn any real money."

"How about..." Margaret started. "Nah, that wouldn't work."

"Hang on," Francesca said, her face lighting up. "My dad has already of-fered to teach me how to drive — I could become a cab driver, just like him. How awesome would it be if he was actually the one ensuring we get away from him, without him even knowing about it?" She flipped open the top of her laptop and started searching for the requirements.

"Yeah, that'd be perfect," Emily agreed. "And also, the evening and weekend shifts are the ones that pay the most money anyways."

"Alright," Francesca started reading aloud. "So, obviously I need to have my license; I need to have a clean record; to master the Norwegian lan-guage, both spoken and written; and..." her heart sank. "Damn."

Tina leaned in closer to see the computer screen. "What?"

"I need to be at least 20 years old..."

"Really? That sucks..." Margaret said, giving her a quick hug. "But hey, don't fret, we'll figure something else out."

Francesca sighed. "Yeah, I guess. Anyway, class is in 5 minutes; we'd bet-ter pack up our stuff and head over." She got to her feet and started putting her computer and notebook into her computer bag.

On the far right corner of the white, rectangular table lay a single piece of paper with something printed on it.

She picked it up, and turned toward her friends. "Hey, did anyone forget this piece of paper?"

Tina shook her head. "Nope, not me."

"Don't think so." Margaret moved in closer. "What does it say?"

Francesca quickly skimmed through the paper. "Richard Storvik, the founder and CEO of *Storvik Enterprises AS* is giving a talk about how he built his business at seven o'clock tonight, here in auditorium number One."

"Yeah, I actually heard about that," Margaret started. "He's that guy who takes businesses on the verge of bankruptcy and pulls them apart in order to build them back up again, isn't he?"

"Cool, we should definitely go to that," Emily said.

"Well..." Francesca hesitated. "I've got ballet class tonight, so I think I'm going to opt out of this one."

"Francesca," Margaret said, her hazelnut brown eyes wide and doe-like, looking down at Francesca from her beyond-catwalk-model-height. "You never know — something good might actually come of it." She looked at Francesca in the same way that her mom had often done — a look so honest it was even capable of convincing her that water was in fact not, nor had it ever been, wet.

Francesca ached for another ballet class; some much needed tension release. That, she thought, was so much more enjoyable than listening to some old guy give a presentation. ...But then again, she found herself thinking; what if, what if it could actually help her in some way? As of now she was completely clueless about what to do about this whole job situation. And she knew this guy Richard Storvik was extremely successful ...so maybe he'd be able to give her some pointers? She definitely needed all the help she could get right now. "Um... alright. I guess I'm in."

*

Through the front door on the left hand side, Richard Storvik entered the large auditorium seating just over 500 people.

The audience put their hands together.

He strode out front and center, stopping right in front of the first row of listeners, smiling confidently as he waited for the applause to fade out. "Wow, guys, thanks for coming out tonight, this is quite the turnout." He contemplated the crowd for a moment; listening to the silence; holding them in suspense for a few seconds.

"Alright," he continued. "Let's get down to business then, shall we?" He unbuttoned both sleeves of his pale blue shirt, and started rolling them up to his elbows. "Now, I'm sure you're all wondering why I'm rolling my sleeves up; thinking it's unprofessional; not very businesslike — right?"

The crowd chuckled.

"Wrong. This is exactly what business is all about: getting your hands dirty and working hard. And, in fact..." Mr. Storvik opened his belt buckle and ripped the black leather belt out of the belt loops of his pants with one swift movement.

Francesca giggled, and leaned over toward Margaret, whispering. "My God, what is he doing?"

Margaret shook her head, and laughed, "Well, I'm sure if he drops his pants he'll be promptly escorted out of here."

He kicked his shoes off, and threw himself into the caster wheel office chair placed behind the professors' desk. "There, that's much better. Now that we're all comfortable, we can finally begin."

"Haha... actually, I suddenly feel a little uncomfortable," Francesca muttered to the girls.

"So, I'm sure many of you expect me to provide you with a recipe for coming up with a buzzworthy idea, and then show you how to use that idea to build your own business?"

Francesca felt a smidgen of hope.

Richard leaned back in his chair, placed his feet on top of the desk, and folded his hands behind his head. "Nah, I'm not gonna do that."

"So, why exactly are we here again?" she whispered to Emily.

"Well, I agree that his presentation is off to a weird start, but let's just give him a minute to see where he's going with this."

Francesca sighed. She knew she shouldn't have come to this damn presentation. She checked her watch.

It was five minutes past seven, meaning ballet class was due to begin in twenty-five minutes.

"All I'm here to do," Richard continued. "Is simply to make you see that if you really and truly wish to achieve something — anything — in your life, then you can. All you need to do is believe in yourself; be patient; and work harder than you've ever worked at anything in your entire life. Trust me, I know." His lips folded out into a greasy-looking grin.

Francesca peered down at her bag on the floor. She had brought her dance gear just in case, and if she left immediately she could still make it to ballet class on time. She slipped her notebook and pencil case back into her bag.

"Allow me to demonstrate," Mr. Storvik said, bouncing out of his chair. "So, let's see..." His gaze slowly scanned through the masses of students.

"Sorry guys, I'll see you all tomorrow," Francesca whispered to her friends, before stooping down low and sneaking out of her seat.

Mr. Storvik pointed and said; "How about you; what's your name?"

Margaret nudged Francesca's arm gently.

Francesca turned toward her friend, and whispered; "what?"

"Look up, he's talking to you," Margaret muttered.

Francesca felt her face turn a crimson red. She lifted her head slowly, praying that Margaret was mistaken.

Richard Storvik was staring right at her.

She turned her head and looked all around, then back at him. "Who, me?"

"Yes, you." He smiled, and walked over so that he was standing right in front of her. But as he got closer his smile faded and he began studying her, narrowing his eyes, like he was looking for something. Then his mouth fell slightly open, as if in disbelief.

His lingering gaze upon her was starting to make Francesca feel uncomfortable.

"I'm sorry," he said, "but... have we met before?"

"Um... no, I don't think so." She tried to sound polite, though mostly, at this point she was feeling kind of creeped out by him.

He blinked a couple of times; lightly shook his head; and repeated; "So, what's your name?"

"Francesca."

"OK, Francesca, why have you come here tonight — what were you hoping to gain from listening to my presentation?"

Francesca felt everyone's eyes on her. "Eh, well I a... I was just curious."

"Aha." He nodded, "...and that's it?"

"Yes."

"I don't believe you."

Francesca was taken aback. "OK... well, it's the truth."

"I think that if you were just generally curious, then you would've stayed on longer — probably even for the full hour. Instead, you've just packed your things and are about to leave already," he paused to check his watch. "—only seven minutes into my presentation." He stuck his hands in his pockets and rocked back on his heels. "This leads me to believe that you're looking for something specific, and seeing as you haven't gotten the information you were hoping for yet, you've decided you've got better things to do. Do you see my point?"

She gaped. "I..."

"Relax, I'm not trying to make you feel bad about leaving — I'm not perfect, and I realize my methods aren't for everyone — rather, I'm applauding what I believe to be your strong determination, and the good sense to not waste any time on bullshit that you don't agree with."

She stared back at him blankly.

"Listen, I'll tell you what; you let me know exactly what kind of information you wanted to get from my presentation, and then I'll tell you if I can provide you with what you're looking for or not. If I can't, then you're free to leave; but if I can answer your questions, then you stay for the entire presentation. Do we have a deal?" He held out his hand for her to shake.

Francesca immediately flashed back to the deal she'd recently made with her dad, and if that experience had taught her anything it was that entering into another dodgy agreement would be unwise.

"So, what's it going to be?" he urged her.

She quickly looked around at the other students, feeling extremely embarrassed about holding up the entire talk. "I'm sorry, but I'm not really clear on why you're doing this...?"

"Well, I'm always ready for a good challenge. Besides, I have a reputation to live up to, and it doesn't exactly make me look good when my audience walks out after I've barely started my presentation."

She hesitated, then glanced up at the clock hanging on the wall to her right. She'd just missed her bus anyway, and would now be late for ballet class if she still decided to leave. "OK." She shook his hand, and then immediately sat back down.

He contemplated her again. "And so, young lady, what is it that you would like me to help you with?"

"Ah, well... My fa—, I mean, someone I know, kinda bet me that I wouldn't be able to get my own business up and running before the end of this year." She bent the truth.

"Aha, so I was right about you — ambitious, and with not a second to lose. And from your desperation to get a away at such an alarming speed I would wager there's a lot at stake?"

Francesca's eyes turned glossy. "Yes, the thing that matters the most to me in the entire world."

"OK, so registering a sole proprietorship is not the problem — that's a quick and easy task. The issue, of course, is creating any substantial amount of revenue in such a short amount of time."

Francesca looked down at her hands, twisting in her lap. She knew how stupid and naive this whole thing made her sound.

"But obviously — I'm guessing — the revenue part is the whole point of the bet, correct?"

"Yes," she muttered.

"And so, you would like me to tell you if your goal is possible or not?"

"Yes..."

"Well, to be honest, my answer is not going to please you... but I would have to say; what you would like to achieve is probably near impossible. However, tell me this brilliant business idea of yours, and how far along you are, and I'll offer up more detailed feedback based on that."

She felt panic strike her — there was no business idea. For every passing second, she felt more and more stupid, but she also knew she needed to come up with something to tell him. "Um, well, I don't really feel comfortable about revealing my idea in front of such a large number of people."

"Alright, fair enough." He reached into his shirt pocket. "But I still promised I'd answer your question as best I could — and I never break a promise — so here." He handed her his business card. "If you want you can call or e-mail me, and then I'll give you my opinion. However, I must warn you that I'm always completely honest, so be prepared for the fact that, most likely, what I'll have to say isn't what you're going to want to hear."

She took his business card. "OK, thank you very much."

"Now, moving on." He strode off to the other end of the auditorium. "Anyone else have any issues they would like to discuss?"

Francesca exhaled, relieved about her quick save. She looked down at Richard's business card in her hands, and it occurred to her that she would be wise to take advantage of the opportunity he had given her.

Now all she needed to do was to come up with one of the most amazingly genius and fool proof business ideas the world had ever seen — ideally within the next couple of days.

Chapter Seventeen

After Richard Storvik's talk, Francesca had hardly been able to sleep at all last night. Her entire body shook as she travelled down the half flight of stairs leading to the school cafeteria, her hand gripping the railing firmly to keep her from tripping. It was lunch time, but she wasn't hungry; her stomach already felt full from all the butterflies.

Francesca and her three best friends gathered around the nearest table.

"Alright, ladies!" Francesca smacked the palms of her hands onto the white veneer table. "So about this business — are y'all in?" She eyed the other girls.

"Yeah, I mean, if we'd actually be able to make it happen then that'd be awesome," Emily said.

Francesca nodded rapidly. "Oh, don't you worry — we will."

"I hear ya," Margaret added. "But exactly what kind of business do you have in mind?"

"Well... I haven't quite figured that out yet... but we will!" Francesca was faking her confidence to the extreme, and felt the muscles around her mouth and eyes cramp up. She remembered having read somewhere that faking optimism was what leaders spent most of their day doing, that that was what made them good leaders.

"OK, so let's get onto that brainstorming," Tina said.

"Yeah, I mean, any kind of suggestion is highly welcome," Francesca assured them. "The key is to just start spewing out every single idea that comes to mind, and then go from there. And please draw on anything useful you might think of from any of our classes like *Enterprise Development,* as well as *Product Development* and our *Marketing and Consumer Behavior* class."

Silence reigned over the four girls for a couple of minutes.

Francesca gulped down her water like she was attempting to hydrate the Sahara desert.

"So... it needs to be something practical," Margaret started.

"For sure, something lots of people would need," Emily added.

"Exactly... a product or service we'd be able to convince the majority of the population that if they had it, would significantly improve their lives," Francesca said.

"Yet, it needs to be quick and affordable to make — remember, time is of the essence," Tina reminded them.

"OK, guys," Francesca attempted to inject another shot of optimism into the group. "So I know that this sounds tough and all, but I believe in us!" she exclaimed. But then heard herself, and realized it was time to take it down a notch.

"How about sock clips?" Margaret suggested.

Francesca leaned in across the table toward Margaret. "What do you mean?"

"You know, to clip pairs of socks together before putting them in the washing machine so they don't get separated — somehow socks always seem to magically disappear while in the wash."

"Nah." Francesca shook her head. "It's already been done. Good thinking, though — that's the kind of simple, yet highly useful product we need to create."

"Ah, dang, I had a feeling I wasn't completely making that up on my own."

"Well, what about edible paper plates?" Emily asked.

Francesca frowned. "OK, I'm gonna need to you to elaborate..."

"Edible paper plates — saving the environment one mouthful at a time. And also, it's safe for all the little kiddies out there, meaning parents don't have to worry about harmful toxins getting released into the food, or their kids chewing on pieces of cardboard plate — I mean, my one year old nephew puts absolutely everything in his mouth."

"Alright, well, not to kill the creative flow that you've got going on here or anything, but to be honest I think I need to veto the plate suggestion. I can't really see what they would be made out of, and then there's the issue of shelf life. Of course, we could pump the plates full of preservatives to make them have the shelf life of a year, but then again, that kinda defeats the purpose as they wouldn't be very healthy to eat anymore. And they'd probably end up being pricey, so I do believe the ever-so-popular recyclable paper plates would definitely whop our asses in that competition."

"How about accessories for your bike?" Tina suggested

Francesca sat up a bit straighter. "Meaning?"

"It could be different things, like for example some kind of extra support system, that you somehow attach to the handlebars to avoid stuff like grocery bags from getting caught in the front wheel."

"Hmm, that's better." Francesca nodded. "Except that snow will be on the ground pretty soon; and there won't be much demand for bicycle add-ons."

"That's true."

"But the whole paper plate thing gave me an idea." Francesca said. "What about paper squares for used gum — like a block of paper where you tear off a piece at a time, kinda like peeling off a post-it note? We could sell them to places like movie theatres and schools and stuff. That way, when kids throw their gum on the floor, at least they'll be packed in wrappers and therefore easier to clean up, instead of kids sticking them on the bottom of their chairs or other places."

"You know, that's not a bad idea," Margaret agreed.

"Yeah, I mean, that'd be cheap and easy enough to make. However, there's no guarantee people would actually use them just because they're there," Tina added.

"True." Francesca nodded. "But at least if they're there then hopefully some people would use them, and that's better than nothing. Especially if we could sell them cheap enough, then maybe some of our potential clients would be interested."

"Yeah, but we would need to sell a ridiculous amount of them in order to make any real money to speak of," Tina pointed out. "And it might just really be more useful to attach miniature trashcans to the movie theatre seats instead. That way they can actually toss all of their trash right away."

"Yeah, that's a valid point. Damn it — this is so hard."

"Still, though, I think we're on the right track about creating a product we can sell to a company, or some kind of chain," Emily weighed in. "If we can just figure out *what* that product is, we're far more likely to succeed in accumulating revenue quickly with a big chain, where they'll hopefully be buying large quantities at a time, as opposed to the average consumer who'll only be buying maybe one apiece. Not to mention the amount of time it'll take to build the much needed word-of-mouth among consumers."

"You're definitely right about that," Francesca said, pulling a notebook out of her bag. "We'll need a company — or preferably companies — to sign a contract with us for a set amount of our product." She jotted down.

"Well, maybe we're just looking at this all wrong," Margaret jumped in. "Maybe we should be less focused on having to come up with some amazing, new product, and instead start looking into an existing product that hasn't reached Norway yet. Because that would mean we'd already be half-way there, and could start importing it to Norway as soon as we have a buyer."

"Absolutely, that's a good point," Tina agreed.

Francesca looked up from her notebook. "Yeah, it is..." She let her eyes drift across the cafeteria, trying to empty her mind. *Come on, Francesca — think*, she told herself. *What was there a general need for...?* She eyed her surroundings carefully for a minute or two, but nothing great came to mind.

All around them, people seemed to be getting out of their chairs and heading over to various auditoriums.

Francesca checked her watch. "Alright, well, I guess our brainstorming session is over for now. But if any promising ideas come to mind, then let me know!"

The girls gathered their things, and stood up to leave. They shuffled off in the direction of their lecture theatre, passing first the cafeteria and then the little convenience store next to it.

Their friend Albert from class stood at the checkout counter in the convenience store.

"That'll be 76 kroner," the clerk said. "Would you like a bag for that?"

"Yeah, sure."

Then a thought suddenly struck Francesca. She felt her face go warm, and slowly shifted her gaze over to her friends. "Oh my God, you guys — I think I might've just thought of a possible business idea."

"What is it?" Margaret asked.

Francesca looked around to ensure that no one was listening. Then she gestured for them to huddle together, before lowering her voice. "OK, what do you guys think about this idea...?" she started explaining

The girls listened intently.

"You know, that might actually work," Tina nodded eagerly.

"Hell, yeah!" Emily agreed.

"Absolutely. I mean, we'd have to do some research first, but so far I'm loving that idea," Margaret added.

Francesca smiled. "OK, awesome. It may or may not end up working out, but if we don't at least look into it then we'll never know — and obviously, it's better to find out sooner rather than later."

"Yeah, definitely," Tina agreed.

"So, what we need to do is present our idea to Richard Storvik in the best possible, most professional way," Francesca continued. "And I think we'd have a better chance of getting a more useful answer if he'd actually be willing to sit down and meet with us. Now, I know he's a very busy man and all, but I'll do some research on the product and then contact him.

Hopefully he'll agree to meet us."

"Oh my god, this is so exciting." Emily grinned.

"By the way, how did you even think of that product?" Margaret asked. You've never been to the US, have you? Or am I missing something...?"

"Nope, never been. I've seen the product on TV. But I'll see what I can find out and then run everything by you guys before I ask him, how does that sound?" Francesca suggested to her friends.

"Yeah, that's great," Emily nodded.

"And let us know what we can do to help," Margaret added.

"OK, cool." Francesca smiled. Her fingers started tingling and her heartbeat picked up its pace. Could it possibly be that this was the solution to her and Jenny's problem? Could it be that this idea would be the thing to finally set them free? At least for now, she allowed herself to feel hopeful.

*

Richard Storvik sat in his office, his frustration mounting. The business he'd acquired almost a year ago just wasn't paying off. Every little change he'd attempted had yielded him nothing but setback after setback. Absentmindedly, he started doodling in the corner of his notebook.

Should he just give up and admit defeat, he wondered? He tossed the pen down onto the notebook, and started massaging his temples.

That would end up costing him gravely, though... not only the substantial sum of money he'd already invested, but also — and more importantly — his pride. He wasn't a quitter. Definitely not. He never would've become this successful had he been the type who just gave up over any little obstacle.

He still remembered the very first time he'd felt defeated beyond repair, like even life itself wasn't worth continuing on with. But then a very special childhood friend had persuaded him otherwise; made him feel hopeful again.

For the majority of his early years, right up until he'd turned 18, she'd always been there for him, always encouraging him to keep trying, to never give up. And even though she'd had a tough childhood herself, she still always managed to help make other people's lives better. It seemed her biggest joy was to be able to help others; to make them happy.

More than anything else in his life, he had wanted to end up with her, and at the time, he had believed that she had wanted him as well. But then... in the end, he'd lost her. It turned out that she'd really wanted someone else more than him. It was like he had lost the only person in the world that really mattered to him.

Could he have done anything differently, he'd wondered so many times? The thought had tormented him; driving him near insane. Why couldn't he stop thinking about her? What was it about her that made every atom of his being long for her?

He took a deep breath, and leaned back in his office chair, rubbing his tired eyes. Until yesterday, he hadn't thought about her in a very long time, not since the day it became absolutely clear that he'd lost her for- ever. That was the day he promised himself to never think about her ever again. And to make up for his loss, he had vowed to never be defeated again; to never give up again. He had buried himself in work, becoming immensely successful in his career ...though not in love.

But then that girl Francesca who had come to his presentation last night had reminded him so much of his dear Anna, and all his old memories had come rushing back. The resemblance was striking, actually. Something about the eyes, and the small, yet roundish shape of her face. And, of course — at least from his immediate impression of Francesca — their shared de- termination. Even though he didn't know the exact age of this Francesca girl, he estimated that she was close to the same age Anna had been the very last time he'd seen her.

He sank down in his chair a ways, closed his eyes, and took a few deep breaths, and then, shortly after, nodded off to sleep.

About an hour later, he was awakened by the sound of his phone ring- ing. He opened his eyes, feeling groggy, and for a moment confused about where he was. After blinking a few times, his surroundings once again be- came clear.

He located his phone and glanced at the screen.

The call was from a number he didn't know.

"Richard Storvik," he muttered, sleepily.

"Hi, Mr.— Mr. Storvik, I'm so— I'm so glad I caught you," a female voice stuttered on the other end of the line. "This is Francesca Hansen calling."

His entire body started racing, as though he had just gotten onto a rollercoaster. "Francesca... Hansen, did you say?"

"Yes, I spoke to you during the presentation you held at the *Norwegian University of Business and Management* the other night. Not sure whether you remember me or not..." She sounded even more nervous.

"Yeah, sure, I remember. And, I apologize about being a little slow here... but you said your last name is... Hansen, correct?"

"Yes, that's right."

His heart started pounding louder, like it was located inside his head, right up against his eardrums. His Anna had married a Hansen. And not just any Hansen, but Phillip Hansen — the guy responsible for making his childhood at the orphanage a nightmare. *Was it possible... could it be that Francesca was in fact their daughter?* He shook his head, and decided he was still delirious from his little nap. After all, what were the odds? Especially considering the fact that Hansen was one of the most common last names in Norway.

"Uh, I'm sorry, is this a bad time?" Her voice trembled. "I mean, I'm calling to get your professional opinion on my business idea, like you mentioned that I could — but I can always call back later if you're busy?"

"No, that's OK, now is fine."

"OK, great! So, here's the basic idea for my business..." she started explaining so fast her words nearly tripped over each other as they came out of her mouth.

"Aha," he said every once in awhile, but he was barely listening. All he could think of was what a bizarre coincidence this seemed to be.

"And, so..." Francesca continued, "We were hoping that maybe you'd be willing to have a short meeting with me and my friends in order to discuss our idea further?"

He considered her request for a moment. Normally, he didn't make time in his busy schedule to meet with students, and his immediate reaction was to turn her down. But then again... it wasn't like he'd ever run into someone who might be the child of the old love of his life, either. Besides, this new business he was working on was causing him a tremendous amount of stress. He could use a break from it all. "Alright," he said, "I'll at least meet with you guys to hear you out."

"You will?" she burst out, unable to hide her excitement. "Oh, thank you so much!"

"Yeah, so..." He paused, checking his schedule. "I've got an opening tomorrow at two o'clock. Does that work for you? Say at Café Fram right by the *National Theatre?*"

"Oh, absolutely!"

"OK, so I'll see you guys then."

"Yes, see you then. And again, thank you so much for your time."

"You're welcome." He hung up the phone, and jotted the appointment down in his calendar.

What if this girl actually turned out to be Anna's daughter? He chuckled to himself. What an incredibly small world that would be. And if she were, in fact, Anna's daughter, then that also meant that she was Phillip's daughter, and... he took a deep breath. How he had hated Phillip when they all grew up at the orphanage together. Just thinking about him, even after all these years, still made his jaw tighten and his fingers curl.

Back then, Phillip had beaten him not only once, but twice. The first time was when a couple had come to the orphanage, looking to adopt a boy. The rumors were that Phillip and Richard had both been among the favorites, so when it looked like they had decided to not choose Phillip, and Richard was the runner up, Phillip just couldn't stand it. It was absolutely unbearable to him that anyone be happy when he wasn't, for anyone to get more attention than he got.

Once he realized that Richard might be the lucky one to get adopted, he had poured water all over Richard's bed right before the couple came in to see his room, making it look like Richard — at the age of 10 — had wet the bed. Phillip had also smeared lumps of mud on his sheets, making it look like Richard had soiled himself, like some kind of wild animal.

At the time, Richard had no idea who would do such a thing, and his face had turned a deep pink as he stuttered to the couple, as well as the people working at the orphanage, that he couldn't explain where it had come from. It was only after the couple had left that he discovered it had been Phillip sabotaging his last chance at happiness; his last chance of getting a family.

Just even thinking about it; remembering the look on the couple's faces, made his own face burn red hot with rage. He clenched his fists. Such behavior was unforgivable, and the act more selfish than anything else he had experienced in his entire life.

Naturally, Richard did not get any parents that day. Or any other day, for that matter. A week or so later, he overheard that the couple had decided to adopt a child from some other orphanage instead.

Then, there was the second time he'd lost to his old archenemy — and that time Anna had been the one Phillip had taken away from him. Anna, the love of his life.

Richard cracked his knuckles. He'd always sworn that if there were ever another time in his life where he came up against Phillip — then that time he would make it his business to beat him.

Chapter Eighteen

Francesca pinched her eyes shut and pursed her mouth as hard as she could in an attempt to force her face to release its nervous tension, hiding the evidence before Richard showed up. She took a deep breath, and reminded herself that the key to achieving any kind of success in this situation was acting confident.

"OK, so remember," she said, turning toward her three best friends sitting around the café table. "This meeting is all about presenting our idea in such a way that he'll approve of what we're trying to do. He's got many years of experience, and has managed to turn lots of struggling businesses around — if he believes our idea's got a chance of working out, then it probably will. And if we're lucky, he might even give us some much needed pointers. However, if he gives us the thumbs-down, then it's back to the drawing board. Or, more likely, I'll need to find a fulltime job that I won't have time to do — which basically means I'm screwed, and I'll end up losing to my dad."

"Hah," Margaret bit her lower lip. "Yeah, so no pressure or anything."

Richard Storvik entered through the big, glass door.

The four girls rose simultaneously from their brown café chairs.

He nodded to signal that he'd seen them, and walked over to their table.

Francesca extended her right hand, and strove to keep her voice as steady as possible. "Thank you so much for meeting with us, Mr. Storvik."

He gripped her hand firmly and shook it, while studying her face intensely.

The other girls followed with their hands, before they all settled back down around the table.

"Yeah, well I don't usually do this sort of thing," Richard started. "But I must admit I was intrigued by your idea ...and, yeah... Anyway, I wanted to hear you out."

"Thank you." Francesca smiled. "And we know you're very busy, so we won't keep you for long, but we've compiled a little PowerPoint presentation on my computer that we would like to show you." She turned her laptop to face him. "Now, as I mentioned on the phone, and as you can see from these pictures, there are basically two different kinds of grocery bag stands: the big carousel stands for multiple bags; and the freestanding single-bag stands."

"I know," he nodded. "I've seen them in the US."

Francesca took a deep breath and glanced discreetly at the other girls, noticing that they were just as nervous as she was. She had never actually seen the stands in real life like he had, she'd only seen them online and on TV. "So, then obviously you know that the concept is for the cashier to ring up all the items and then — rather than sending each item down the conveyor belt for the customers to bag up themselves, like they're currently doing — the cashier instead places them directly into the bags on these stands, thereby saving the customers a lot of time, and reducing the queues considerably, meaning everyone benefits."

"Yes, like I said, I've seen them before."

"OK, so what we'd really like to know is whether or not you think we'd be able to sell these stands here in Norway?"

"That depends."

"Yes, of course." Francesca nodded and looked around at her friends.

The four girls waited for him to elaborate.

He contemplated them, but remained silent.

Tina cleared her throat. "So, specifically, what are the factors that you would consider the sales dependent on?"

"Well, I do believe it's a perfectly saleable product if you have the right contacts and therefore the right buyers." He laid his hands out in front of him on the café table and folded them. "Therefore, of course, my question for you is: who are your contacts, and who are your buyers?"

Francesca's heart fluttered like a butterfly with ADHD. "Um, well we don't exactly have any buyers just yet... but we're definitely working on it."

"I suspected as much." He sighed. "So, realistically — how exactly do you believe four 19-year olds without any contacts or experience will be able to profit from this idea by the end of the year?"

Francesca screwed her eyes shut and took a deep breath, making herself feel brave. "What I believe is that I have no other choice, and so my only option is to succeed. For me, that kind of attitude usually means that I do end up succeeding."

He smirked. "Oh, is that a fact?"

Francesca fixed her eyes on him. "Yes, that is a fact." She was sick of all these men putting her and her ideas down. Of course, in this particular case she knew he was absolutely right — although she didn't dare show him that.

"And what about the rest of you," he said, gesturing to the other girls. "Are you the silent partners?"

"Well, basically," Margaret spoke up. "It's Francesca's idea. But we're helping her."

"OK, and what kind of help have you been able to provide Francesca with so far?"

"Er... You know, we've done some work with... Or, rather..." Emily attempted, but then frowned, before deciding to shut up.

"Listen girls, I'm not looking to trample on your idea here, I'm just trying to make you be realistic about your options."

"Yes, we know it'll be hard, but we've got a plan." Francesca put forth her most optimistic tone of voice.

Richard leaned back in his chair. "Brilliant — walk me through your plan."

"OK, so we realize we need to get some sort of chain to sign a contract with us — and, really, the bigger the chain, the better — if we want to reach any kind of sales volume that would be worth our while."

"Well," Richard jumped in, "remember also, though, that the larger the chain, the longer time it'll take them to reach a decision on whether or not to buy your product, as it'll necessarily need to go through more managers and more levels of discussion before any decisions can be made."

Francesca instantly felt a couple inches of her optimism get shaved off.

"And have you guys considered issues like customs and transportation fees? We're not part of the EU, you know — and that complicates matters. As well as Incoterms and other important factors related to doing business with an overseas supplier, for example in the US or China — what happens if you get screwed over?"

Francesca racked her brain in an attempt to remember if she'd ever heard about Incoterms before, and if so, what the heck they were. "Of course," she nodded. "We would read up on all that stuff first."

"You'd also need to invest a certain amount of money to cover start-up costs."

"OK, so how large an investment are we talking about?"

"That just depends on a lot of things, like the scale of the deal, etcetera." He shook his head. "I'm sorry, ladies, but my professional opinion is that this just isn't going to work out by the end of the year."

Francesca sighed. "Right."

"That is," he added, smirking discretely. "It isn't going to work out unless you've got a whole lot of help from someone who knows exactly what they're doing, and who they need to be dealing with."

Francesca sat up straight and glanced over at her friends. "OK... so, do you have anyone specific in mind, or are you just speaking in general?"

"Well, actually, you guys are in luck," he started. "Because at the moment I'll be putting one of my current projects on the backburner for a little while, meaning I've just freed up some of my time. And more than that, this will give me the opportunity to find out for sure whether or not..." His voice phased out. "Anyway." He cleared his throat, and turned his gaze back to Francesca. "Obviously, I've got contacts, and ways of putting your idea out there quickly to test the waters to find out whether there'll be any takers."

"OK," Francesca blocked out the surrounding café noise. "So, are you saying what I think you're saying?"

"If you're interested, I could look into helping you out."

"Really?"

"Yes, really."

"Oh, wow, that's so great — I mean, that's just absolutely fantastic! Thank you!"

"You're welcome." He smiled. "Although, the way I see it, if I were to help you guys out, it would basically mean I'd be doing the majority of the work."

Francesca was getting a bad feeling about where this was going. "I mean, I guess you'd need to be doing a fair share at least, but—"

"Let's face it, most of the work you wouldn't have a clue how to go about doing because you're young and inexperienced. I don't mean any disrespect; I'm just telling you the honest truth."

"Yeah, well—" she started.

"So," Richard interrupted her, "that also means that if I'm doing most of the work, then of course I'll also need to be collecting the majority of any future profit."

Francesca suddenly got the sensation she'd taken a wrong turn and stepped right into quicksand. "Right..."

"I trust you understand I can't afford to be taking this risk and wasting my valuable time if I don't know it's going to pay off."

"OK, so how big of a cut are we talking here?"

He crossed his arms. "I'll be needing 75 percent."

"75 percent?" Francesca blurted out. "Are you serious? This is *our* idea we're talking about here."

"Yes, that's true. But it's also my time; my good name and reputation on the line; my knowledge and experience; and, I'm assuming, my money covering start-up costs — so I think 75 percent is more than reasonable."

Francesca looked over at her friends, openly displaying her disbelief over Richard's nerve.

"Listen, I'm not saying you have to agree to do business with me — obviously, it's up to you. And, of course, I won't be stealing your idea and using it on my own — all I'm doing here is presenting you with this opportunity, which, I believe you would be wise to take."

"So then how do I know we'll actually end up making any money by the end of the year?"

"Well, I can't guarantee anything for sure — considering we haven't even looked at any monetary figures yet — but I'd say based on my past 25 years of experience that it'll probably be worth your while." Richard glanced down at his watch, and then rose from his seat. "I have a meeting to attend in half an hour so I've got to go. But you have my card — think about it, discuss my offer among yourself and get back to me, OK?"

Francesca was astounded by what he had just told them, as well as the way he followed his words by wrapping up their meeting in a mere two seconds. Nonetheless, in a zombielike haze, she got to her feet as well and shook his hand. "OK... thanks for your time."

"No problem." He again shook the other girls' hands and started walking away. Then he stopped, turned his head and looked back at the girls, "Oh, and remember; for there to be any chance of us getting this project up and running by the end of the year, I'll be needing that decision as soon as possible."

Francesca nodded. "Yes, we'll let you know by the end of tomorrow."

Chapter Nineteen

Francesca watched as Richard Storvik made his way toward the exit, waiting for the glass door to clang shut behind him. Then she turned back toward her friends, wheezing; "He wants 75 percent of our profit — what the hell?"

"Yeah," Margaret sighed, "we didn't exactly see that scenario coming."

"No, but really, we should have, though," Tina pointed out. "He's just doing what he does for a living — why should he treat four random students any differently?"

Francesca banged her forehead lightly against the brown, wooden table. "How about in order to be nice — doesn't anyone do stuff just to be nice anymore?"

"Not if they know they can make a profit from it instead," Margaret said.

"Fuck," Francesca groaned.

"Yeah, there's no sugarcoating this one," Emily agreed.

"OK, so... what do you wanna do?" Tina asked.

"Alright, let me think for a sec here." Francesca drummed her fingers on the table. "I mean, we've really got *no* way of knowing at this point whether or not the whole thing will actually pay off."

"True," Margaret agreed. "but then again, what we absolutely *do* know for sure, is that if we don't agree to work with him we'll never be able to get anywhere by the end of the year... Or probably even by the end of next year, for that matter."

"Yeah..." Francesca sighed. "Damn — I hate it when my seemingly brilliant plans just fail spectacularly."

The girls sat in silence for a couple of minutes.

"I just wish we had a way of looking at some numbers, you know?" Francesca said. "Just to get a ballpark idea of the profit we'd be looking at here. I know he's super successful and all, but basically, we don't have any insight into to what he's thinking, or what he's capable of achieving for *this* project by the end of the year."

"But Francesca, in any case, he is right about that one thing, you know." Margaret said.

"What thing?"

"We're the silent partners — this whole business is your idea. And seeing as the remaining profit will probably be limited after he takes his cut, at least to begin with, then maybe... Maybe it's better if the rest of us just back out for a while."

Francesca felt a familiar stab of abandonment. "What?"

"Margaret's right," Tina added. "You're the one who really needs the money."

"But... I don't want to do this alone — I need your help."

"Basically, what you need right now is Richard Storvik's help," Tina continued. "And, of course, we'll be there to support you, but this is your deal and you need to be making that money so Jenny can come live with you."

*

Francesca stood outside the entrance door to Adrian's apartment building, hoping he was at home. But in a way, also hoping that we wouldn't be home.

The last time she'd seen him, they'd ended up kissing. Neither one of them had mentioned the kiss after the fact, though, and she wanted to keep it that way.

Of course, she really, really liked Adrian. Over the years she'd attempted to convince herself otherwise many times, but her heart had always called her bluff. And seeing as she didn't believe in relationships, and hadn't for quite a few years now, she knew it was very risky for her to come over to his apartment because something might happen between them again. But... it was just that she really wanted to see him.

Her father had always warned her to not get too attached to anyone, not even family, because all they'd ever do in the end was hurt you and leave you behind.

At first, Francesca hadn't believed him. Or, at least, she hadn't wanted to believe him. She had actually pitied him for thinking that way. But through the years, his words — repeated over and over — had gradually started sinking in, and now she had come to realize that he'd been right all along.

Every member of her family had somehow lost the people who'd meant the most to them; everyone had been abandoned at some point or another. Both sets of her grandparents had deserted her parents — left their own children at orphanages. Then there was her mom, who in the end had chosen to leave her dad. Why Anna had done so, Francesca had never gotten a clear answer to. But she always remembered hearing about how much they'd loved each other in their youth, and how happy they had once been.

That was what scared Francesca the most. How could two people who loved each other so deeply, all through their childhood, all of a sudden just stop loving each other? Weren't you supposed to become physically addicted to being together after all that time? She didn't understand what had happened between them. Maybe she never would. But what she did understand was that she never wanted that to happen to her. She'd seen how bitter it had made her dad.

Even though she and Adrian had always cared for each other so much, for most of their lives, she was terrified that if she gave in to her feelings and started a relationship with him, then one day Adrian might suddenly stop needing her — stop loving her — and then Francesca would end up like her dad ...resentful and too heartbroken to recover. When it came to Adrian, she couldn't afford to take any chances.

She had already experienced being abandoned; even Anna had left her and Jenny in the end, though, not on purpose, of course. And although Francesca didn't believe in curses, she'd gradually become convinced that the people in her family just didn't get happy endings. After all, it hadn't happened to a single family member that she knew of.

For this very reason, Francesca knew she could never leave Jenny. She needed to be different — better — when it came to Jenny. They needed to stick together.

She took a deep breath, attempting to clear her head. *Yes*, it was risky going over to see Adrian in his apartment. But then again, she couldn't bear being in the same house as her dad. Not tonight. She needed to be around someone objective about this whole business idea. Someone who could provide her with some unbiased advice, and Adrian — he was her man for the job.

On the collective doorbell, she punched in his apartment number followed by the button with a picture of a bell on it.

It rang three times. Then his voice sounded over the intercom. "Hello?"

She felt her relief manifest in a smile. "Hey, it's me, Francesca."

"Hey, what's up?"

"So... do you mind if I stay over at your place tonight? I've got a lot on my mind, and I really don't want to be around my dad at the moment."

"Nah, 'course not, come on up." He buzzed her in.

"Thanks." Francesca pulled the door open, and climbed the stairs to the second floor.

Adrian greeted her with an exaggerated grin, his charming dimples making their usual appearance. "So, how are things, kiddo?"

She stepped inside, shutting the door behind her. "Ah, just building a business from scratch in my spare time in order to steal my sister away from my dad — you know, the typical life of a 19-year old."

"Oh yes, I remember that age. Lots of fun."

"Yeah, and I can hardly wait till I'm old like you to see what life has in store for me," she teased.

"Oh, you better start getting excited – there ain't nothin' like the golden age of 22," he said, and ruffled her hair.

"Hey, you're wrecking my do." She stuck her tongue out at him, and patted her hair back down."

"So, I was just about to watch a movie. Do you wish to partake?" He turned and headed back over to his couch.

She followed, and plopped down beside him. "Sure. But first I have a few questions I'd like to ask you."

He grinned. "You always do."

"'Course. You're my legal adviser."

"Alright, shoot."

Francesca started filling him in on the events of the day.

Adrian listened carefully, nodding every so often.

"...so, basically, what I'd like to know is: Could he technically end up screwing me over if I agree to do business with him."

"Technically — yes. But, obviously, a contract between the two of you would have to be drawn up, so I'll need to look into all the details and do some research first in order to see what we'd need to include on your behalf. Of course, he's definitely going to demand an airtight contract, and our job is to make sure that contract doesn't only protect him, but that it also protects you equally."

She nodded, and took notes on her phone.

"And have you made a final decision yet on whether or not to include the girls?"

Francesca sighed. "Yeah, I've been back and forth a few times, and even though doing it by myself will mean a lot more work on my part, I think they're right — I need all the money I can get."

"Although, you know, if Mr. Storvik starts working on this now, and you don't end up making any money until next year, then you can't expect him to suddenly give up the project when he's already invested such a large amount of his time and energy, not to mention money."

"Of course, I realize that."

"And if that turns out to be the case, then you may be making money next year, but you'll have lost Jenny."

She rolled her eyes. "Adrian, don't you think I've considered that fact?"

"All I'm saying is at this point it's basically a roll of the dice in relation to how it'll all pan out time wise."

"Yeah..." Francesca started biting her nails. "But maybe I can just keep looking into other jobs at the same time, you know, as a safety net."

"To be honest, I don't really see how you'll possibly have any time left over to work more hours, considering you still need to get to your classes *and* start working on this business, all at the same time. And I also know you've started taking more ballet classes again."

She flung herself backwards onto the couch pillow. "So, then the whole issue of whether I should be having the girls help me out or not, basically comes down to whether I'd like to be making a larger sum of money, assuming everything works out according to plan; or if I'd prefer to have a bit of extra time left over to figure out a plan B. Of course, I could never ask the girls to help me out for free; they've got their studies and their own lives to worry about."

"Unless..." he started, "unless you stop going to ballet class, just for a little while right now when everything is so ridiculously hectic? That would at least free up a bit of time."

Slowly, she sat up straight, and turned to look at Adrian. "No," she shook her head. "I can't give up ballet. Don't get me wrong, I love Jenny and I'm doing this for her, but in all this madness I need some part of it to be just for me as well — for once in my life I need to be thinking about my own needs, too. Not to mention, it's the one thing that makes me feel connected to my mom. My dad was able to stop me from going to ballet class once, but I won't let anything that has to do with him stop me ever again."

Adrian repositioned himself on the couch, and his hand accidentally landed on top of her fingers. He made no attempt to move his hand away from hers. His eyes gave her a slight smile. "I understand."

Francesca felt his hand warm her cold fingers, and realized her breathing was getting shallower. She forced herself to remain focused, and cleared her throat. "Um, so maybe I need the girls to help me out with at least some of the work after all then, in order to free up a bit of my time."

"Obviously, it's up to you and the girls, but it probably wouldn't be a bad idea. And also, once I start looking into this contract business—"

"So you're definitely gonna help me with that, then?" Francesca interrupted him.

"Well, who else have you got? Just admit it — you're lost without me, kiddo." He winked at her.

She laughed. "Well I must confess you do come in handy at times."

"Anyways, what I'm trying to say is that when it comes to drawing up the contract I'm sure Mr. Storvik will demand that it specifies exactly who he's doing business with — whether that means just you, or the four of you girls together."

"Yeah..." Francesca paused, and gazed out into the living room. "Alright, so I'll talk to the girls first thing tomorrow morning and try to convince them they need to help me. And hopefully they'll still be willing to."

"Sounds good." He reached for the remote control. "So for tonight, how about this movie watching?"

"Yeah, let's do it."

Adrian hit play, and leaned back on his couch.

Francesca bit her lower lip and shot him a sideways glance.

He turned his head toward her. "What?"

"What do mean *what*?

"I caught ya looking at me."

"No, no, I wasn't looking — I have no idea what you're talking about."

He smiled slightly. "OK..." his gaze on her lingered for a couple of seconds before he went back to watching TV.

Then, not long after, they both turned toward each other simultaneously, and this time it wasn't funny anymore. Francesca looked into his moss green eyes, and that's when she knew. She knew it was wrong; that she would end up regretting it. But she also knew there was nothing she could possibly do to stop herself.

They threw themselves at each other. They were so close; closer than they'd ever been before. Kissing like she'd never kissed anyone before. Him touching her in a way she'd never been touched before. All she could think of was how much she wanted him, and how much she'd wanted him for a very long time.

Although she'd known subconsciously that it was inevitable that this would happen at some point, she realized that at the same time she'd been praying, silently, to please make sure that it wouldn't. They could never go back, and Adrian meant way too much to Francesca for her to risk losing him.

They tore each other's clothes off, and Francesca heard one of the seams in her shirt rip. Yet it still felt like it wasn't happening fast enough. She needed him. Right now. She gasped for air, and was suddenly convinced that she wouldn't be able to breathe properly unless her lungs, and the entire front of her body, were right up against his. She pulled him as close to her body as was physically possible. Instantly, she felt better. More normal. More like herself.

Together, as one person, kissing continuously — their lips parting for no more than a millisecond at a time — they stumbled toward his bedroom, launching themselves onto his bed.

*

Francesca lay on her side in Adrian's bed, her back facing him. He had draped his arms around her waist; reaching — longing — for her body.

Fuck, she mouthed, pinching her eyes shut. *What had she done?* Now she'd definitely blown it. *Fuck, fuck, fuck,* she repeated silently to herself. How could anything feel so good, yet so wrong at the same time?

She sighed, desperate to get up and leave. Not wanting to make things worse than they already were. Obviously there was no going back to exactly the way things had been between them; yet her brain was working overtime, attempting to come up with some sort of brilliant plan for how they could still go on as friends — even if that meant a more distant kind of friendship — but nothing came to mind.

...Or maybe, she thought, *maybe they could simply pretend that this had never happened? Yeah*, she took a deep breath; *they could do that, right? Surely, he didn't want things getting weird between them, either.*

She rolled slightly backwards in his direction. "Hey," she tried sounding casual, though she suspected she'd never seemed less carefree in her entire life. "So, um... I just want to get one thing straight. This doesn't change anything between us, and we're still just friends, right?

His arms around her immediately loosened, then slunk away from her body. "What?"

"We're both adults here, so we can get past this lack of judgment and pretend it never happened."

He sighed, and rolled onto his back. "You're kidding, right?"

"Adrian..." she started, but closed her mouth after a couple of seconds. She really didn't know what to say.

"What're you so afraid of — why do you keep pulling away from me? Are you so terrified of being happy for once in your life that you won't even give us a chance? You know how great we are together — and don't even try pretending otherwise, because I know you feel it, too. I've seen it in your eyes, and I felt it from your body just a few minutes ago. I don't want you to think of this as a mistake. I mean... I really want to be with you."

"Please, don't..." she begged, her voice about to break.

"And, to be completely honest..." he continued, "I think that... that I love you."

She felt tears begin to spill out, and was desperate to get away from him and his apartment. Right now. "I've gotta go," she whispered, and scurried into the living room, gathering her clothes from where they lay strewn eve-rywhere and quickly pulling them on. She didn't dare look back; she didn't want him to catch her crying.

"Francesca," he called from his bedroom, "please don't go."

She could hear him getting out of his bed, heading for the living room.

She flung his front door open, bolted down the two flights of stairs, and out onto the street.

The tears had now completely conquered her eyes; leaving her with no choice but to surrender, and though her vision was blurred, she continued racing down the street just in case Adrian decided to follow her.

*

Adrian sighed, and noticed that his face felt raw; like it had just been slapped, at least emotionally. He walked over and shut his entrance door after Francesca had fled his apartment like he was a madman about to hurt her. He would never hurt her. He loved her.

Then he dropped down onto his couch, and used the palms of his hands to gently massage his face.

Why was she so afraid of being happy? He knew she loved him, too. Why couldn't she just admit that to herself?

Adrian had never done anything to suggest that he would ever abandon her. But... he also knew that he wasn't the one who had made Francesca this way. He blamed *Phillip* for her insecurities; the fact that she was so un-willing to trust anyone.

Even though Adrian realized that, in a way, he should've been relieved knowing this wasn't his fault, somehow his conclusion about Phillip only made things worse. The possibility of helping Francesca let go and trust people didn't lie with Adrian. It was up to Phillip and, as of now, Phillip was only making his relationship with Francesca worse.

He sighed and flung himself back onto the couch pillow behind him. It was impossible to say how long it would take Francesca to start trusting people again. After all, her outlook on life had been colored by her dad her entire life, and that was a stain unlikely to come out very easily.

Maybe there was something Adrian could do to help. Maybe there wasn't. He didn't know for sure yet. But what he did know was that he wasn't able to give up quite yet. He still wanted her. Francesca deserved better, and if he could find a way, then he really wanted to take part in helping her realize that.

He would need a little time alone in order to gather himself, as well as come up with a strategy for moving forward. But for now, he still knew that he would recover from her rejection relatively quickly. After all, it hadn't been his fault; it was Phillip's fault.

Chapter Twenty

Phillip studied his face in the bathroom mirror. Today's meeting with his boss was very important, and it was essential that he look sharp.

He washed his face and applied shaving cream. With a slightly shaky hand, he pulled his razor in short, downward strokes all along his square jaw line. As he moved over to his chin, the razor slipped a little in his wet hand, and he accidentally nicked himself. The shaving cream seeped into his cut, causing it to sting terribly. "Ah..." he gasped. "Damn." He splashed cold water on his face to stop the bleeding.

He took a deep breath, and whispered to his reflection in the mirror; "You can do this." He had to remain calm and confident for long enough to ask his boss for a raise — he needed that raise.

Phillip knew he had failed as a father, and when Francesca ended up losing their bet at the end of the year he would have to get it together so he could become a better father for Jenny. A higher salary meant he'd finally be able to work fewer hours and therefore have more time to spend with her.

Maybe, he hoped, working less would also help him relax more, preventing him from losing his temper quite so often. And then, when Francesca saw how good his relationship with Jenny had become, hopefully she'd want to come over and spend some time with them as well, and they'd finally become a happy family.

He put on a clean white shirt, and tucked it into his navy-blue pants. He took one last look in the mirror, running his fingers through his thinning blond hair, before heading out his bedroom door.

He started making his way down the long, narrow hallway.

Halfway down the hall, on his left hand side, the door to Francesca's room was ajar.

He checked his watch.

It was almost nine o'clock.

She should've been in class by now, and she knew their deal about not cutting classes or letting her grades slip. And Phillip knew she'd never leave her door open after she'd left the house — in fact, she always locked it to make sure he didn't go in there.

He knocked gently on her door. "Francesca, are you in there?"

She didn't reply.

"Francesca?" he repeated.

Still nothing.

He pushed her door open, and peered into her room.

Her bed was unmade, but she was not in the room.

Phillip continued down the hall.

There was an odd sound coming from the girls' bathroom.

He put his ear up against the door.

There it was again, that same hurling sound.

He realized Francesca was in there throwing up. "Francesca, are you alright?"

She scrambled around for a moment, then turned the faucet on and gulped down some water. "Yeah, I'm fine."

"You don't sound fine to me."

"Well, I am. Don't worry about me. Just head off to work."

He knew he needed to leave within the next 10 minutes in order to make it to his boss's office on time. He walked toward the end of the hall, and started travelling down the flight of stairs. When he'd reached the kitchen on the first floor, he continued walking until he got to the front door. Then he shouted loud enough for her to hear, "OK, goodbye, see you tonight."

"OK, bye," she yelled back at him.

Phillip opened the front door and, while still remaining in the house, slammed the door shut harder than necessary in order to make sure she heard it and would think that he had left.

Then he slowly snuck back across the floor, taking care to avoid the floorboards that he knew creaked. He travelled back up the stairs, and again listened outside the bathroom door.

Francesca sobbed; gently at first, and then the crying grew louder.

Phillip immediately felt a soreness materialize in his chest. It was stuff like this — things like leaving the girls by themselves when they needed him the most — that was a big part of what made him a bad father.

On the one hand, it was incredibly important that he make it to his meeting; but on the other hand, this would probably be his last chance to comfort, and really be there for Francesca — something he knew he'd never done enough of. Come January she'd probably be leaving for good, even though it meant leaving without Jenny.

In the bathroom, Francesca got to her feet, and flushed the toilet.

Phillip backed away from the door.

She stepped out of the bathroom.

"Hi," Phillip said.

She jumped. "Dad?" She looked away, attempting to hide her puffy, red eyes. "What're you doing here, I thought you'd left?"

He placed the back of his hand on her forehead.

She pulled away from him, but not until after he'd managed to register that she was burning up. "You told me you were fine, but you're not fine — you've got a fever. I'm staying home from work."

"But Dad, you can't—"

"Yes, I can. Now, march back into your room, and I'll go get a cold wash-cloth for your forehead."

She stared at him blankly, her mouth hanging open.

He pointed toward her bedroom. "Get back to bed."

She turned, slowly, and wandered back down the hall.

He watched to make sure she'd closed the door behind her before he hurried back downstairs.

He pulled his cell phone out of his pocket and dialed his boss's number, holding his breath as he waited for him to pick up.

"Hello?"

"Hi, Mr. Selmer, this is Phillip Hansen. I'm so sorry, but er, unfortunately I won't be able to make it to our meeting today."

"Excuse me?"

"You see, I'm sick and—"

"How can you all of a sudden be sick?" Mr. Selmer yelled into the receiver. "You, yourself, called me up yesterday afternoon and practically begged me to meet with you as soon as possible."

"Yes, I know. And I really am sorry, but I must've gotten food poisoning or something," he lied.

"I'm a busy man, and I cancelled another meeting because you claimed it was so important that you talk to me right away — and now you're too sick to even leave the house for an hour? This just adds up to the strikes you've already gotten from customers filing complaints on you. You're treading on thin ice here, Hansen, do you understand me?"

Phillip closed his eyes, realizing he couldn't expect a raise anytime soon. "Yes, sir, I understand." He hung up and slipped the phone back into his pocket.

He sighed, opened the top cabinet above the sink and pulled out the largest bowl they had. Placing the bowl on the countertop for a moment, he let the water run in the sink until it was ice-cold. He filled the bowl and dumped a tray-full of ice cubes into the water. Wrapping a kitchen towel around the base of the bowl, he lifted it from the counter and headed for the stairs.

A phone started ringing, barely audible, like it was muted.

Phillip set the bowl down again, and checked his phone.

The screen was completely blank.

He looked around, and noticed Francesca's bag by the foot of the stairs. He unzipped the bag, grabbed the phone and started to put it into his other pocket to bring up for her. But then he froze. What was that name on the screen? It couldn't be... He looked at the screen again. What were the odds of it actually being him, after all these years? And if by some crazy coincidence it was him, how the hell did he possibly know Francesca? Phillip felt his blood pumping; felt it pounding in his head. With a trembling finger, he answered the call. "Hello?"

"Hi, this is Richard Storvik calling. I'm sorry, I was trying to reach Francesca Hansen, do I have the wrong number?"

Phillip immediately recognized his voice. 20 years had probably passed since they last spoke, but that was definitely him; there was no doubt about it. "No, you've got the right number, alright. This is her father, Phillip Hansen — do you remember me?"

"Ah," Richard sneered. "So that means my hunch was right all along, then. Though, how could it not have been, Francesca looks so much like Anna I thought I'd gone back in time."

"How did you even get my daughter's number?"

"Oh, now I understand," Richard continued. "So you're the one she's trying to beat."

"Excuse me?"

"Your daughter told me she needed my help to start her own profitable business by the end of the year in order to win a bet. Now, blackmailing your own daughter does sound like something you would do."

Phillip was having a hard time breathing. "You stay out of this," he warned Richard, making sure he kept his voice down so Francesca wouldn't hear. "This is a family matter, and it doesn't concern you."

"Oh, I think it does. See, I like winning over you, and I'm really looking forward to beating you at something that truly matters to you."

"Oh yes, that's right, you just want to beat me because you're still sore from that time I won Anna. Seems to me that was a pretty big win."

"You're just jealous because I managed to build a successful career and, from what I've heard, you're still stuck driving people around like a common working-class servant."

"And you're jealous because I got the girl, as well as the full family package," Phillip hissed. "And you probably still haven't found anyone willing to spend more than two minutes with you."

"Hah, don't make me laugh. What family package? Your wife is dead, and for some reason, your daughter is doing whatever it takes to beat you through starting her own business — yeah, you sure do have the perfect family life."

"You know nothing about my family."

"Well, what I do know is that things just got interesting. To be honest, I was only looking at this whole business thing as a minor project on the side, like a hobby. But guess what — now I'm going to make it my personal goal to defeat you. And, as we both know, I usually do succeed in building businesses. So, good luck to you in trying to stand in our way."

"Oh, yeah? Good luck to you, asshole. I'll win this round; you'll see — when it comes to family I always do." Phillip spat, and hung up.

Chapter Twenty-one

Phillip paced the kitchen floor like a storm was coming. He knew Richard was dangerous; there was no doubt about it. "Fuck. What am I going to do?" He muttered to himself, and sat down at the bottom of the stairs. Then he got up again. He grabbed Francesca's phone from the kitchen counter, and copied Richard's number onto his own phone.

Francesca was waiting for him, and he knew he needed to get back up there, but he was so pissed off he was afraid he wouldn't be able to stay calm and rational.

How the hell could she do this to him — how could his own daughter go so far as to team up with his old archenemy? He cleared his throat, preparing his voice for the longest screaming marathon of its life.

But as he started climbing the staircase, he remembered how Richard hadn't even known for sure that Francesca was his and Anna's daughter until their phone call just now. And if Richard wasn't completely sure, then he hadn't talked to Francesca about it yet, meaning Francesca most likely had no clue who Richard was, either. Maybe he should just pretend he hadn't answered Richard's call, and that he didn't know about their business?

He climbed a few more steps.

Then he realized that she might see his call on the call log of her phone. Besides, if he didn't let her in on the conversation he'd just had with Richard, then Richard definitely would. He needed to beat him to the punch; needed to make Francesca see what a horrible guy Richard really was before he managed to tell her ridiculous lies about her own dad. And then, hopefully, he could make her agree to back out of the business.

He continued up to the second floor, walked down the hall, and knocked softly on her door.

"Come in."

He pushed the door open, grabbed the chair by her desk and pulled it up next to her bed. "So, how're you feeling?"

"I'm OK. I must've just caught a stomach bug or something."

He drenched the white washcloth in the cool water, wrung it out, and placed it on her forehead.

She raised her upper body slightly, supporting herself on her lower arms. "Why are you doing this?"

He looked down for a second or two. Then he looked back up at her. In his opinion, Francesca had always been overly sensitive; a very emotional girl. So he realized that if he wanted her to stop working with Richard, he needed to appeal to her sensitive side; to take a softer approach than he usually did. "Because you're my daughter, and... I love you."

She flinched. "Dad..." she started. "I can't even remember the last time you told me that."

He removed the cloth from her forehead, and once again dipped it into the bowl of water before returning it to her forehead. "I know, sweetie, I'm sorry. From now on I'm going to start saying it more often."

Francesca laid back down, her confusion visible in every minor expression flitting across her face. Her whole life she'd done this whenever she was in deep contemplation — almost as though she created tiny furrows all over her face, one at a time, releasing each one before moving on to the next, until she'd covered every area of her face. Phillip suspected, though, that she was not aware of it herself, and he wasn't about to reveal one of the secret ways in which he was always able to read her face.

Then she cast her gaze back up at him, not saying a word.

He could tell she was unsure whether or not to trust him.

She took a deep breath and said, "Dad, I know we're not in a good place, and that things have gotten a little out of hand lately, but for what it's worth I... I still love you, too, no matter what happens."

He felt her words soften him; warm him. In his head, he slowly counted to ten in order to build up the courage for what he needed to ask of her. "So, then, don't do business with Richard Storvik."

She gaped. "What?"

"I know what you're planning on doing, and I need you to stop."

"How do you...?"

"When I was downstairs, your phone rang and I answered it."

She sat up straight, the washrag plummeting into her lap. "What the hell? You have no right to answer my calls."

He put his hands up in the air. "I know, I know — and I'm sorry. The only reason I did is because I recognized Richard Storvik's name on the screen, and he is by far the worst man that I have ever known."

"What're you talking about?"

"Him; your mom; and I all grew up at the orphanage together, and he would do really nasty things — anything he could — in order to keep your mother and I apart."

She huffed, and crossed her arms in front of her chest. "Well, it doesn't exactly seem like he did a very good job, considering the two of you ended up getting married."

Phillip sighed. What could he possibly say to make her stop working with Richard? He needed to be creative, and to choose his words carefully, even if it meant lying to her. "I know, sweetie, but in part he's also responsible for your mom's death," he lied. He knew it was risky, and that it might backfire on him, but he had to put a stop to this business somehow.

She stared at him; her eyes big, blue and watery. "I don't believe you — Mom died in a car crash."

"Yes, she did. However, he was in his own car chasing her when she crashed."

"The next time I see Richard, I will ask him if what you're telling me is actually true."

Phillip's heart rate increased so fast it felt like his heart was about to shoot right out of his chest. "Please, I'm begging you to not do business with that man."

Francesca continued to stare at him. "So does that mean you're giving up and letting Jenny come live with me, then?"

"Absolutely not."

"Alright, then you leave me with no other choice than to carry on as planned. Besides, I already signed a contract with him, and there's no getting out of that."

Phillip pushed his chair back and got to his feet. "I cannot believe you are doing this to me."

"Ditto."

He stormed out of her room. He needed time to think; needed to come up with a way to sabotage their plan. And, the worst part of it all, when Francesca asked Richard about Anna's death, she would know for sure that Phillip had lied to her — resulting in Francesca trusting Richard more than her own father.

All he ever wanted was for Anna, their two daughters, and him to be one happy family, but then Anna, the love of his life, gave up on him. She started to do so the minute Francesca was born, though at that point, Phillip was the only one who could really tell. But the moment when she'd completely given up on him, and the thought of them all being a family — given up legally, for all the world to see — was when she became pregnant with Jenny. And now his two daughters — the only family he had left — were about to do the same thing.

Was it possible that Richard knew anything about what had happened right before the accident? No, Phillip shook his head, the only people who knew were himself, Anna, and her new boyfriend — and that bastard died in the crash as well. To his knowledge, Anna and Richard hadn't kept in touch after Phillip and Anna had gotten married 20 years ago, and if that was the case, then Richard probably didn't know that he and Anna were separated at the time she died, either.

Phillip continued down the hallway, and passed Jenny's bedroom.

On her door hung five wooden letters painted in different colors, spelling out her name.

His eyes lingered on the letters. Maybe Jenny was the key to making Francesca listen? Francesca had made it quite clear that she would never believe another word he said. And the person who mattered the most to Francesca in this world was Jenny — Jenny was the only one who could persuade Francesca to see that what she was doing was wrong.

The next time Francesca went off to see that boyfriend of hers, or wherever it was that she went in the evenings — that was when he would make his move. He would get Jenny on his side by finally telling her what Anna had done; how she'd refused for him to have any contact with his very own daughters. Maybe that would make them see that their mom wasn't so great after all. He hadn't wanted to before — he hadn't wanted to let them know just how terrible a person she had been. Even after all this time, even after what she had done to him, he still loved her more than he'd ever loved anyone else. But now he was left with no other choice; it was time to tell them.

Chapter Twenty-two

For Francesca's *Marketing and Consumer Behavior* class at the university, they had been given the assignment of looking into and analyzing an aspect of their choice related to either marketing or consumer behavior. The task was extensive. This was a test, their professor had said. An initial experiment to see how much these first year students knew about the subject, as well as how their minds reasoned in the process of reaching a conclusion.

Naturally, Francesca had chosen to analyze consumer behavior and preferences when shopping for groceries, focusing on the end of the shopping experience at the checkout counter.

The assignment counted for 30 percent of their grade, and each student was allotted one 60-minute session with the professor in order to ask questions and seek guidance related to any issues they might have.

Francesca had scheduled her session for nine o'clock tomorrow morning. She desperately needed some help in order to make her seem professional for her first business presentation with Richard in a few days.

She thought about how she would be showing her preliminary analysis to her professor tomorrow, and noticed an involuntary contraction in her stomach. After all, he was an expert and she was a newbie. Her nervousness, though, couldn't compare to how excited she was about soaking up as much golden information as possible. Without her confidence charged to the max for her part of the business presentation with Richard, she wouldn't get far.

But more than that, what she felt nervous nausea about was the situation with Adrian she had so stupidly put herself in. By sleeping with him she'd ruined everything, and she already knew that her only option was to cut him completely out of her life; to never see him again. She hadn't even talked to him since she ran out of his apartment a couple of weeks ago.

Of course, he'd tried calling and texting her several times — all of which she'd ignored.

Well... that wasn't completely true. As far as Adrian knew, she'd ignored his attempts to get hold of her, insofar as she hadn't picked up the phone or responded to any of his texts.

Her heart, though, hadn't been able to ignore him. Each time she saw his name pop up on her phone screen, her heart screamed with longing for him. And for the first time in her life, she didn't know how to shut it up.

So far, he hadn't tried coming over to her house. But if he all of a sudden did decide to show up at her door, she knew she'd be in trouble. Right now, she was way too shaky to be able to refuse him.

Due to her heartache, spending lots of time working on the business, and then having been sick for a few days, she hadn't taken a single ballet class for more than two weeks now. Although her stomach wasn't feeling completely back to normal, at least she hadn't thrown up for the past two days.

In order to be able to get ready for her meeting with her professor tomorrow morning, as well as to help her stop thinking about Adrian continuously, she first needed to get rid of all of her nervous tension. Then she could begin rebuilding her strength. And there was only one way she knew how to do that. She grabbed her ballet bag and headed out the door.

*

Francesca took a deep breath, cracked her knuckles, and looked at her three best friends. "Alright, chicas; this is it."

Margaret smiled, and gave her a hug. "Don't worry, you'll be fine."

"Yeah, I hope so. At least Richard's already got a few of the franchisees interested, so now all I need to do is make sure I don't change their minds and blow our chances," she sighed. "I just wish you guys could be in there with me."

"Yeah, although Richard's got a good point. After all, we really are the silent partners, and if they're already a bit skeptical about the fact that you're so young, then having three more young ladies just sitting in there watching wouldn't exactly make the business seem any more professional," Tina added.

"No, I know."

"I can't believe Richard managed to set up this meeting with 29 people in such a short amount of time — I mean, they are franchisees for one of the largest grocery store chains in Norway," Emily whispered, her eyes gleaming.

"Well..." Francesca started. "Something happened last week that made him become extra motivated."

"Like what?" Tina asked.

Francesca looked around, and gestured for her friends to gather in closer. "I haven't mentioned this to you guys yet because I was really trying to avoid giving it too much thought. I didn't want it to end up clouding my judgment. But, it turns out Richard grew up with my dad at the orphanage. And apparently they were mortal enemies or something."

"Oh my God!" Emily blurted out. "What're the odds?"

"Yeah, it's crazy, right?"

"Wait, so how did they find out about both having a connection with you?" Margaret asked.

Francesca lowered her voice to a whisper and recounted the conversation she'd had with her father.

Tina raised her eyebrows. "Damn."

"So, have you talked to Richard about what your dad said?" Margaret asked.

"Not yet. I'm sure he's already guessed that my dad's told me everything, but I haven't wanted to bring it up. I'm at least going to wait until today's meeting is over. I just can't take any more drama and conflict making me even more nervous right now."

Richard stepped out into the hallway where the girls stood waiting. "Francesca, you ready?" He checked his watch. "We only have 15 minutes until the meeting starts, and I'd like to go over some last-minute items before heading in there."

"Yeah, of course."

He turned and headed over to a small empty room.

Francesca whispered to her friends. "OK, wish me luck."

"Good luck!" the three girls chorused in low voices.

Shaking slightly, she followed Richard.

He held the door open, allowing her to enter, before closing it behind her. Then he turned toward her. "Now, remember," he said, his face turning rigid. "Just because a couple of franchisees agree to buy our stands, doesn't mean we'll end up making any real money to speak of. Even though the individual stores need to look nearly identical to each other, we're not talking about a one-for-all deal when it comes to these freestanding racks — every franchisee makes the decision for their own store on whether or not they want to make this local investment," he said, and started pacing around the small room.

Francesca watched him, and realized he was just as nervous as she was.

"I wish we could have done it differently, and instead aimed for another chain to make a large collective investment in the carrousel racks for every single one of their stores," he continued. "But that means completely changing out their existing cash registers, and there simply isn't enough time to run our idea past a slow-deciding board of directors. So, like I said, for our current situation we just really have to convince as many franchisees as possible. And then ideally from there, we'll eventually be able to turn these stands into a standard and permanent solution for the entire chain's cash registers — by really making them feel deep down in their bones that they truly need our product."

Francesca nodded eagerly, attempting to commit every single one of his words to memory. "Right."

"One thing we can use to our advantage, though, is that franchisees tend to be ambitious and competitive types — in fact, they have to be in order to succeed within the franchise business model. So, what we need to do is to discretely put them up against each other in a kind of friendly rivalry when it comes to winning the customers over. Of course, they're already used to that. When the chain has various campaigns going on, then the different stores always compete amongst themselves in order to see which store can earn the most money, resulting in a bonus for the franchisee — remember, these are money-driven people." He stopped pacing, and looked over at Francesca. "Are you following my train of thought here?"

"Yes. Absolutely."

"Good. Now, this time around we're focusing on the grocery stores located in Oslo, and for today's meeting we've got people representing almost fifty percent of all the chain's stores in Oslo. And then, assuming all goes according to plan, we'll move on to other cities and counties after that."

Francesca swallowed hard, feeling both proud and terrified at the thought of what was about to go down. "OK, sounds good."

"So, remember what we agreed on: your job is basically to be the inspiring, visionary, young go-getter; and then let me answer the technical business questions, alright?"

She nodded. "Yes — understood."

He smiled and patted her on the shoulder. "OK, go show them what you've got — show them that you have the same entrepreneurial spirit they do; make them feel that you're just like them, and that they can relate to you. And, most importantly, give them a compelling reason to buy our product."

Francesca stood up straight on the outside, while shrinking slightly on the inside. "I'll do my very best."

Then, he just stood there watching her, for what seemed like almost thirty seconds.

Francesca was starting to feel uncomfortable. She didn't like it when people stared at her; like they could see straight through her exterior and into her soft and vulnerable side — allowing them to judge this part of her. If they managed to enter, she wouldn't be able to defend herself anymore.

"Hey," he finally said. "I'm proud of you, and I know you can do this."

Francesca felt his words instantly zap away the worst of her nervous tension. Was he really proud of her? It was such an unfamiliar sensation to have an adult support and root for her like that. The last time she remembered feeling this way was more than ten years ago, before her mom had passed away, and she almost didn't recognize what Richard's words were doing to her. Yet, she found herself believing him — he never would have put his good name and reputation into this business if he didn't think she, and they together, were capable of succeeding.

Sure, Richard was also trying to beat her dad, but then again, he had actually agreed to work with her before he even knew who her father was. Maybe her dad had been wrong — maybe Richard wasn't so bad. After all, it wouldn't be the first time her dad had told her lies in order to get what he wanted. She smiled back at Richard. "Thanks, Richard, that means a lot."

"So, are you ready?"

She nodded confidently. "Yes, I'm ready."

"Alright then, let's get in there." He opened the door, and led the way toward the meeting room.

Francesca followed him down the hallway, and together they filed into the room alongside a few chatting franchisees. As she and Richard made their way to the small table and two chairs located at the front of the room, she noticed some of the franchisees looking as if they were trying to size her up.

Little by little, the others settled into the two rows of chairs placed opposite Richard and Francesca's table.

Richard counted the franchisees as they entered the meeting room, and when the number matched the 29 that he had on his list of attendees, he walked over and shut the door. He checked his watch. "Ladies and gentlemen," he said loud and clear. "Since everyone has arrived, I trust we're all ready to begin?"

A couple of them mumbled their agreement.

"Welcome to this meeting. We'd like to thank you all very much for showing up on such short notice. And, as you already know from having spoken to me on the phone, my name is Richard Storvik. So, without further ado, let me introduce my main business partner, and the initiator of this grocery bag stand idea; Miss Francesca Hansen," he gestured toward Francesca.

Shaking, Francesca gave a few nods all around. "Hi."

Some of the franchisees nodded or replied back.

Richard glanced at Francesca.

She had fixated her gaze down into her lap and was breathing heavily, scrunching her eyes shut a couple of times, before forcing them back open.

He turned back toward their audience, and noticed some of the franchisees whisper and point at Francesca. "So," he began, raising his voice to the point of almost shouting in an attempt to zap all the whispering, and squelch any doubts they might have about her. Just like Anna had stood up for him, and squelched the many doubts people had had about him while they were growing up. "Now, this girl right here is hardworking and brilliant," Richard continued. "So don't let her age fool you — she knows what she's doing. And as she was able to wow me — and trust me, I've pretty much seen it all — I'm sure she'll knock your socks off as well. So, Francesca; kindly explain your vision behind the grocery bag stands to these lovely people."

She took a deep breath, and closed her eyes for a moment, imagining herself back on stage performing. Just like when she'd been dancing ballet full time. In her performance mode, she was usually able to find her confidence. All she had to do was picture her audience out there in the dark, where she wouldn't be able to see anyone's faces in case they judged her. And if she couldn't see them, then she could pretend they weren't even there, and she was able to just be herself, allowing her to say exactly what she wanted and needed to say. "Thank you for the grand introduction, Richard — I'm glad you haven't given them insanely high expectations of me or anything!"

A few people chuckled at her lame attempt at an opening joke.

"Anyway," she cleared her throat. "Let me share my vision with you." She left her seat behind her table, and stepped out in front of the franchisees. "Please imagine a busy Saturday afternoon, with lots of tired, stressed-out people everywhere — a really good mix of rushed families with screaming, young children; hung-over people in their twenties; impatient workaholics; and slow moving seniors." She paused for a couple of seconds, allowing them to fully develop the image she was describing. "And what do all these people want?" she continued. "Probably to either just go back to bed, or have some time off after a long week to relax and read a book, or the like. But what do they all need?" she asked the franchisees.

"Basically, they all need the same thing: groceries. It might be the full week's worth of shopping, or just a frozen pizza, but whatever it is; we all need to eat, am I right?"

The crowd nodded in agreement to her obvious statement.

"Now, no offense to you guys and what you do for a living, but let's be honest here: no one actually likes to go grocery shopping — or, at least, I don't think I know a single person who truly enjoys shopping for groceries. Yet, there's no way around it, it's just one of those things that has to be done, like getting out of bed on a Monday morning." Slowly, she took a couple of steps toward her audience, while straightening her back and letting her shoulder blades roll slightly down and back.

"And so where's the main problem, or the main holdup if you will, when it comes to shopping?" She looked a couple of the franchisees in the eye. "Of course; the main holdup in a grocery store on any busy Saturday — and most afternoons and evenings for that matter — will always be at the checkout area. And why is that?" she asked, pausing for a second, before going on to answer her own question. "It's because the customers usually wait until all their groceries have been rung up, before paying, and then finally getting around to packing up their goods. The groceries pile up at the end of the conveyor belts; and then many customers tend to be a bunch of slowpokes when it comes to bagging their stuff; meaning the clerks have to wait before they can send the next customer's groceries down the conveyor belts. All this creates a bottleneck effect, leaving the other customers stuck waiting for a lot longer than necessary. Do you agree?" she asked the franchisees.

"Yeah."

"Sure."

"Obviously, that's how it is."

"OK," Francesca continued. "Now, we've conducted a short random sample survey, asking 400 consumers. The two questions we asked are as follows: *If you had to define the number one thing that could help make your day easier, what would it be?*" She pointed toward the PowerPoint presentation on the screen behind her. "And, as you can see, almost 90 percent of the people asked, answered: *Having more time.* People just don't feel like they have enough time in their hectic day-to-day lives." She looked back out at the franchisees, attempting to make eye contact with a couple of them. "And, I don't know about the rest of you, but personally, I can definitely relate to that." She hit a button on the little remote control in her hand, taking her to the next PowerPoint slide. "The second question we asked was:

What's your least favorite thing about shopping? And guess what; the predominant answer by a whopping 83 percent was: *Standing in line.*"

The crowd murmured among themselves.

"Our solution to both of these problems is of course the shopping bag stand. When the clerks ring up each item and then place the items directly into the grocery bags — that are conveniently held open, and supported in a sturdy position with the help of these stands — the clerks can then pass the already packed bags down the conveyor belts for the customers to pick up right before leaving the store. Shortening the time spent at the checkout counters will naturally reduce the lines leading up to them as well. The result: saving the customers time and frustration, which ultimately leads to happier customers. Do you see the benefits of these stands?"

A general consensus was murmured.

"And just to further demonstrate my point here; there are actual studies conducted on the act of waiting in line, and just how much this particular activity is capable of irking us, to the level of causing extreme irritation." She paused, taking a deep breath.

"So, then the ultimate question you need to ask yourselves is this: why would customers choose your store over any other store in the same basic area? Most smaller grocery stores like yours have the same general selection of groceries, and usually the prices are quite similar, etc. These things are all points-of-parity and, naturally, all else being equal, these will not be the deciding factors for the customers. In today's competitive market, with a grocery store on almost every corner, the customer's experience is critical to the survival and growth of the business. Therefore, you need to make sure you surprise customers and exceed their expectations by really providing service beyond what they expect, and beyond what they get when shopping at other stores." She took a few more steps toward her audience, preparing for her grand finale.

"What you need to be looking at are the points-of-difference — the things that really make your store stand out from the others. These grocery bag stands are the points-of-difference that you need. And I say this with confidence, because studies show that the memory of an event is far more important than the actual experience — as future behavior is, in fact, based on that memory. And what part of an experience is it that we remember the most?" she asked the franchisees.

"The end," a man on the front row said.

"Exactly — the very end!" Francesca exclaimed. "Therefore: get the point-of-difference working for you precisely where you need it, and where the customer will remember it: right at the end of the customer's shopping experience, at the checkout counter, in order to ensure they return again and again." She took a second to catch her breath, and then smiled at the franchisees. "Also, one concern we've identified that some customers might have about others bagging their groceries for them, is the way in which the goods are stacked inside the bags — as in accidently putting, say, a heavy watermelon on top of a carton of eggs. As a final note, I would therefore like to add that we can also offer basic training for your clerks in how to bag groceries in the most beneficial way, should any of you be interested."

A few of the franchisees nodded or murmured their agreement.

"So, I'd like to thank you all very much for listening to me," she said, and turned slightly, gesturing to her business partner. "Richard, back to you."

He rose from his seat, and stepped out in front of their table. "Yes, thank you Francesca for that compelling presentation. Now, moving on to any questions you might have."

Francesca sat back down, and, as previously agreed, let Richard take it from there. As she sat there waiting, her entire body went numb. She registered that the franchisees were asking Richard a bunch of questions, which she had no doubt he was able to answer perfectly. Although, what the questions were about, she didn't catch, as her ears seemed to have momentarily blocked out all sound.

Wow, Francesca thought to herself. She'd done it — she'd actually managed to get through this. Sure, she'd had an out-of-body experience for the majority of the time she was speaking, and she was so nervous she couldn't remember exactly what she'd said, but she felt like she'd given a decent presentation — hadn't she?

After a little while, she wasn't sure just how long, she snapped out of her haze, and again became fully conscious of what was being said within the meeting room.

"As there are no further questions, let's wrap this meeting up," Richard's voice was loud and clear. "You've all had about a week to look at the figures as well as the terms and conditions that I've e-mailed you. And as you've been informed earlier, there's a 10 percent discount for those of you willing to put your order in today before you leave this meeting. Now, there's a list over here on this table, so if you are interested, you can come on over and place your order. Thank you all for your time and attention, and we look forward to doing business with as many of you as possible," Richard finished off.

The franchisees put their hands together, before beginning to discuss quietly among themselves.

Richard turned and gestured at Francesca to come join him down by the door.

Francesca hurried over, and when she was standing right next to him, whispered. "So, how... how was...?"

He looked at her, and smiled subtly. "You did great, kid."

Her eyes glistened. She had done it, and she had done it well. Out of the corner of her eye, she saw a couple of the franchisees crowding around the piece of paper, and more of them kept heading over to the table. Just exactly how many of them had actually placed orders she didn't know for sure yet, but as she attempted to count, she realized it must be at least eight or ten already. The only two emotions she was able to register were overwhelming amounts of relief and happiness. They were in business; there was no doubt about it. And soon, she and Jenny would finally be free.

Chapter Twenty-three

After all the franchisees had left the meeting room, Francesca slowly counted to ten in her head before rushing out the door and down the hallway to meet her three best friends. "My God, ladies, it was a total success!" she exclaimed.

"Awesome, tell us more — we need details!" Tina urged her.

"OK, so 14 of the franchisees already signed up to order the stands, averaging five stands apiece to begin with, and then they may order more if they find that they like them. Of course, the remaining franchisees might also buy the stands as well, and then we're gonna start looking at other cities soon and, ah..." she let out a sigh of relief. "There's just so much work to be done from here on out, but we'll be getting into exactly where we're at in terms of monetary figures, and timeframes, and investments and all tomorrow, so I'm gonna need you guys with me for that."

Richard started walking down the hall toward the girls, a grin covering his face.

"Hey, Francesca, Richard's heading over here," Emily whispered.

Francesca turned around to face him, and smiled. "Thanks again, Richard. You have no idea how much this means to me."

"Oh, I think I do."

"Well, I couldn't possibly have gotten this far so quickly without you, so..."

"I couldn't have done this without you, either — I never would've been able to hit him where it hurts the most if it weren't for the fact that you're his own daughter."

Francesca felt like she'd been slapped across the face. "Ah... yeah, I heard you used to know my dad and all but—"

"I can't believe a helpless loser like him managed to raise such a strong, independent daughter."

She felt her entire body heat up. "Hey, he's not—" she heard herself begin to say, but stopped midsentence, noting her own surprise at the fact that she was actually defending him.

"You know, you remind me so much of myself at your age — so

determined and goal-oriented, willing to do whatever it takes to win."

She took a deep breath. "Listen, I know you've got a history with my dad, but I'd really prefer to just keep this business on a professional level between the two of us, if you don't mind?"

He managed to keep a straight face. "Yes, of course. In any case, I think we make a good team."

"It would appear so, yes."

"OK, well I've got to go," Richard said. "But, I'll see you all tomorrow morning, then?"

"Yes, tomorrow at 10 o'clock," Francesca confirmed.

"Great." He put his hand casually in the air, then turned and walked away.

The girls watched him until he had exited the building.

Francesca exhaled. "Geez..."

"Yeah, I guess he's not a huge fan of subtlety," Emily noted.

"I mean, I know I'm eventually gonna have to ask him about what my dad said when it comes to my mom's car accident," Francesca muttered, staring at the floor. "But I just didn't want to spoil this moment right now, you know? I just really wanted to savor this little bit of success for today."

"Of course." Margaret reached out and gave her a sideways hug. "And what an amazingly successful achievement it is!"

The girls started making their way toward the building's front door.

"So, do you wanna go somewhere to celebrate?" Tina suggested.

"Yes, a celebration is definitely in order. However, I promised Jenny I'd pick her up from school and tell her how the meeting went, so how about we grab some pizza at our usual place at, say, six o'clock?"

"Yeah, sounds good," Tina agreed.

"Cool, see ya later." Francesca exited through the front door, and made a right, heading in the direction of Jenny's school.

*

"Francesca!" Jenny called out, grinning, as she ran across the schoolyard toward her.

"Hey, J-love!" Francesca held her arms out, and wrapped them around her sister. She kissed the top of Jenny's head, before letting go of her. "So, what's up? How was your day?"

"Good." Jenny put one hand in her sister's, and the other hand on her hip. "But I think the real question here is: what happened at the meeting, and have you managed to save me yet?" She raised one eyebrow.

Francesca laughed. "When did you become so grown-up all of a sudden, huh?"

"I *am* grown up — 11 is old, you know. I can feed myself, tie my own shoes, read and write. What more does a girl need?"

"You're right — you don't need saving." Francesca winked.

Jenny put her other hand on her hip as well. "Yes, I do! And you didn't answer me yet... So, will I be able to come live with you or not?"

Francesca bent down to her sister's eye level, and winked at her. "Yes, Jellybean, you'll be able to come live with me."

Jenny leapt up and flung herself around her sister's waist.

Francesca lost her balance and staggered a few steps backwards. "Whoa, easy there, kid."

Jenny looked up at her sister. "I love you."

"Love you, too."

Then Jenny let go of Francesca's waist, and once again grabbed her hand.

Francesca smiled. She knew she was doing the right thing for her little sister. "So, you wanna go home?"

"Yeah, let's go."

"Hey, guess what, I'm going out for pizza with the girls tonight to celebrate. Do you wanna come, too?"

Jenny's eyes lit up. "Yeah, can I?"

"'Course, it'll be a little Friday night treat."

"Cool!"

They crossed the street, reaching a busy intersection.

"Hey, J-love, let's not tell Dad about this just yet, OK? We'll keep it a secret for now, is that alright?"

"OK."

"Good girl."

"Hey, Francesca...?"

"Yeah."

"Dad told me something last night when you were at ballet class."

Francesca's pulse rose slightly. "Really, like what?"

"He said that Mom had gotten a new boyfriend right after she and Dad broke up. Did you know that?"

"Ah, yeah, I actually met him briefly once or twice. But she wanted to keep the relationship a secret for awhile, at least until it became really serious."

"Well I think it was getting pretty serious, because Dad said that Mom and her new boyfriend had been over to talk to Dad right before they were in that car crash, and that they'd gotten into a huge argument. Dad said that that's probably why Mom had crashed the car, because their argument had upset her so much that she wasn't able to pay attention to the traffic very well."

"What was the argument about?"

"They'd told Dad he was no longer allowed to see us. They'd said they were going to make sure that he lost all visitation rights, and that her boyfriend would be our new dad."

Francesca turned to face Jenny. "Jellybean, are you sure about this? Is there any chance he could've been lying?"

"I don't think so. He was crying when he told me — I've never seen him cry before."

Francesca felt nauseous. "He was crying?"

Jenny nodded. "Yeah."

"Did Dad say anything about why they wanted to keep us away from him?"

"Mom had told him that she didn't love him anymore, and that she'd never really loved him; that she'd only used him because she wanted to have kids, and to finally have a family of her own. And then she'd told Dad that she'd never felt loved by him either, and said how he couldn't possibly become a loving parent all of a sudden, seeing as he still hadn't learned how to love. She said her only option was to take us away from him and give us a new, emotionally stable dad, so we wouldn't become damaged like Dad was."

Francesca covered her mouth, and felt her eyes sting. "Those are terrible things to say."

"I know, I started crying too when he told me. I couldn't hold it in when I saw how sad he was."

Francesca took a deep breath, trying to decide whether or not to believe the story her dad had told Jenny. She realized there was a possibility that he'd been lying to her, banking on the fact that Jenny would tell Francesca, making her stop what she was doing with the business. She didn't know for sure, though. She'd never gotten the full story of why her parents had broken up in the first place, or what had happened right before her mom died. "OK, um... I think it's still very important that we don't tell Dad about the meeting today, or anything else about the business, alright?"

"Yeah, I promise."

Chapter Twenty-four

Richard pulled a notebook out of his brown leather briefcase. "Alright, let's see what we've got here."

Francesca looked Tina in the eye, and gave her a single, subtle nod.

Tina nodded back, and let her eyes hang over Richard's book and calculator as he worked out the figures.

Francesca knew it was a wise move to place Tina next to him. That girl was a born mathematician — if Richard decided he wanted to pull a fast one on them, Tina would stop him dead in his tracks before he could even think about punching another digit into his calculator.

"So far we've sold 72 stands," Richard said. "This means that after taxes we're looking at a total profit of..." He started doing the calculations. "just shy of sixty-three thousand kroner. And since you'll be receiving a twenty-five percent cut, that means..." he paused to calculate again. "fifteen thousand six hundred and sixty kroner for the four of you to share this time around."

Francesca grinned. "Alright!" She slapped Emily's hand five. "Not bad for only having had our first meeting."

"Yeah, we're doing OK so far," Richard said. "However, that money won't last you long."

Francesca nodded, her grin quickly slipping off her face. "No, I know."

"So, what are your expectations, more specifically? I mean, I don't know the details, as well as which criteria need to be met in order for you to have won this bet you've got going on."

Francesca figured the less Richard knew about Jenny and all the rest of it, the better. The only part of the deal she'd made with her dad that she was interested in discussing with Richard was the money aspect. "I'm going to need to be making a minimum of twenty-five thousand a month after taxes."

"Alright, and what about the rest of you three girls? How much do you expect to be making?"

"Well," Margaret spoke up. "As specified in our contract, we decided that Tina, Emily and I will work on an as-needed basis. So, obviously, as you and

Francesca are the faces of the business, then we'll handle any customer service work, like placing orders to our supplier in China and answering e-mails. Initially, we're thinking that working one hour a week each — as in having someone there for customer service one hour every Monday, Wednesday and Friday — would cover our needs at this stage. And then we can always work more as demands increase. We also decided on an hourly wage of two hundred."

Richard smiled. "So I understand Francesca isn't the only clever one in the group. I'm glad to hear you've given it this much thought," he said, and started jotting down notes. "OK, well that sounds fair enough to me. You're cheaper than the people I have on staff, and in any case, they're all really busy at the moment with more advanced stuff, working out the kinks and legal issues for this other business we acquired last year. And you should hardly need any training at all for simple tasks like placing orders and answering e-mails. Besides, it's really up to you guys how you want to split that twenty-five percent profit."

On hearing Richard approved of the deal the four girls had decided on among themselves, Francesca registered that the tension in her stomach eased up a bit. "So, with these figures, how many stands do we need to be selling each month?"

"Hang on..." he bent back down over his calculator and notebook.

Tina followed discreetly.

"Based on what you've just told me," Richard said, and looked back up at Francesca. "The minimum number of stands we need to sell each and every month is 125 stands."

"OK — 125 is the magic number, then." She looked at her friends, and then back at Richard. "So, is this actually feasible?"

"Yeah, it's feasible."

Francesca grinned. "Awesome!"

"Though, not for an endless number of months, obviously."

"No, of course, I understand. But do you have an educated guess as to how many consecutive months we'd be able to pull off this kind of sales volume?"

"Considering this particular chain's number of stores throughout Norway, and assuming they each purchase an average of five stands like our current customers have, then, hypothetically, the maximum market potential is about twenty-seven months with the amount you're talking about — so two years and three months."

Francesca's jaw dropped. "Are you serious?"

"Yes, I'm serious. However, this is all hypothetical — we can't assume every single one of this chain's stores in Norway will want to buy our stands. All franchisees need to pay for these local investments themselves, they can't count on any financial support from their franchisor. Although, since the franchisor is an old personal friend of mine, I happen to know he's encouraging his franchisees to meet with us and buy our stands, as it'll most likely lead to happier customers and ultimately higher profits not only for the franchisees, but for him as well."

"OK, so at least we have the market potential as well as the franchisor on our side."

"Yes." Richard nodded. "But what concerns me, though, is the rate at which we'll need to sell the stands. We've got our work cut out for us, and it definitely won't be easy."

"Right, I understand," Francesca said. "But I also hope you know that I'm an extremely hard worker, and ready to do whatever it takes to make this happen?"

"I've got a fairly good idea, yes."

"OK, good. So, what's the game plan?"

"We need to start booking meetings with the franchisees — as many meetings as possible, and as quickly as we can in order to get the ball rolling. The franchisor has given me a list of the names and contact information for all the franchisees, and he's also already sent them all e-mails with information about us and our stands in order to prepare them before I begin making the calls."

"Wow, that's great." Francesca glanced at her friends, attempting to digest the opportunity they had been presented with.

"Fantastic!" Emily agreed.

"Well, yeah, obviously having the right contacts is everything when it comes to doing business," Richard stated matter-of-factly.

"For sure," Tina nodded.

"Now," Richard looked at Francesca. "I think it's extremely important that we both go to every single meeting. We're going to be needing my professional experience and know-how, but I believe it's equally important to have you there to present your compelling speech, so they don't feel like this is just another stunt by some sleazy businessman — they've all seen that before. Our new twist with you as the young visionary is bound to create some interest."

"OK, yeah, absolutely."

"Good. So before I start making calls I need to know what your schedule is like, and when we can be setting up these meetings."

Francesca pulled out her day planner. "Ah, well the thing is that I still need to be making it to the majority of my classes. I mean, I could take a few sick days, but basically—"

"Yeah, that's what I was afraid of. What time in the afternoon do you finish?"

"That varies a bit... however," she paused, knowing what she was about to say probably wouldn't go down very well with Richard. "I'm also hoping to make it to a couple of ballet classes a week, so..."

"I'm sorry, ballet class?"

"Yeah, it's a long story, but it's pretty important to me."

"Geez..." he shook his head. "Well, you've got to make time for these meetings at some point."

"OK, so except for the meetings we'll be holding in Oslo or the immediate vicinity, we'd need more time to travel, right?"

"Obviously."

"Alright, how about we in general aim for booking our meetings for Saturdays? And then whatever meetings held within the general Oslo area that can't be done on Saturdays we can book for afternoons instead, meaning I'll just have to skip ballet class on those days — does that work for you?"

"It does, yes. But what really matters isn't what works for me, but what works for our customers."

"Yes, of course," Francesca said, sitting up straight and feeling brave. "But I suggest we try it this way first, and if it doesn't work out then I'll just need to be more flexible with my afternoons — is that OK?" She smiled hopefully.

Richard gave her a grudging smile. "I guess I won't need to put any time into teaching you how to act like a tough business woman; it seems like you've already got that attitude down."

"I do try my very best."

"OK, I'm not promising anything, but I'll see what I can do. It may in fact be that Saturdays work better for some of the franchisees because they're so busy during the rest of the week, but I'll have to get back to you on that. And if Saturdays turn out to be a no-go then I expect you to be ready to work more afternoons instead."

"Yes, sir."

"And another issue is the fact that Norway is a very topographically challenging country, and therefore quite expensive to travel around in. The more we need to travel, the more expenses we'll accumulate, meaning we'll be needing to sell a bunch more stands, so be prepared for that as well. We can't expect our potential customers to travel any great distances to get to us — we need to reach out to them where they are. And that includes every little rural area if we need to. So remember, let's focus on selling as many stands as we possibly can in the bigger cities, and on our first visit over there."

Francesca nodded. "Gotcha."

"Alright, so do you have any questions?"

"Not at the moment, no. Everything seems pretty clear to me so far. How about you guys?" Francesca asked her friends.

The girls shook their heads.

"OK," Richard said. "Well, you've all got my number in case you think of anything. Oh, and by the way, Francesca, are there any weekdays that are better for you than others, in case the whole weekend thing doesn't work out?"

"Ah, let's see…" Francesca leafed through first September and then October in her day planner, searching for patterns of what would be the best days of the week to give Richard.

He started drumming his fingers impatiently on the table. "You finding anything?"

She gasped.

"What?" Richard asked.

Her heart started beating faster and faster. It wasn't about what she was finding, it was about what she wasn't able to find. "Um… nothing," she uttered, her voice high-pitched. She held her breath, and noticed that she was becoming more nauseated by the second. What the hell had happened to her period? Was it possible… could it be that she was actually *pregnant*? She clenched her fists in her lap underneath the table, and took a deep breath. *No, that couldn't be — absolutely not — her tired mind was leaping to conclusions. The missing period was just due to stress.* She cleared her throat. "How about Tuesdays, would that work?"

"Yeah, I guess Tuesdays are as good a day as any."

"Great."

"OK, so I'll make some calls and get back to you as soon as I know more."

"Perfect."

*

"Good meeting, huh?" Francesca knuckled Emily's upper arm on their way out of Richard's office building.

"Ah," Emily rubbed her arm. "What's up with you and your freakish up-per-body strength all of a sudden — did you morph into a dude from doing business with the guys or something?"

"Oh, I'm sorry... I didn't think it was that hard."

"Relax, I'm fine."

"So," Tina started, trying to catch her evasive glance. "Why are you so jittery all of a sudden?"

Francesca waved her hand through the air. "Oh, it's nothing. You know, just thinking about how crazy my schedule's going to be from here on out."

"Yeah..." Margaret said. "But at least it's going to be worth it in the end when you get Jenny."

Francesca nodded. "True." She took a deep breath. "And thank you for being there for me today, guys, and also for helping out with the future cus-tomer service work — it really means the world to me."

"'Course, that's what family's for," Emily said casually. "Besides, it won't exactly look bad on our resumes, either."

The four friends continued walking down the street in silence. After about a minute they reached a big mall.

"OK, well I'm gonna run in here and pick up a few things," Margaret said, pointing at the white warehouse-looking mall building.

"Yeah, you know what, I'll actually come with you," Francesca added.

"OK, bye ladies," Tina said.

"Yeah, see ya later." Francesca put her hand up, giving a single wave, and watched Tina and Emily for a moment as they headed toward the bus stop, before trotting to catch up with Margaret. "I think I've got a problem," she whispered.

"Oh, honey," Margaret said, patting her on the shoulder. "Yes, you've got quite a few problems you're working through this fall, but it'll all turn out fine in the end, just you wait and see."

Francesca frowned. "No, I'm talking about a whole brand new issue I wasn't aware of this morning."

"Like what?"

"Looking through my day planner during the meeting I noticed that I haven't had my period in about six weeks."

Margaret halted. "OK, well six weeks really isn't that much. Are you al-ways completely regular?"

"Maybe not always exactly on the day, but I'm usually fairly regular."

"Right. But you know, you've been super stressed these last few weeks and all, so maybe—"

"Margaret?" Francesca cut her off.

"Yeah," Margaret nodded. "We better stop off at the drugstore and get a test."

*

Francesca broke the perforation at the top of the box and squinted down at the foil-wrapped at-home pregnancy test. "Great," she moaned, rolling her eyes at Margaret. "Just what I needed to offset my success — peeing on a stick in a mall bathroom."

Margaret grabbed the instructions. "OK, let's see..." she scanned the printed paper. "You've got to hold the color change tip in the urine stream for five seconds, and then put the cap back on and wait for three minutes, and then... then you'll know."

"You know," Francesca looked at Margaret. "I hate my life so much this year — I really do."

Margaret seemed to be attempting a smile, though the end result kind of made her look like she was sucking on a lemon wedge instead. "Well, it's probably best that you take the test before you start completely freaking out."

Francesca sighed. "Margaret, I don't know what I'll do if..." her voice crumbled, and her eyes started tearing up.

Margaret rushed over and hugged her. "Hey, first things first, OK?" She brushed the tears off Francesca's cheeks with her finger.

Francesca took a deep breath, and nodded. "Yeah, first things first." She peeled the foil off the test and disappeared into the nearest stall.

Margaret got her cell phone out. "Let me know when I should start the timer."

Francesca put the plastic cap back over the tip. "OK, go ahead," she called out to Margaret, and was suddenly overcome by nausea. Whether it was from actually being pregnant, or just from the fear that she was, she didn't know yet. She flushed the toilet, and exited the stall. Her hands shaking, she placed the box on the flat edge of the sink, before resting the test on top of the box. She washed her hands, praying for a miracle that was the opposite of the miracle of life.

"30 seconds to go," Margaret said.

Francesca paced the bathroom floor, afraid to look, yet at the same time realizing just how hard she had to work to restrain herself from glancing over at the test.

"OK, it's time," Margaret announced after a little while.

Francesca sighed. "Alright," she said, but didn't move a muscle.

"Do you wanna be the one to look, or do you want me to do it?"

"Ah..." Francesca cracked her knuckles. "I don't know..." she paced back and forth some more. Then she stopped cold. "No, I've gotta be the one to do it."

"OK."

Francesca held her breath and peered down at the test. Her eyes immediately bounced back up, like she'd been blinded.

"What did it say?"

Francesca turned her head toward Margaret, without really looking at her. "It's positive."

Chapter Twenty-five

Francesca sat on Margaret's bed, hugging her knees to her chest.

Margaret sat next to her and stroked her friend's back. "Either way, I'm here for you. You know that, right?"

Francesca stared straight ahead. "Yeah, I know."

"So... can I get you anything or...?"

"A time machine would be nice."

"OK, I'll get right on inventing one of those for you."

Francesca rested her throbbing head on top of her knees. "What am I going to do?"

"Well, ultimately, only you can make that decision. And I know you're not talking to Adrian right now, but maybe... maybe considering he's the dad, you might need to get over your issues and just see what he thinks, too?"

"Yeah, that's kinda part of the problem as well..."

"What do you mean?"

"Well, the baby could be his... But then again, Eric might also be the father."

"Eric? That guy from your birthday party?"

"That's the one."

"But, I didn't know the two of you... Why didn't you tell me?"

"I was too embarrassed — I didn't even know him. And I just desperately wanted it to not be true, because he was actually a pretty sleazy guy..." She paused to take a deep breath. "And besides, I don't feel ready to face Adrian yet."

"OK... so may I ask what Adrian did that was so terrible? All you told me was that you slept together; then had a huge fight, and that you didn't want to talk about it at that point. But it's been a few weeks now, so... do you want to tell me what really happened between the two of you?"

Francesca sighed. "Do I have to?"

"No, of course not. But Adrian seems like a pretty good guy to me, and I find it hard to believe that he would do something truly horrible to you. I mean, I've always gotten the impression that he really likes you."

"Yeah, that's the thing... he does like me. And he actually told me... he actually told me that he thinks he loves me."

Margaret frowned. "...and this is why you're never speaking to him again?"

Francesca rolled her eyes. "I know it sounds stupid when you put it like that, it's just... I just know that if I give in to him, then somewhere down the line he's going to end up leaving me."

"And what exactly makes you think that?"

"Oh, come on, Margaret, you know I don't believe in happy endings. Maybe it's possible for some people, but it just hasn't ever happened to anyone in my family, so..."

"Well, I seriously doubt that your family is jinxed somehow. Besides, happiness does exist, you know ...if you just let it. And even though you've never admitted it, at least not to me — I'm pretty sure you really like Adrian, too."

Francesca pinched her eyes shut. "Of course I do, I feel the same way about him as he feels about me." She immediately covered her mouth, realizing what she'd finally admitted out loud to her best friend.

"OK, so what's the problem? All you're doing is making your life miserable for absolutely no reason at all. Of course, if you do end up deciding to keep the baby, then you and Adrian will be connected for life. I highly doubt he'll just up and leave you guys somewhere down the line, like you fear. And you never know... being with him might actually turn out to be all you've ever wanted."

Francesca banged the palm of her hand against her forehead a few times. "OK... so I'm not saying that I'm going to keep this baby... But suppose that I did ...and then the baby comes out with dark hair, when both Adrian and I are blond."

"OK, well were there any of the times that you didn't use a condom?"

Francesca sat up straight, stared at Margaret, and raised her voice. "Of course we used a condom both times — how stupid do you think I am?"

Margaret put both hands up in the air. "Hey, only trying to help here."

Francesca felt nauseated again. "I know. I'm sorry."

"I know this is a really sucky situation... but I guess the only thing I can tell you is to just give it some thought, and then I'm sure the right decision will come to you within a couple of days or so."

"Yeah... although, I've really only got one option. I mean, the way I see it, it's either Jenny or the baby. I can't afford to take care of both, and I definitely don't have time for both what with going to school, and the business and all. And taking a break from all of that in order to have a baby means breaking the deal with my dad, so... I'm gonna have to get rid of it..."

"Are you sure?"

Francesca sat motionless for a moment. Then she shook her head. "No... how can you ever be sure about something like this? But... I've given Jenny my word, and I can't go back on that."

"Are you going to tell Adrian first?"

Francesca sighed. "I don't know. I guess it would be the right thing to do, but I just don't think I can face him right now."

"Yeah... But he probably has the right to know. I mean, if I were the guy I think I would've liked to know."

"In a way he does have the right to know, but then again, if he's not the father then it doesn't really concern him."

"True. But he loves you, I'm sure he—"

"Exactly, Margaret — he loves me." Francesca felt her entire body tensing up. "And that is why nothing good can come from me telling him. If I were to have the baby and it turned out to be Eric's, then Adrian would hate me. But then again, if I tell Adrian about the baby and he decides he wants it, and then I still go through with the abortion anyway — because, let's face it, that's the only possible solution — then he'll also end up resenting me. No matter what I do I just can't win."

"OK." Margaret nodded. "I understand."

But then Francesca had a horrible thought. "What if he somehow ends up finding out later? What if he finds out I was pregnant, possibly with his baby, and then had it taken away without even telling him?"

"Well, I guess that's just a risk you'll have to take, although, I really don't see how he'd find out unless you told him."

"I won't tell him — at least not now. Maybe there's a tiny, minuscule chance I'll change my mind about telling him at some point in the faraway future, but I guess I'll have to deal with that if and when it happens," she muttered. Noticing how tired she was getting, Francesca closed her eyes for a moment. "But," she suddenly remembered, opening her eyes. "I've already sworn to never see him again, so I guess there's no real danger of him finding out."

Margaret again displayed that forced, awkward smile that made it look like she was sucking on a lemon wedge. "Well, ultimately, that's your call. My honest opinion is that cutting him out of your life forever is not the best way to go, but obviously I can't change your mind."

"Margaret, you've gotta promise me," Francesca said, holding her pinkie out. "that you won't tell anyone about this — least of all Adrian."

Margaret looked amused by her friend's childish way of sealing a promise, but wrapped her little finger around Francesca's nonetheless. "I promise."

"Thanks." Francesca reached out and hugged her friend. "I just wish my mom were here so I could talk to her about this, you know? I really miss her."

"Yeah, I know."

"Although," it dawned on Francesca. "If she were here, she'd probably tell me to keep it. All she ever wanted was to have kids and a family of her own — in a way, all she ever wanted was to have me. And she was only 21 years old when she had me."

"Yeah, but sweetie, this is kind of a different situation than the one she was in — the two don't really compare."

"Tell me about it; if she hadn't just gone and died on us, then I never would've been in all of this mess with my dad in the first place."

Margaret's eyes moistened. "She never wanted to leave you, you know."

"No, she just wanted to make sure my dad would never be able to see us again."

"But then again, your dad might not be telling the truth about that."

Francesca sighed. "Yeah, I just wish I knew for sure." She pulled her fingers through her hair. "Can I tell you a secret?"

"Of course."

"This whole story my dad told Jenny about my mom got me thinking — I think I'm actually starting to resent my mom a bit. Maybe my dad is right; maybe she wasn't such a great person after all. I've always looked up to her more than anyone else, and I don't want to suddenly start hating her now, 10 years after she passed away, but I just don't know what to think anymore."

"Well, I think it all comes down to how she made you feel. Maybe she said some bad things, maybe she made some bad decisions, but in the end, no matter how you look at it, she also did a lot of good things."

"Yeah, I guess."

"Of course she did. You're always telling me how strong she made you feel, how she made you realize you could do anything you wanted to — well, look at what you're doing right now for Jenny by building your own business. This might come as a surprise to you, but not many people can pull that off. And your mom planted that strength in you from the day you were born, just like you're planting that same strength in Jenny."

Francesca wiped her eyes, and choked down a sob. "That's true."

"But most importantly, she made you feel loved. And my personal opinion is that love is something you need to really feel and experience in your bones from a young age in order to fully understand it. Now, what could possibly be bigger or more important than love?"

Francesca nodded. "I think you're right. I think that's why my dad is the way he is, and does the things that he does — I don't think he's ever really understood love."

"Unfortunately, he probably hasn't."

Neither of them spoke for a couple of minutes.

"So... would you maybe go with me to the doctor when I have the thing done?"

"Of course."

*

Francesca left Margaret's house and started making her way back home. The crunching noise from the frosty leaves being crushed underneath the weight of her shoes made her wince with every step she took. It felt like the cold November air swaddling her body was stealing the life right out of her, replacing it with a frozen resignation.

Of course, she had never wanted to not be part of a loving family anymore. She had never asked for that to happen, for her mom to die.

And yet, it had happened. So abruptly. Her life was ripped apart in such an unforgiving way, and she still could not comprehend how it was possible for something so big and important to change so drastically within mere seconds.

She continued down the sidewalk, rubbing her hands together in front of her mouth, blowing frosty smoke onto her stiff fingers in an attempt to warm them, if only slightly. As the frosty smoke evaporated, she noticed the frosty leaves on the trees, twinkling in the rays of the lampposts.

Gazing up at the streetlight directly above her head as she passed underneath it, she was surprised to catch herself dangerously thinking... could it be that this pregnancy might be a chance for her to once again become part of a real family? Her chance to once again find what she secretly needed? A need she had never admitted to anyone else — and hardly even to herself. But still, if she remained quiet and undistracted for long enough... then a little voice would whisper from deep down inside of her: *I long to be loved; I long to be held. I long to again be a part of something special; to find a deep and meaningful connection with another person.*

Of course, she and Jenny already had an incredibly special bond — and they always would. That was one of the few things in life Francesca was absolutely sure of.

However, she'd heard that voice several times now, and recently, it had come to her more frequently. And maybe, she had begun to quietly suspect... maybe she did indeed need more, after all?

She sighed, and continued walking in a steady rhythm, stomping her feet down onto the asphalt harder than necessary in an attempt to make the noise drown out the sound of the thoughts in her head.

Eventually, she reached her dad's house. As she stood on the doorstep for another moment, she noticed that second voice she'd heard so many times before — many more times than the other voice that she'd just worked very hard to shut up. And she heard this familiar voice reminding her what it felt like to lose someone she loved, and instantly she knew that she'd never be strong enough to go through that again. True, she was strong. But not strong enough to take Adrian walking out on her. She would have to do what was best. She would need to stick to the plan and put Jenny first.

Chapter Twenty-six

Francesca peered over at the big black-rimmed clock hanging next to the door in her lecture theatre.

Only a couple more minutes until it struck twelve o'clock, signaling lunch break.

She bent down and pulled her phone out of her bag.

There was another missed call from Adrian.

Although it made her feel horrible, she again ignored his attempt to get hold of her. Right now, she had a more urgent phone call to make; she needed to schedule a doctor's appointment. It had already been two days since she found out about her pregnancy, and for each passing hour, she was finding it harder and harder to cope with the fact that... she needed to give it up.

How far along could she be? How many weeks did she have left before she would no longer be able to have a say in her own future? She needed it done, and she needed it done as quickly as possible. It was bad enough that she was so tired and emotional all the time, but she was also starting to become paranoid — thinking that people were already able to tell that she was pregnant, just by looking at her.

"OK, that concludes our lecture for today," their professor said.

"Yes," Francesca whispered to herself. This was her signal. She grabbed her brown leather bag by the straps and flung it over her shoulder before bolting for the door.

"Hey, Francesca, wait up," Emily called out.

"Damn it," Francesca muttered under her breath, and turned around. "Ah... Hey... I just need to run to the grocery store real quick, I didn't bring any lunch today, so..."

"What's wrong with the cafeteria?"

"You know, I'm just sick of everything they have there."

Emily raised one eyebrow. "You do remember that they offer a different hot meal selection every day, right?"

Francesca started laughing eerily, but then heard how fake it was sounding, and immediately stopped. "Yes, that's true. But, uh... the grocery store is just so much cheaper and, as you know, I've gotta be saving as much money as I possibly can... So, anyway, I'll just head right over, and I'll be back in a few minutes."

"Hey, I wouldn't mind getting some lunch from the grocery store as well," Tina said, joining the conversation. "I'll just come with you, then."

"No!" Francesca and Margaret cried out in unison.

Tina covered her ears. "Geez... what was that?"

"Yeah, something's going on, for sure." Emily looked suspiciously back and forth between Francesca and Margaret.

"No, it's nothing," Margaret started. "It's just that... Well, why do you have to be so nosy all the time?"

Emily put her hands on her hips and took a couple of steps toward Margaret. "What are you guys hiding from us?"

Margaret rolled her eyes, and whispered. "Well, if you must know, seeing as it's someone's birthday soon," she darted her eyes in Tina's direction, "Francesca is just heading over to one of the stores around the corner to check something out — OK?"

"Ah, OK, I see," Emily winked at Margaret. But then her face suddenly dropped, and she whispered. "Wait, so does that mean that you're getting her something without me this year?"

"No, 'course not. Just play along, I'll fill you in later."

"OK, yeah..." Emily took the bait. "Hey, Tina, I've been meaning to show you this super funny video I saw on YouTube the other day," she said, directing Tina toward the nearest university computer.

Francesca turned toward Margaret and mouthed: *Thank you.*

Margaret gave her a little nod.

Francesca hurried down the sidewalk, watching the cars and people passing by her. She envied them; so seemingly carefree as they went on with their lives. ...But then again, she realized, they, too, might be hiding secrets of their own, just like her.

All she knew was that for now, until she had gotten rid of it, she was just going to pretend that everything was exactly like before; attempting to convince herself that nothing had changed — although, she knew very well that everything had just changed.

She walked up to a bench in a small park area and sat down. Then she realized that someone might come by and sit down next to her. She'd really prefer to have this conversation in private. Getting up, she walked over to a group of tall, slender bushes, with a narrow opening leading into the middle. She knew it would look a bit suspect if anyone saw her disappearing into the bushes like that, but at least she'd be by herself in there.

When she'd reached the center of the shrubbery, where she was covered on all sides, she pulled her phone out of her bag. Her finger shaking slightly, she scrolled through her contacts until she found the number for the women's clinic at Oslo Central Hospital that she'd found on their website and saved on her phone last night.

She stared at the number for awhile, just waiting, and hoping to soon wake up from her nightmare. But unfortunately... this was the kind of nightmare where she was already awake. She took a deep breath, and hit dial.

"You've reached Oslo Central Hospital's Women's Clinic," an elderly woman's monotone voice played out in the other end.

Francesca listened intently, waiting to hear a selection of extensions.

The line was silent for about five seconds.

"Hello, you've reached the Women's Clinic, how may I help you?" the monotone voice repeated.

"Oh, sorry, I thought that was an automatic answering machine..." Francesca's voice trailed away. She cleared her throat. "Hello, my name is Francesca Hansen, and I would like to schedule an appointment with one of your doctors, please."

"OK, we're quite fully booked at the moment, so I'm going to have to set you up for an appointment in about... let's see..." the woman paused while flipping through the pages of an appointment book. "in exactly two weeks from today, on November 24th — will that work for you?"

"No!" Francesca burst out. "I mean, no, I'm sorry, but I really do need something sooner than that."

"May I ask what the appointment is for, and then I'll see if there's anything I can do to squeeze you in sooner?"

"Well," Francesca instinctively looked around, though, of course, she wasn't able to tell whether or not anyone was close by from where she stood hiding in the center of the tall shrubbery. She lowered her voice. "I think I'm pregnant, or rather, I'm quite sure I'm pregnant. I haven't had my period for about six weeks now, so..."

"And do you tend to be regular?"

"Yes."

"OK, and have you taken an at-home pregnancy test?"

"Of course, and obviously it was positive," Francesca huffed. "With all due respect, ma'am, this is not a prank call."

"Miss, I do understand your situation, however, you still can't be more than somewhere between four and six weeks along. We don't usually schedule a check-up before the pregnancy is quite a bit further along than that."

"No, but you don't understand. I don't want it — I want it... taken away."

"Alright, but you've still got about another six weeks before the ordinary cut-off time for such a procedure."

"You're kidding, right? I'm supposed to walk around feeling like this until then?"

"Listen," the woman said, paging through the appointment book again. "We've just had a cancellation for next week. Now, Dr. Karlsen told me she'd prefer we leave that appointment open if possible, as she had some business to attend to, but I guess I could fit you in there if you really want?"

"Yes, perfect — I'll take it."

"OK, I'm scheduling you in for November 18th, at 3:30 p.m."

Francesca pulled a pen out of her bag and wrote the time down on her left hand. "Great, thanks."

"What did you say your name was?"

"Francesca Hansen."

"OK, Tuesday November 18th at 3:30 it is, then," the woman repeated. "Goodbye."

"OK, bye." Francesca hung up, and slipped her phone back into her bag. She sighed, relieved that the worst part of her day was over. Checking her watch, she realized she needed to hustle if she wanted to have time to pick up something for her rumbling stomach before returning to class. She vacated her hiding spot amongst the tall bushes and returned to civilization.

"Ring, ring..."

Francesca placed her hand up against the outside of her bag.

The bag vibrated underneath the palm of her hand.

She reached for her phone, and checked the display.

It was Richard.

"Hi Richard, what's up?"

"What's up is that I've already managed to book another meeting with more franchisees."

"Wow, that's great!"

"Yeah, apparently some of the remaining franchisees for the Oslo stores heard about our successful presentation on Friday and now they, too, want to hear what we have to say — nothing better than word-of-mouth."

"Absolutely. So, when is it?"

"Next Tuesday at four o'clock. And it'll be in my usual meeting room again, same as last time."

"OK." Francesca pulled her pen out again. Then she glanced over at her left hand, and immediately felt her stomach contract. "Wait, you don't mean Tuesday the 18th, do you?"

"That's the one — as far as I know each week only comes with one Tuesday."

"Ah... I don't suppose there's any chance we could reschedule, is there?"

"I know you said you'd rather do Saturdays, but unfortunately the Franchisees I've talked to couldn't make it next weekend. So, whatever you've got planned, cancel it — this is more important."

Francesca sighed. "Right."

"Listen, if we want potential customers to spend their money on us then we've got to jump when they say jump, you understand?"

"Yes, I understand."

"Good. And the best thing about it is that the presentation will be held in Oslo again, so we don't even have to travel anywhere. Now, in the meantime I'll make sure to distribute the time and place to as many of Oslo's remaining franchisees as possible."

"Great," Francesca mumbled.

"Hey, you don't need to sound too excited or grateful or anything."

"No, I'm sorry," Francesca tried to make her voice sound perky. "I am grateful, I really am. Just let me know the specifics and I'll be there with bells on."

"That's the spirit. I'll keep you posted."

"OK, cool!" Francesca hung up. "Fuck." She banged the top edge of her phone against her forehead repeatedly.

Chapter Twenty-seven

Francesca dragged her feet a few steps back in the direction of her university. "Man, I just cannot catch a break." She walked over to a grassy area just off the sidewalk, and sat down on a large rock, letting her head drop into her hands.

"OK, let me think for a sec here..." she muttered to herself.

Maybe, she would just keep her doctor's appointment for now, and then she'd come up with a solution by next Tuesday. Was it possible that she could make both her appointment and their business presentation?

No... she shook her head. She was no expert, but suspected her check-up would probably take around thirty minutes, or at least not much less than that. Besides, the hospital and Richard's meeting room were on completely opposite sides of town.

Then, maybe... Could she call in sick for their business presentation?

Nah, that was too risky. It would make her — and thereby as an extension of that, Richard, and their business as well — seem unprofessional. And they could end up losing out on money — money she desperately needed within a clearly set timeframe. Besides, Richard would know she was faking it.

"Alright..." Francesca said to herself. There was really only one thing to do. And the receptionist had said that technically she still had about six weeks until the cut-off time — so what was another two weeks from now, right? Until then, she would just find a way to be strong, and focus on what was important: Jenny and the business.

She got her phone out, and again called the hospital.

"Hello, you've reached Oslo Central Hospital's Women's Clinic," the same woman with her monotone voice answered the phone.

"Hi, this is Francesca Hansen calling again. You might remember me from just a couple of minutes ago?"

"Yes, I do."

"Anyway, I'm really sorry, but something's just come up, and unfortunately I won't be able to make it to my appointment next Tuesday."

"OK, and you're absolutely sure about this now before I erase your name?"

Francesca sighed. "Yeah, I'm sure. And, is there any chance that other appointment on November 24th that you gave me first is still available."

"Yes, it's still available."

"OK, great, I'll take it."

"OK, November 24th at nine a.m., then."

"Thanks. Oh, and could you please let me know if you have any cancellations between now and then?"

"OK, in which case can you be reached at the number you're dialling from now?"

"Yes, this is my cell phone number. Thanks."

"OK, goodbye."

Francesca sat motionless on the big rock off the side of the road for a moment. Eventually, she managed to pull herself together, slinging her bag over her shoulder, and shuffling back out onto the sidewalk.

Less than a minute later, she quickly caught up with a mother and her young daughter sauntering along at a painfully slow rate in front of her on the sidewalk. They held hands and blocked the entire width of the narrow sidewalk, leaving no room to pass without stepping out into the busy road.

Francesca was gradually becoming more and more annoyed with herself for being too polite to ask them to get out of her way, and instead, forcing herself to take baby steps in order to avoid walking right into them. Baby steps, for which there was no time if she wanted to feed the baby inside of her before her next class — her baby who kept demanding her to eat an increasingly larger amount of food each passing day.

That thought stopped both her heart and feet cold. Yes — it was *her baby*. Ever since she'd found out she was pregnant, all she'd referred to it as was *this thing* growing inside of her.

She contemplated the little girl walking in front of her for a moment, guessing that she was probably around three years old.

The girl dropped her stuffed bunny rabbit on the asphalt sidewalk, but didn't seem to notice.

Francesca bent down and picked up the yellow stuffed bunny. She studied it, remembering that her very own first stuffed animal had been a rabbit as well, only it was a pale pink color.

Francesca walked up to the mother, and tapped her on the shoulder. "Excuse me,"

The mother turned around. "Yes?"

Francesca looked at her face.

The woman seemed quite young — probably very early twenties.

"Sorry, I think your daughter dropped this." Francesca held the stuffed animal out in front of her.

"Oh, thank you so much!" the mother said, looking relieved. "You just saved me from what could've been a very long night. She loves that thing, can't sleep without it."

Francesca smiled and bent down, handing the little girl her bunny rabbit.

The girl's hazel eyes lit up. She took her toy, held it tight to her chest and giggled softly.

Francesca smiled, and didn't know if it was her hormones spinning out of control from being pregnant or not, but she suddenly felt her heart go warm, along with an urge to reach over and hug the child. She realized that would be inappropriate, though, and managed to refrain from doing so.

The woman looked at her daughter. "So, what do you say?"

The girl studied her mother for a second with her mouth hanging open, then turned to Francesca and said, "Thank you," before giggling again.

Francesca smiled. "You're very welcome."

The mother turned toward Francesca. "Thanks again."

"No problem."

"Now, wave goodbye to the nice lady."

"Bye," the girl said, waving her chubby little hand.

Francesca waved back. "Bye." She stepped out in front of them on the sidewalk and hurried along in the direction of the cafe near her university to grab a quick bite before class.

She thought about how young that mother had looked, and all of a sudden caught herself wondering... young mothers who were still students, weren't they entitled to receive some financial support from the government due to not being able to work? And what about young student mothers who were also single — weren't they maybe entitled to an even larger amount of money?

She shrugged. Obviously, this was all irrelevant to her — she was having the abortion. But still, she thought, it couldn't hurt to simply do some research in order to find out what the rules were — just out of pure curiosity, of course.

Chapter Twenty-eight

Phillip walked into the cab central and started getting ready for his 8:00 a.m. shift.

"Phillip," his boss called after him as he passed through the corridor. "A word, please."

Phillip quickly glanced around, "Who, me?"

"Yes," his boss muttered, looking down at the floor. "Please step into my office for a minute."

He hesitated, racking his brain in attempt to remember whether or not they had scheduled a meeting that he'd forgotten about, but nothing came to mind. "Uh, OK," he said, and followed his boss into his office.

Mr. Selmer cleared his throat. "So, I'm going to make this quick... Unfortunately, we've received another customer complaint about you, and as I've warned you before, another strike and you'd be out, so..." His voice trailed off.

Phillip felt his face burn with shame; he couldn't believe it. He'd really cleaned up his act lately, tried his hardest to be polite. At least, much more polite than he'd tended to be in the past. "But, Mr. Selmer, I..."

"I'm sorry, Phillip. But I've been told from a couple different people that your attitude has given the company bad word-of-mouth on a few occasions, and the industry is getting increasingly competitive, so you've left me with no other choice. Please pack up your stuff today."

Phillip's eyes stung, and he suddenly felt very dizzy. He turned slowly toward the door, and made his way out of the office. He emptied his locker and left, without a single word to anyone. What was he going to do now? If what Mr. Selmer had claimed was actually true, then he wouldn't likely get a job at another cab company in Oslo, either.

He sighed, and got back into his private car. He had a few contacts that he could always try calling. Of course, working for them would mean having to make some changes. ...But then again, what choice did he have? Maybe that was exactly what he and Jenny needed — a fresh start?

*

The wind encircling Francesca's face felt chilling, yet refreshing at the same time. It was mid-November, and Oslo had just received its first snowfall of the season a couple of days ago.

She looked down, and realized that her mitten-covered right hand was lightly stroking her stomach through her gray woolen coat.

Francesca pulled her hand away, shook it, and instead used it to check the map on her phone to make sure she was still heading in the right direction.

She had done some online research about what kind of financial support a young student mother was entitled to, but the specifics were all quite confusing. And for certain issues the stuff she had read online had just been downright contradictory. She needed help from an expert.

Francesca turned the corner, and followed the busy downtown street until she reached her destination. She stopped and looked over at the red and white sign hanging on the left hand side of the big, glass entrance door, and read: *The Norwegian Labor and Welfare Administration.* Usually, she would've needed to wait a lot longer to meet with one of their advisors, but she'd told them about her situation, and that time simply wasn't something that she had a lot of.

Francesca took a deep breath, and pulled the heavy door open.

A short hallway led into a large, open waiting room.

She looked around and found an empty seat across the room, next to a woman in her thirties and her three young children.

The air was stuffy, and the people were noisy.

She attempted to drown out everyone and everything else, and started going over the questions in her head that she wanted to make sure to remember to ask.

A couple of minutes later, a stocky, bespectacled woman entered the waiting room. "Francesca Hansen," she called out.

"Yes, that's me." Francesca rose from her seat, and started walking in the woman's direction.

Francesca took the woman's hand and shook it. "Hi, nice to meet you."

"Likewise." The woman's eyes smiled from behind her square, red-rimmed glasses. "Please come along with me." The middle-aged woman gestured with her hand, and led the way down a corridor. She stopped at the third door on the left, and held it open for Francesca.

Francesca entered, and gazed around at the sterile office. She immediately got the sensation that she'd been bad, and had been taken to the principal's office to explain herself.

"Please, have a seat." The woman nodded at the two red upholstered office chairs on the visitor's side of the pinewood desk.

"Thanks." Francesca smiled politely.

The woman sat down in her chair on the other side of the desk. "So," she began, peering first at her computer screen and then back at Francesca. "I understand that you're pregnant, correct?"

Francesca looked down at her hands twisting in her lap. "Yes, that's right."

"OK." The woman nodded, and scrolled down the screen of her computer, before turning back to Francesca. "So, in your case, you are definitely entitled to child benefits and financial support from the government."

Francesca smiled. "OK, that's good."

"Now, the exact amount that you'll be entitled to per month depends on your circumstances, so I'm going to ask you a few questions, alright?"

Francesca sat up straight. "Yes. Of course."

"OK, so will you be a single mother, or will the father also take part in the caring for and raising of the child?"

"Well, I'm not quite sure about that. You see... I haven't exactly told him yet."

"The reason I ask is that as a single parent you will be compensated enough to be able to support both you and your child by yourself. However, if the father is involved, and you're living together, then you'll need to rely on him for a substantial amount of the financial support for your family of three."

"What if he's a student and doesn't have a lot of time to work?"

"Obviously he'll still be receiving his student loan each month, and a small amount of extra compensation will also be given between the two of you due to the fact that you're both young students. However, the way the system works is that when there are two parents providing for a child, there will naturally also be two people in a position to earn money, thereby splitting the cost of living — and consequently you would be receiving quite a bit less money from the government each month. So the situation between the two of you needs to be clarified before you can go ahead and apply for any kind of financial support."

"OK." Francesca nodded, and pulled her notebook out of her bag.

"Another important factor is how much money you'll have earned next year, by the time the baby comes. Do you have a job at the moment?"

"Yes. Well, I just recently started my own business together with another business partner, so I don't know for sure yet how much we'll end up making during the course of the coming year."

"OK, so just so you know, there is a transitional benefit available once the baby has come. However, this amount starts decreasing quite rapidly from the moment your annual salary exceeds more than forty-three thousand."

Francesca stopped taking notes, and looked up at the woman. "Forty-three thousand? Well, that's not very much."

"So you think you'll definitely be making more than that, then?"

"Well, yeah, I pretty much have to, because I'll be supporting my younger sister liv..." Francesca stopped herself.

The woman slid her glasses down along the bridge of her nose, and peered at Francesca. "Your younger sister?"

Francesca felt a nauseating pang in her stomach. Was this baby stripping her of all common sense as well — why the hell did she mention Jenny?

"Ah… Well, what I meant is that we'll probably be having sleepovers every once in a while — you know, sibling quality time."

The woman continued to look at Francesca over the top of her spectacles.

Francesca all of a sudden noticed how incredibly warm the office was. And she was also getting an increasingly stronger urge to go and push the woman's glasses right back up in front of her eyes where they belonged.

"Francesca, does your sister live with you?"

"No, of course not." Francesca waved her hand back and forth. "Why would she live with me? No, no, don't be silly — she lives with our dad." It's OK, Francesca attempted to reassure herself; she wasn't lying — at least not quite yet.

"And you're sure about that?"

"Well, in a way you're right; my sister and I are living together, but that's only because I'm also living with our dad at the moment." Francesca laughed and slapped her hand onto her thigh, in a weak attempt to show how funny and absurd she thought the woman's question was.

The woman started typing on her keyboard. "OK, because if it turned out you were having an underage sibling living with you as well, then that would be a cause for concern, and we'd need to have someone from child care services investigate why she was staying with you and not your parents. Especially considering the majority of your attention would be on the baby once it's born. And, of course, you having the baby and receiving financial support from us would mean you'd be in our files and we'd be able to find out if anything out of the ordinary were going on."

Francesca gulped. "Understood."

Chapter Twenty-nine

Francesca felt like her head had just been drenched in a bucket of ice water, and she was now more awake than ever to the reality of what was actually going on.

Although the advisor at the Norwegian Labor and Welfare Administration had eventually switched over to other topics than Jenny, Francesca hadn't been able to fully concentrate on what she'd said after that.

She hadn't considered the fact that somebody — a neighbor, or a parent at Jenny's school, or someone else — might alert the child care services to the fact that Jenny was living with her. Of course, this probably wasn't very likely. But she couldn't be completely sure that it wouldn't happen, either. And for there to be any point in Jenny moving, they would have to change her address and everything. It couldn't just be for pretend-getting-away from their dad — It would have to be for real.

Maybe that lady would be their downfall? How ironic was it that they were this close to succeeding; this close to escaping; but then right at the very end, Francesca — and not Phillip — was the one to screw it all up, all by herself? She pursed her lips, until the inevitable words exploded from her mouth, stating the obvious: "God, I'm so stupid."

But then it suddenly occurred to her... through the very nature of the advisor's job, she must be bound by client confidentiality — meaning she couldn't tell anyone anyway, right? Francesca instantly felt a little better. It was OK, she told herself; all was not lost yet.

She crossed the street, and reached a frosty bench right by the National Theatre. She plopped down onto the bench.

But then again, it dawned on her, maybe if the advisor felt concerned enough about what Francesca had almost revealed — maybe she was then allowed to disregard her confidentiality, and still alert the child care services so they could at least investigate what was going on? Francesca noticed that she was shaking — and not just from the slightly below freezing temperature.

The lady at the Labor and Welfare Administration had made her realize quite clearly what her two options were. No matter how Francesca tried calculating the variables of her situation, the bottom line was: she could either have Jenny — assuming no one found out about Jenny living with her — or; she could keep her baby. There was no right answer to her dilemma, and that was making her furious... pushing her to the verge of insanity. Usually, she could resolve the majority of her problems through working hard both at school, and especially through her ballet classes. But not this one; this dilemma was different.

Though at least when it came to Adrian, she knew she'd made the right choice in deciding to cut him out of her life. Well... she was almost totally sure that that was the right thing to do; like ninety percent sure.

She'd noticed that along with the decision to stay away from him, a part of her seemed to have died, somehow. Was that actually physically possible, she wondered...? It must be — at least emotionally possible. For there she was, her heart feeling less whole; saddened and weakened. Even though no one had actually died, the death of an almost lifelong personal relationship had occurred.

But more than that, if she had let her feelings rule and entered into a relationship with him, then the constant worry that their relationship might someday end would be more unbearable than anything else she could imagine. And so to carry the death of cutting him out of her life now seemed like the lesser of the two pains. She would recover at some point. She would have to.

She dragged her feet slightly from side to side across the icy cobblestones, and observed the people passing by.

An old man wearing a brown cap walked slowly past her, supporting himself on his wooden cane. He wore his sadness on his face; around his mouth and his eyes. He suddenly paused as if to gather his strength. Glancing around, his eyes landed on Francesca.

She immediately felt embarrassed that he'd caught her staring, and was about to look away, but then she decided to give him a big smile instead.

He smiled back, although he still appeared to be in pain.

Maybe he was all alone, Francesca wondered. Did he have any family, or had they all passed away? Maybe he'd never had any kids?

It struck her that her dad would end up being in that situation when he grew older. She and Jenny would always have each other, and they would always love each other; their dad wouldn't have anyone.

She put her hand on her belly and caressed it gently.

Luckily, it hadn't started growing yet, but still, there was no escaping the fact that, soon, it would.

Then she thought about how much her dad had changed lately, ever since he realized he could end up losing the girls forever. He'd been there for her when she was at home with morning sickness, although, of course, none of them had known the reason for why she was throwing up at the time. She remembered how surprised she'd been when he had stayed home from work to take care of her — he'd never done that before. And he hadn't needed to at this point — Francesca hadn't asked him. She was 19 years old and could take care of herself. He'd only done it because he wanted to be there for her, to spend time with his daughter.

Suddenly it occurred to Francesca that, even though Phillip had taken the wrong approach; almost every argument and discussion she and Jenny had had with him lately had basically been about their father wanting to spend time with his daughters — yet, they had brushed him away every time. He had even told Francesca he loved her when she was sick, despite the fact that he already knew she was teaming up with Richard. He had finally been a real father — the father they'd always wanted and needed.

She caught herself wondering if maybe it wouldn't be so bad for Jenny to live with him after all? Maybe Jenny would be fine now that their dad had changed so much?

Francesca felt her eyes fill with tears, and started blinking over and over again, quickly wiping away the tears as they started to fall. Yet as soon as she'd wiped the old ones away new ones appeared, taking their place. She wasn't sure whether it was her hormones wanting to sabotage the promise she'd made to Jenny, but she was beginning to realize how every day it was becoming increasingly harder to have to give up her baby. She sighed, letting her head drop into her hands.

Even though she knew it would be hard to raise the baby, and that she'd probably have to do it on her own, she still knew that she was capable of doing it if she really wanted to.

Maybe there was a reason for her previous doctor's appointment and their second business meeting falling on the exact same day, at almost the exact same time — maybe it was meant to force her to reschedule, giving her a chance to change her mind and keep the baby after all?

Then it dawned on her; if she had the abortion and put Jenny first, then she would have to continue putting Jenny first for the next seven years, until she turned 18. She'd been so strong ever since their mother had passed away — maybe the time had come for Francesca to stop playing substitute mom for Jenny?

The problem, of course, was how she'd convince Jenny that she needed to continue living with their dad. Francesca had already told her that the business was going to work out, and that she would be able to come live with her, like they had both hoped.

Although, Francesca thought, surely Jenny must've also noticed just how much their dad had changed during the past month or so?

Still... she would need to come up with a plan in order to persuade her sister that this was the best solution for everyone.

Francesca could suggest that the three of them get out of the city for a weekend trip, just like they'd done that summer five years ago when Phillip and Francesca together had taught Jenny how to swim. Whenever Francesca looked back and thought about the happiest moments of her life, that weekend had always ranked right up at the top of the list. Another trip like that would help them all become closer. Except, maybe this time they could go away to some cabin in the mountains and teach Jenny how to ski?

She got out the calendar on her phone, and counted the days until her doctor's appointment.

She had 22 days to convince Jenny she needed to continue living with Phillip. And if worse came to worst, Francesca could always confide in her sister that she was pregnant, and that that was the reason for Jenny having to live with their dad. And maybe Jenny would even be happy about becoming an aunt? Francesca knew she'd always hated being the youngest family member, and always being bossed around; too young to have a say in any major decision. Now, Jenny wouldn't be the youngest anymore; now she'd finally have the right to decide and boss over someone else for once in her life.

Francesca started biting her nails. That plan had at least a small chance of working out, right? *Yes*, she convinced herself, it would work out — it *had* to work out. She had no other choice.

As for Adrian, even though she cut him completely out of her life, she was pretty sure he'd still manage to find out about the baby somehow if she ended up keeping it. And if and when that happened, she had no idea how to go about telling him that he might or might not be the father of her child. But she would just have to come up with something when she got that far. First of all; she needed to persuade Jenny.

Chapter Thirty

Francesca stood on the doorstep of her dad's row house and unlocked the front door. She entered, closed the door behind her, and checked the time on her phone.

It was 5:27 p.m.

She sighed. She was going to miss ballet class — which, unfortunately, seemed to be happening quite a lot lately — but it just couldn't be helped tonight. She only had 22 days to turn the future living situation with Jenny and her dad around, and every day that she didn't make any progress was another day closer to having the abortion and losing her baby.

Today was Thursday and if the three of them were going away for a weekend bonding trip at all, then this coming weekend would have to be the time to do it. Francesca had already promised Richard to keep all her future Saturdays open for potential business meetings, and this coming weekend was the only weekend between now and her doctor's appointment that she, at this point, absolutely knew for sure they wouldn't be having any meetings.

She realized it might be a bit ambitious to hope for a full weekend away together — especially considering that she had no clue what kind of shifts her dad was supposed to be working these next three days. But hopefully they'd at least be able to pull off a day trip somewhere, or maybe even staying overnight at some place.

Francesca walked over to the bottom of the staircase. "Jenny?" she called up to the second floor.

Except for the slight creaking of the floorboards underneath her feet, there was complete silence.

"Dad?" she tried instead.

Again, there was no response.

She ran up the staircase, and knocked on Jenny's bedroom door.

Still nothing.

She pushed the door open.

Jenny wasn't there, and neither was her backpack.

Francesca searched the room for clues that Jenny had been back at the house since she'd left for school that morning.

Her bed was still made, just like Francesca had taught her some years back that all big girls do before they leave the house in the mornings. Mainly, this had been to avoid giving Phillip a reason to chew Jenny out when he was cranky after work... and teaching Jenny how to do it meant Francesca wouldn't have to be the one to do it anymore.

Francesca walked over to Jenny's desk.

There was no homework floating around, and Jenny's favorite story-books, that Francesca knew always gave her comfort when she was feeling lonely or scared, remained neatly stacked in her bookshelf above her desk.

"Where is that girl? School finished a couple of hours ago." She grabbed her phone and hit the speed dial for Jenny's number.

The phone rang several times, before going to voicemail.

She felt her heart start to race... What was going on? Then she tried her dad's phone as well.

It was switched off.

Francesca began pacing Jenny's bedroom floor. Then she stopped abruptly, and sat down on Jenny's bed. She took a deep breath, and racked her brain for any piece of information she might not be remembering at the moment. Had Jenny said anything about having plans with friends or something like that tonight? Francesca started rubbing her temples with her fingertips.

Nothing came to mind.

Considering Jenny kept mostly to herself, and with the exception of Francesca, didn't tend to let anyone get too close, it seemed unlikely that she would've spontaneously decided to go over to some friend's house — especially without letting Francesca know where she was.

She could always call Jenny's school to see if they knew anything.

But then again, she realized, at this point it would be too late in the evening for anyone to be there to pick up the phone.

She scrolled through the contacts on her phone, and found the number for the operator at her dad's cab central. Francesca knew he hated it when she called that number, but at the moment she didn't really care what he thought.

The phone rang twice before a woman answered. "Hello, you've reached Oslo Central Cab Service, how may I help you?"

"Hi, this is Francesca Hansen — Phillip Hansen's daughter. Is there any chance you'd be able to tell me what time his shift finishes tonight? You see, I've tried his cell but he's not picking up."

"OK, one moment please." The woman tapped away at her keyboard. "Yes, is this regarding the family emergency?"

Francesca immediately thought of Jenny, and felt all the blood drain from her face. "What family emergency?"

"I'm sorry, but I don't have any specific details. All it says here in our system is that he left this morning. It had something to do with a family emergency, and that most likely he'll be away for a certain period of time."

"OK, thanks." Francesca immediately hung up, before trying Phillip's number again.

His phone was still switched off, and again went straight to voicemail.

She got to her feet and continued pacing the floor again, waiting for the recorded message to finish up so she could leave her own message after the beep. "Dad, what's going on? Where are you, and where's Jenny? I called your work, and they said something about a family emergency — call me as soon as you get this."

Francesca threw herself onto Jenny's bed.

Had something terrible happened to Jenny? Maybe she'd been in some kind of accident and was at a hospital right now — maybe that was why Phillip had been required to turn his phone off? And if so, why hadn't Francesca been notified?

The waiting was unbearable.

She rolled around on Jenny's bed, constantly changing positions.

Then she looked over at Jenny's bookshelf, forcing her mind to distract itself with other thoughts, and started reading the titles on the spines of the books. As she reached *Beauty and the Beast* — Jenny's absolute favorite storybook – Francesca remembered something Jenny had told her one evening some years back when Francesca had read the story aloud to her. With a knowing smile on her face, Jenny had said: "Belle has been taken prisoner by the beast, but it's OK, Francesca, don't worry — she will be free in the end. They only need to learn to love each other first. You'll see; when they love each other then Belle will be free, and the beast will not be a beast anymore."

Francesca got up and walked over to the bookshelf. She pulled the book out, and brought it back over to Jenny's bed with her.

She settled down in a cross-legged position, and opened the book to the very first page.

"Ding, ding." Her phone sounded. Francesca's eyes darted over at her cell phone. She immediately picked it up from where it lay next to her on Jenny's bed, and flipped the front flap of the blue cover aside. She opened and read the text: *Hi Francesca. Dad picked me up from school today. He has packed some of my things and says we are going on a trip, but I don't know where. I'm a little scared. Love you, Jenny.*

Chapter Thirty-one

Francesca stared at the text message, rereading it at least 10 times. Suddenly, she felt something start to work its way from her stomach and up toward her chest.

She covered her mouth and ran for the bathroom.

Just in time, she managed to fling the toilet lid open before hurling into the bowl.

She sat there on the bathroom floor for a moment, breathing heavily and resting her forearms on the toilet seat. Both her stomach and her chest were cramping up, like they were trying to strangle her torso. The sharp, sudden pains made her wince with every contraction in her midriff. How could she have been so stupid as to believe that her dad had really changed? He was still playing games with her, just like he'd done her entire life.

Her eyes started burning. Jenny wasn't the only one who was scared. Francesca had been through a few scary moments before, but the thought of not knowing if and when her dad would come back with Jenny — that frightened her more than anything she'd ever experienced.

She slammed the palm of her hand into the gray tiles on the bathroom floor. What the hell had she been thinking going up against their dad in a crazy bet like this? After living with him for 19 years, she should've known that he would end up resorting to a cowardly move like this. She was supposed to protect Jenny — why hadn't she managed to prevent this from happening?

Francesca got to her feet and turned the faucet on, letting the cool water pour all over her face and into her mouth. She reached for a towel, wiped her face, and stared at herself in the mirror. "OK, Francesca; think."

Her phone lay on the counter next to the sink, still displaying Jenny's message across the screen.

She grabbed her phone and reread it again, lingering on Jenny's words toward the end of the message; *I'm a little scared.*

The words carved themselves onto her retinas. She knew Jenny hated to make her worry, so when she said she was *a little scared*, Francesca realized Jenny must be absolutely terrified.

She needed to text Jenny back; she needed to comfort her; and she needed to try to get more information about where they were going.

She wrote: *J-love, don't be scared. I promise you everything's going to be OK. Remember what you said about 'Beauty and the Beast'? You said that Belle would be free in the end — all she needed to do was to love the beast.* Francesca paused. That's it — that was the clue. She continued writing the text: *Jenny, tell Dad how much you love him, OK? I think that might help.* She held her breath, and hit send.

Francesca stared at her face in the mirror again.

She looked tired.

She was tired — exhausted, actually. Exhausted from fighting with her dad; from having to be so much older and stronger than a 19 year old should ever have to be.

She pinched her eyes shut, wanting to disappear.

"Ding, ding." Her phone sounded.

Slowly, she moved her finger across the screen of her Smartphone, opening her message from Jenny: *Dad says he loves me, too, and that's why we have to go away so that you can't take me away from him.*

Francesca felt the nausea building again. She realized her plan had back-fired. Just a simple statement of love from Jenny to Phillip wasn't going to be enough to make him admit defeat and bring her back to Francesca — on the contrary, this might've only made him more determined to stay away and never come back.

But Francesca couldn't just let him get away with kidnapping Jenny, either — not when she knew how terrified Jenny was; and not when she knew giving up might mean her hardly ever seeing her sister again, depending on how far away from Oslo he was taking her.

Then it dawned on Francesca that both she and her dad actually wanted the same thing. What they both wanted more than anything was a chance to be able to keep their own child — to not have their child forcefully taken away from them.

And then she thought about her grandparents whom she'd never met, and whom Phillip, himself, had no recollection of either, and how they had been so very different from both Francesca and her dad. How they had *not* wanted to keep their child, giving him away so easily ...their own son. ...or, at least, that was the story her dad had always told her.

She was at a complete loss about what to do in order to get Phillip to come back home with Jenny, but maybe... maybe his parents might some-how be the clue? After all, they were the reason Phillip had become this way in the first place, were they not?

She wondered whether there was any way she could track them down to get the story of what had really happened when they gave him up 42 years ago? Maybe if she could just get him together with at least his biological mother he would discover that she, for some reason, had no choice but to give him up? Maybe that would finally help him find some peace in his life, possibly even change him for the better?

She grabbed her phone again, and started searching online for any useful information she could find. "OK, let's see..." She skimmed through the results, and found something that might be able to answer her question.

Regarding children who have grown up in orphanages, and/or have been adopted, Norwegian law states that only the person in question is entitled to information about their biological parents — and only they, and no other family member — can request access to details about the case. In the event that any information about the biological parents should exist on file, this information can be obtained by writing a letter to the Children-, Youth- and Family Affairs, as well as including a signature that is verified at a government office and then stamped with a municipality stamp.

"Damn..." There was no way she'd ever be able to contact her grandparents.

She felt her desperation begin to mount, and as she sat there staring into space, she became aware of the fact that she was willing to try absolutely *anything* that might make her dad come to his senses.

Of course, this was 2015, it's not like she wouldn't be able to track them down somehow. However, he still had the parental rights, and even if she found them, and actually moved to wherever they were, then Phillip could always just up and move somewhere else whenever he felt like it. Francesca was in no mood to play the apartment version of the musical chairs game all over Norway. They would need to come back to Oslo.

But maybe... she suddenly had another thought. Maybe she could lie, and tell her dad that she'd done some research and had actually been able to find his birthmother?

But then again, he might've looked into the rules at some point himself, and would therefore know that Francesca was bluffing. And if not, then all he needed to do was perform a quick internet search in order to uncover Francesca's lie.

Unless... she brainstormed. Unless, she told her dad that, say, his biological mother had all of a sudden showed up at his house, wanting to see him?

She tapped her forehead with her fingertips while she evaluated her own idea. Of course, he'd probably see right through that. Besides, it was most likely against the law for his birth mom to look him up after having given him away all those years ago. And who knows, she might not even still be alive. And would Phillip even *want* to see her?

She rubbed her hands over her face. If he *had* wanted to find out about his parents, then he probably would've by now. And considering the current situation between Phillip and Francesca, what were the odds of his mother showing up at the exact same time as Francesca was trying to make him come back home with Jenny?

She paced the floor again, for what felt like close to ten minutes.

It was a lousy plan... But, whatever the outcome, she could see no other idea likely to work out any better. She didn't have to tell him the details of how and why his mother had suddenly shown up at his house — it was enough to just spark his interest, and to hopefully give him a reason to want to talk to Francesca. Even if he didn't believe her, at least Francesca might be able to plant some ideas in his head to get him thinking about his parents.

Francesca knew the situation was no longer in her hands. Phillip was in control, and only he could decide to come to his senses and bring Jenny back.

She tried Phillip's phone again.

It was still switched off.

She realized her only option was to text Jenny: *Jenny, tell Dad that his biological mother is at our house right now.*

Chapter Thirty-two

Francesca checked her phone again, just like she'd done pretty much every other minute since she'd texted Jenny, telling her to let their dad know that his birth mother was at their house.

Almost an hour and a half had passed. Yet, she still hadn't heard back from either one of them.

That was it, she decided. She needed to talk to her dad somehow, and she couldn't afford to wait any longer. It was going on eight thirty in the evening — who knew where they might be by now if they'd left town at around noon or so. She called Jenny's cell phone and held her breath.

The phone rang once; then again; and then a third time.

Francesca cracked her knuckles as she waited.

"Hello..."

Francesca gasped. "Dad?"

"Yes, what do you want?"

"Why are you answering Jenny's phone? Where is she — is she OK?"

"Since when does your sister have a phone? I know I didn't give it to her." His voice was cold and steady.

"No, that's right. I gave her my old phone."

"And why would you do such a thing without my permission?"

"I gave it to her so she could feel safe; so she knew she'd always be able to reach me whenever she needed to."

"And who's paying the phone bill?"

"I am."

"Interesting..." Phillip sneered.

"What does that mean?"

"From now on you can save your money. I'm confiscating the phone from Jenny — she's too young to have a cell phone."

"You can't do that — it was a gift from me."

"I'm Jenny's father, and I know what's best for her. I'll mail the phone back to you when we reach our destination."

Francesca felt her entire body heat up. "And so what's best for Jenny is for you to kidnap her, thereby pulling her out of school and away from her friends and life in Oslo? That's a great way of putting her needs first, Dad."

"I've been offered a new job with higher pay and better hours. Don't you worry — Jenny's needs will be met."

"So you lied to your boss about having a family crisis and being gone for a certain amount of time, when really, you're never coming back?"

"Obviously, my boss knows he's fired me — the operator at the cab central does not."

"Where's your new job?"

"I'm not telling you that."

Francesca felt her eyes burn and her knees give way, forcing her to plop down onto the edge of Jenny's bed behind her. "So that means I'll never be allowed to see my sister ever again — the person who means more to me than anyone else in this world? How is that fair?"

"Francesca, I understand that you're upset, but it's for the best. And life isn't always fair. In fact, the world is usually a very unfair place, and the sooner you realize that, the easier it will be for you to accept future disappointments as well."

She felt her hatred for her dad pounding through her like a marching band. "What about the house?" she said through gritted teeth.

"I'm selling it."

"Dad," she sobbed. "It's very important that you and Jenny come back home."

"And why would that be?"

She dried her eyes. "Because... because your birth mother is here."

"Oh, really?"

"Yes, didn't you get my message from Jenny?"

"Oh, I got the message, alright. I just didn't respond because I know you're lying."

"I promise you," Francesca begged. "I promise you I'm not lying."

"OK, I'll believe you if you can tell me her full name."

She panicked. "Do you know her full name?"

"I do."

"OK," she sniffled, surrendering. "I lied, she's not here. I'm sorry."

"You know, it's interesting that you don't think I know you well enough to realize when you're lying. And especially about matters where your young mind just doesn't yet have enough experience to comprehend how it all fits together."

"Well, will you at least tell me what her name is? She's my grandmother, you know."

"A woman who abandons her child without another thought does not deserve to be called a mother, nor a grandmother. I will never tell you her name — I don't want you to go looking for her."

"So that at least means that she's still alive, then?"

"That isn't what I said."

"Have you ever met her?"

"I have not."

"But, aren't you at least just a little bit curious about why she gave you up? She might not have had any other choice."

"Francesca, if you want something badly enough, then you always have a choice — you find a way to make it work."

"Then... then, there is another reason you need to come back home."

"I'm not playing any more games with you, Francesca," he said, raising his voice. "You need to stop it right—"

"I'm pregnant, Dad," she interrupted him. "I'm pregnant, and I don't know what to do."

Chapter Thirty-three

Phillip sighed. "Francesca, what is wrong with you?"

Francesca felt every single muscle in her body fire up. "What's wrong with me — are you serious right now?"

"Of course I'm serious."

"You really think I got pregnant on purpose?" she shrieked.

"What I think is that you're lying to me again."

Francesca couldn't hold it in anymore, and she burst into tears. "Lying? You... you think... that I would actually kid about... about a thing like that?" She gasped for air.

"I don't know what to think anymore. Clearly, you've demonstrated that you'd say and do anything in order to get us to come back. But you know I'll never do that as long as you're trying to force me to let you inherit Jenny as if she were an old hand-me-down."

"You're the worst father in the world, do you know that? It's not fair; you're always in a car — why couldn't it have been you that was in that accident? Mom didn't even have a car of her own — why was she the one who had to die?" Francesca shouted. Then she immediately covered her mouth. She knew she had crossed the line.

"Seeing as that's the way you feel, then at least I know you won't miss me. And if you want, now you can even pretend I was the one to have died, as you won't have to see me ever again."

"Dad... I'm sorry, I didn't mean to..."

"All you've done is tell me how you really feel. And now that makes me feel less guilty about you not having a father in your life anymore."

Francesca let her forehead drop into her left hand, uttering a little prayer out loud. "Dad, please come back home. Please."

"Surely, by now you realize I'm not going to change my mind?"

Francesca dried her eyes with the back of her hand, and took a deep breath. "You know, Dad, it's the very end of an experience or happening that matters the most — that's the part that really sticks in your memory and informs your future decisions."

"What's that supposed to mean?"

"It's just something I learned while doing research for my business speech, and something I think it's worthwhile for you to remember. And you know what? You really had me there for awhile, and I really thought you'd changed — I was even going to admit defeat and let Jenny continue to live with you. But then, in the end you go and kidnap her, and so it's what happens at the end that'll really stick in my memory and inform my future decisions, meaning now I'll never stop trying to fight to get her. And remember, our deal is still valid — when I succeed then you'll have to hand her over to me, whether you want to or not. Just you wait and see, we'll manage to finally be free from you once and for all," she said coldly, and hung up.

Francesca noticed that her entire body was shaking. She had been counting on a different reaction from him toward her pregnancy. It had been her last resort; her final card that she could think to play. She was now completely out of ideas for what to do. It had actually never occurred to her that he wouldn't even believe her.

...Although, given her bluff about his mother, she now realized that she'd been stupid to expect him to react in any other way than he'd just done.

Francesca moaned, and pulled her hands through her hair.

If Phillip had just believed her then he also would've known for sure that, now with the baby, Francesca wouldn't be able to take Jenny away from him anymore, and he therefore might've decided to come back home.

Now, how was she ever going to get them to come back?

Francesca let her gaze flit around Jenny's room, glancing at the door, the closet, the desk and the bookshelves above it. Then she looked at Jenny's alarm clock on her night stand.

The seconds hand ticked steadily along as it chased the minutes and hours, never stopping, never giving up; the rhythm almost hypnotizing her.

It struck her that if Phillip and Jenny wouldn't come to her, then she would need to go to them. She would need to chase after them herself.

But how could she possibly chase them down when she had no idea where they were going?

"Ring; ring; ring." Her phone sounded.

Francesca jumped. She tipped her phone toward her so she could see the screen.

It was Adrian.

She muted her phone, but continued to stare at the screen.

After a few more seconds the ringing stopped, and the message of one missed call from Adrian appeared across the screen.

Francesca exhaled, and ran her finger around the frame of her phone.

Then it started ringing once more; and again, it was Adrian.

She hesitated, but then realized she couldn't keep avoiding him forever. Considering he wasn't taking her hint about leaving her alone, she at least had to tell him assertively once and for all that they needed to end their friendship, or whatever confusing relationship it was they'd built up over the years. She owed him that much, though how to do so, and how to act, she had absolutely no idea. Hopefully, the right way of telling him would come to her as they spoke. She cleared her throat and put on a pretend smile, as though he was actually able to see her. "Hello." Her voice came out a fake cheerful.

"Francesca?"

"Yes?"

"Ah, finally." He let out a sigh of relief. "Listen, I know things got really weird the last time we saw each other, but... I don't want it to be this way."

"Like what?" Her voice was high-pitched.

"Francesca, I know you know what I mean. And... can we at least get together and talk about this, just once? Just one time — that's all I'm asking. And then I promise I'll leave you alone after that ...if that's really what you want me to do."

"I can't... I... I need to go away for awhile, need to leave town."

"What? Why?"

"My dad has kidnapped Jenny, and he won't come back. I've got to find them."

Adrian sighed, and muttered through gritted teeth; "Why does he have to go and ruin everyone's lives?"

"What?"

"Let me come with you. I can help."

"Adrian, I don't think that would be a good idea."

"Why not?"

Francesca felt her heart crumble. "We..." She pinched her eyes shut, and let the tears drip out like she was wringing out a wet rag. "We can't be together, OK — it's just never going to work out."

"Where are you?" Adrian's voice was clear and sharp as a whistle.

"Didn't you hear me? Please stay away from me."

"Oh, I heard you alright, but I know you well enough to realize that this isn't what you want."

She shook uncontrollably. "What *you* need to realize is that you have to respect my wishes when I say that I don't want you in my life anymore."

"I know you love me."

Francesca's eyes were so clouded by tears that she couldn't see. She took a deep breath, and shook her head. Her neck was stiff, and her head felt like it was going to explode. "I don't love you."

"You're lying."

"I'm not lying."

"I won't leave you alone until you tell me to my face that you don't love me."

"Adrian, stop it..."

"Where are you? At your dad's house?"

"No..." she lied.

"I know you're there. Stay where you are — I'm coming over." He hung up.

Francesca panicked. She couldn't let him see her like this. And she couldn't ever let him find about the baby. Whether she kept it or got rid of it — either way, she ran the risk of him leaving her at some point. Everyone always did. Even her dad had taken her sister and left her today. That was enough for one day. She had to get out of there before he could see her. She needed to leave him before he had the chance to leave her.

She bolted out of Jenny's bedroom and into her own room. She yanked her closet open and grabbed a large duffle bag.

What would she need to bring? Her brain was so foggy she couldn't think straight. She started pulling her clothes off their hangers — anything and everything she could see — and throwing them into her bag.

Downstairs, the front door opened, and then clanged shut.

She froze, her ears alert.

"Francesca?" Adrian called out from the first floor.

"Oh my God," she whispered. "How the hell did he manage get here so fast?"

She sprinted over to her bedroom door and locked it. Horror-struck, she looked around for a way out. Her eyes landed on the window.

She flung her bag over her shoulder and opened the window wide enough to be able to get out.

It was dark outside, and she could barely see the ground below. But she was only on the second floor — it would be OK to jump, wouldn't it?

"Francesca." Adrian said, knocking firmly on her door three times. "I know you're in there. Please open up."

Francesca studied the frosty grass on the ground as it glittered in the light from the lampposts. Suddenly, she felt dizzy. What if she wouldn't be OK, or worse; what if something were to happen to the baby?

Adrian knocked again. "Francesca."

She opened the window even wider, and started getting ready to climb out.

"I just want to talk to you — I love you."

Francesca felt his words paralyze her. She remembered many a time standing at this very window while looking out at the driveway, watching her dad get into his car and leave, each time wondering whether or not he'd ever come back.

She had always resented her dad for what he'd done to her and Jenny, and now she was doing the same thing to Adrian. She felt her nausea well up again. She wasn't any better than her dad.

"Francesca, I really do love you," Adrian repeated.

What was she doing? Adrian loved her. And while she wasn't certain about much in her life, at least there was no question about the fact that — even though the only person she'd only barely admitted it to once was Margaret — she really did love him, too.

She placed both hands on her stomach, and looked down at her hands.

On the road just beyond their driveway, the cars zoomed past noisily in a steady stream.

Francesca looked up and out of the window, lost in thought for a moment.

The cars' taillights looked like a succession of shooting stars as they whizzed past, one after the other, in the dark.

It would be so easy to just leave, to hitchhike somewhere with one of the many cars passing by.

The cold air flowed in through the window, and chilled her entire body.

She shivered, and then it hit her; If she ran away from Adrian while taking her child with her — a child that might very well be his — then she would be doing the exact same thing to Adrian that her mom had tried to do to her dad ten years ago; taking his child away from him without letting him have a say in the matter.

"Please, let me come in," Adrian said again.

Francesca took a deep breath, and closed the window.

She walked over to the door, unlocked and opened it.

Adrian looked at her, his eyes unwavering.

Francesca took a small, hesitant step toward him.

He stood there perfectly still, waiting patiently, letting her move at her own pace.

Then she took two more steps toward him and slipped her shaking arms in around Adrian's waist, letting her head rest up against his chest, and her tears stain his navy-blue cotton shirt.

He held her tight and kissed the top of her head.

It almost felt as though he had placed his hands gently around her heart. Just holding it there within his palms; telling her that everything would be OK. His hands were soft and warm, and after a minute or two, the invisible coil that had wrapped itself around her heart over the years — squeezing the life right out of it — gradually began to loosen. She felt like she was finally able to breathe again, although it wasn't until this very moment that she even realized she'd been holding her breath in the first place; that her heart had been holding its breath. Slowly, it grew softer. Slowly, it opened itself back up.

From where her head lay on his chest, she felt Adrian's own heart beat steadily underneath his clothes. "Adrian, I love you, too," she whispered; finally daring to say it. The skin on her entire body suddenly became extremely sensitive to his touch. "But..." she continued, "there's something I need to tell you."

Chapter Thirty-four

Francesca let go of Adrian's waist and instead took his hand, leading him toward her bed. "So, um, I think maybe you should sit down for a minute."

He followed, and sat down beside her, placing his arm loosely around her. "OK, so tell me what's going on."

"Ah..." She felt her eyes begin to water, and looked away.

"Hey, it's OK; you know you can tell me anything, right?"

She sniffled, then nodded.

"Good," he said, rubbing her back. "Now, just take all the time you need."

Francesca took a deep breath, and wiped her eyes. "OK. So, you know how we... er... slept together some weeks back?"

"Yeah."

"OK... so, uh... I actually haven't had my period since then."

Adrian looked down at her stomach. Then he looked back at Francesca's face, his eyes wide. "What, so you're... I mean, surely you're not..."

Francesca nodded. "Yes, I'm pregnant."

Adrian let go of her, and buried is face in his hands. "Wow."

She swallowed hard. "Yeah..."

"OK, so now what?"

"Well... I was kinda hoping you could help me clarify that part... I mean, I've been back and forth, and then back again, and... I've just never felt so helpless before in my entire life."

Adrian got to his feet and starting pacing the floor, looking anywhere but at Francesca. "OK, well I cannot make that decision for you."

"It's not just my life that would be changing, though. It's your life, too, you know."

"It's too late to talk about change, things have already changed — our lives won't ever be exactly the same again, no matter what choice you make."

"OK, so what're you saying...?"

"This isn't about change, it's about doing what's right for you — and for us — now and in the future."

"But... I don't know what's right for me, and for us, now and in the future. I just don't—"

"What do you want, Francesca?" Adrian interrupted her. He stopped pacing, and stared right at her. "What is it that you want — what is your heart telling you to do?"

She gazed right back at him. "I want the baby."

Adrian nodded, and put his arms out to either side. "OK, then there's your answer."

Francesca shook her head. "No, that's not my answer."

"What're you talking about?"

"What I want is one thing. But a completely different matter is what's the *right* thing to do"

Adrian sighed. "I just asked you what you thought the *right* thing to do was, and you said you didn't know."

"It's not about what's right for me anymore — it's about making the right decision in order to help Jenny."

"Yeah, well maybe the right thing to do for yourself would ultimately be what's best for Jenny as well."

"How could that possibly be? Having the baby means giving Jenny up."

"I realize that. But Phillip is her father, after all, you know."

Francesca stared at Adrian. "Have you lost it or something?"

"Nope. I just know what I want, and I'm going for it."

"OK, so what is it that you want?"

"Isn't it obvious? I want you."

Francesca felt her cheeks turn a deep pink, and she looked down into her lap. "OK, so does that mean you'll still love me no matter what I choose to do?"

Adrian sat down next to her on the bed, and held her hand in his warm hands.

Francesca's stomach instantly became alive with butterflies.

He gently lifted her chin up, and looked into her eyes. "Everything will work out, I promise."

She frowned. "That's not exactly an answer to my question."

He smiled weakly. "I think you already know my answer to your question. And, as I said before; it's your decision — I can't make it for you." He leaned in to kiss her.

Francesca pulled away. "OK... so, that basically means that you don't care whether or not you become a father?"

"No, that's not true."

"Ah, alright... Well, you're gonna have to be more specific than that."

Adrian shrugged. "Listen, I've known about you being pregnant for what, five minutes, tops — I haven't exactly had enough time to process how I feel about it yet."

"OK, so what if after I make a decision, then you all of a sudden change your mind, and realize you would've wanted me to have chosen the other alternative?"

"Well, we'll just have to cross that bridge when we get there, won't we?"

"What?" Francesca got to her feet. "There isn't going to be a possibility for bridge crossing in the future, buddy. Let me tell you something; we've definitely reached the bridge on our path right here — the bridge crossing is right now, and it'll be too late later."

Adrian stared right at her, not blinking once. "Is that baby even mine?"

Francesca felt like his question had instantly paralyzed her. She had no idea how to respond. "What?"

"You heard me; is it mine? Or is that other guy the father?" His face had hardened.

She opened her mouth, but nothing came out.

He tried to catch her eye. "Well?"

She looked down at the floor. "I... I don't know for sure."

He pulled his hands through his hair a couple of times. "And if you do decide to keep the baby, will we know who the father is before the baby is born?"

"I don't know... I don't think..." Her voice trailed away.

"Francesca...?"

"I already did some research, and it's against Norwegian law to have DNA testing done on a fetus. The reason for this being that it may be harmful to the baby, as well as the concern that the results will sway the mother to have an abortion if it turns out that the father is not the father she would've wanted it to be..." she mumbled.

He rubbed his eyes, and sighed. "Of course..."

Francesca stood watching him in silence, feeling his pain; feeling her own pain; and doubting whether she had made the right decision in telling him after all.

He stared aimlessly out of the window.

"Adrian, I never planned on this happening. And that other guy... he was just a drunken mistake when I was in a vulnerable position — I never wanted to hurt you."

He took a deep breath. "No, I know. And I know we hadn't even... you know... yet, at that point, but it's just... It's just all a bit too much."

"Yeah..."

"And, you know," Adrian paused, looking like he was starting to get pretty nauseated himself. "Please, just let's not mention that guy anymore, alright?"

Francesca nodded. "'Course."

"OK, so how much time do we have before a decision needs to be made?"

"My appointment for the examination is in 11 days, on November the 24th."

"11 days? Geez, they don't put top priority on these things!"

"Yeah, seriously," Francesca said, rolling her eyes. "It's like we're living in the dark ages here — I can't believe you have to wait this long to have an abortion in a country like Norway," she huffed. "But, trust me, I've already chewed out one of the secretaries at the women's clinic and, according to her, there's still an ample amount of time and this is the standard procedure in Norway."

He nodded. "OK, well at least that'll give us some time to talk and figure things out."

"Yeah."

They both fell silent, and remained so for a couple of minutes.

Then Adrian looked over at her. "So, how're you feeling?"

She sat back down beside him on her bed, shaking her head. "Not great. On top of everything else, the pregnancy has made my emotions even crazier than they were before when I only had Jenny to worry about; I've been throwing up quite a bit as well; and just feeling really exhausted most of the time."

"Hey, come here." He scooted backwards across the bed, leaned up against the wall, and gestured for her to lie down on her side in front of him.

She kissed him on the lips, before curling up and getting as close to his body as possible.

He wrapped his arms around her.

"Adrian?" she whispered.

"Yeah?"

"I'm sorry for putting you through this."

"Well, you didn't become pregnant on your own, so I'm sorry, too."

Neither of them spoke for about a minute.

Then Francesca broke the silence with a yawn, before adding sleepily. "I'm so tired."

"It's been a rough day for both of us, and it's almost 11 o'clock. We should try to get some sleep."

Francesca yawned once more, and pulled her covers over the two of them. Then she thought of how she had no clue where her sister was sleeping tonight, or what their dad's plan for her was. "Adrian," she whispered again.

"Yeah?" he whispered back.

"What about Jenny?"

"We'll find them, and get them to come back to Oslo."

"But... what if they don't come back?"

"Somehow, they will. And if your dad doesn't start using some common sense soon, then I'll make it my business to help him change his mind about that."

"Adrian... it's not really up to you. He doesn't even like you, you know. He thinks you've always meddled way too much in our family issues; he says it doesn't concern you... which, in a way, is actually true..."

"Well, he's wrong. When he hurts you — the girl I love — and strips you of the ability to trust that I'll be there for you, just because he's always been too cowardly to do the same, then that's when it becomes *my* business, too."

*

"Ring; ring; ring."

Francesca pried her eyes open, condemning her phone and its frequent calls — usually bringing her bad news.

"Ring; ring; ring."

She slipped out from underneath Adrian's arm, and located her phone on the nightstand. She immediately muted the sound, and looked at the screen.

It was from the women's clinic at the hospital.

She gasped and peered over at Adrian, before hurrying out into the hallway, closing her bedroom door behind her. "Hello, this is Francesca Hansen," she said, making sure to keep her voice low, while rubbing the sleep out of her eyes.

"Hello, I'm calling from Oslo Central Hospital regarding the examination you've got scheduled for November 24th."

"Yes."

"We've also put down a comment about you wanting to be notified should any cancellations occur between now and then."

"Yeah..."

"Well, we've just had a cancellation for today at three o'clock. Would you like to change your appointment for today instead?"

"Ah..." Francesca checked the time on her phone.

It was 9:17 in the morning.

"Um... Yeah, could I just get you to hold that appointment for me, and then I'll call you back within the next 10 minutes or so if I find that I won't be able to make it after all?"

"OK, so unless notified otherwise during the next little while, that means you'll be here at 3 o'clock this afternoon, then?"

"That is correct."

"OK, that's fine."

"Thanks. Bye." Francesca hung up.

Chapter Thirty-five

Francesca stood in the hallway outside her bedroom, tossing her phone back and forth from one hand to the other. "So much for Adrian and I having a decent amount of time to talk things over before my doctor's appointment," she muttered to herself.

However, if she definitely ended up deciding to have the abortion, then the sooner the better, really.

She snuck back into the bedroom, and sat down on her bed next to where Adrian lay sleeping.

He stirred.

She stroked his arm gently, and kissed him on the cheek. "Adrian?" she whispered.

"Hmm?"

"You need to wake up."

"Nah, you need to come back to bed," he mumbled, and slipped his arms around her waist.

"I'm serious. They just called from the hospital and offered to switch my appointment for today. At the moment they're holding both appointments, but I need to let them know within the next ten minutes if I want to keep my old appointment after all. If not, then today will be the day."

Adrian's eyes flared open. "That piece of information is as good a wakeup call as any alarm clock," he said, and started pulling himself into the upright position, leaning up against the back wall. "OK, so talk to me."

"I think I should go today, rather than wait another 10 days."

He nodded. "OK."

"I mean, no matter what, just because I have an examination doesn't mean I definitely need to have the abortion or anything. I'd just like to... you know, I'd just like to feel that I'm at least moving one step closer to making a decision — whatever that decision might end up being."

"Right."

"So..." Francesca scooted in closer toward him. "How do you feel about this?"

"Ah... Well, it's just all so sudden, and... to be honest I'm still not quite sure how I feel."

"I understand."

"But, I mean, if you want to go today, then I think you should."

"Really?"

"Yeah, 'course"

Francesca nodded. "OK, then I will." She looked down at their hands lying next to each other on the bed. She hesitated for a moment, before reaching over and interlacing her fingers with his. "But, um... do you think... would you maybe want to come with me?"

"Well, are you sure you'd want me there?"

"Yeah, I think it would be better — easier — having you there supporting me."

He draped his arms around her, and kissed her forehead. "Alright, I'll be there."

*

"OK, Francesca." The young female doctor smiled, and gestured toward the chair. "Please, get undressed and then settle yourself in the chair," she said, continuing to prepare the ultrasound device.

Francesca did as she was told and noticed that she was starting to feel a little dizzy. As she gazed at the doctor's blindingly white uniform and her squeaky clean appearance, all she could think of was how the hospital's annual budget for bleach and disinfectants must be ridiculous. "Thanks." Francesca trembled as she climbed up into the chair realizing that it was not made for those who were shy about their bodies.

Adrian looked paler than snow as he settled down in a chair on Francesca's right hand side.

"So," the doctor said. "What I'm going to do is perform an ultrasound, and based on that we'll be able to confirm that you are in fact pregnant, as well as how far along you might be. So if you're ready then we'll just get started."

Francesca nodded. "OK, I'm ready," she said, and felt her hand inch toward Adrian's hand.

The doctor turned the machine on, and started the examination.

Francesca half watched her, and half occupied her mind wondering what she'd do if the extreme nausea she was feeling decided to make itself visible.

Adrian took her hand and squeezed it gently.

"OK," the doctor continued. "So what this ultrasound is telling me is that you're definitely pregnant. And the way we define how far along you are, is to look at when you had your last period. So, you said the first day of your last period was on September 29th — is that correct?" The doctor looked up at Francesca.

"Yes."

"Alright, so that means that you're six and a half weeks pregnant."

"Six and a half weeks already?" Francesca blurted out.

"That's right. However, for a menstrual cycle that is completely regular, ovulation is about 14 days after the first day of your period. And based on this ultrasound I can see that you ovulated — and that therefore the actual conception took place — on probably either the 15th or the 16th of October. So, in reality—"

"The 15th or 16th?" Francesca interrupted her.

"Yes, so mid-October, as opposed the very end of September when you had your period."

Francesca looked at Adrian, her eyes glistening and a soft, relieved smile spreading across her face.

Adrian gazed back at her, looking puzzled.

"You're the dad," Francesca mouthed.

He stared at her blankly for another millisecond, before he lit up, and instantly seemed to shed most of his tension.

"So, actually," the doctor continued. "This means that you're really only just over four weeks pregnant, even though in medical terms we define you as being six and a half weeks pregnant because, as I said, we always count starting from the first day of your last period."

"Aha..." Francesca was only half listening.

"OK, so if you'd like to get dressed, then we can discuss your options."

Francesca snapped to again. Right... she still needed to make a decision. She'd been so relieved to hear that Adrian was definitely the dad. She shuddered to think what a catastrophe it would've been for their future relationship had Eric turned out to be the father. At least this new piece of information might make her and Adrian's relationship stronger.

She slipped behind the white screen in the back corner, and quickly pulled her clothes back on. Then she rejoined the other two, and peered over at Adrian.

He seemed to be in deep thought, not really noticing that she was standing right next to him, and a crease was beginning to form between his eyebrows.

Francesca felt like she'd been punched in the stomach. Could it be that she was wrong after all? Could it be that, maybe, the fact that the child was definitely his would make it that much harder for him to accept her having an abortion? Might he grow to resent her down the line if that was the option she ended up choosing? Would he, then, maybe end up leaving her?

Or... was Adrian maybe thinking the exact opposite, instead — that he was nowhere near ready to become a father?

"Alright," the doctor said, gesturing at the two chairs on the opposite side of her desk. "So if you'll just come join me over here at my desk, then I'll talk you through the procedure."

Francesca grabbed the chair on the left hand side, still keeping an eye on Adrian as he settled down next to her.

"So, the majority of the women who choose to call us directly to schedule an examination here at the hospital — as opposed to going through their doctors at the doctor's office first — have often already decided that they're going through with the abortion. Now, have you decided for sure yet, or do you need more time?"

"Ah... well, we haven't really..." Francesca peered over at Adrian.

He leaned in toward her, rubbed her arm a couple of times, and lowered his voice. "I know this is really tough, but I still think that ultimately, it's your call."

Francesca looked at the doctor again. "Could you please just go through the details of the procedure first? I read something about there being two different alternatives..."

"Of course." She smiled. "And you're absolutely right — there are two different methods for terminating a pregnancy. One way of doing it is the medical abortion, which is a type of non-surgical abortion that is induced by using abortifacient pharmaceutical drugs. And the other option, then, is the surgical abortion."

"Which one would you recommend?"

"For you, as of right now, it would have to be medical abortion. The surgical abortion wouldn't be an option until you're a bit further along, so not until another week or two from now."

Francesca nodded. "OK."

"And the medical abortion works by first swallowing a preparation at the hospital under the supervision of a doctor in order to stop the development of the fetus. Then two days later you'll insert some pills — either by having us do it here at the hospital, or by doing it yourself in the comfort of your own home — causing your uterus to contract and then complete the abortion. This is a very safe procedure, and the most common alternative of the two."

"And you would recommend having the medical abortion right away, then, as opposed to waiting a week or two for the surgical abortion?"

"Oh, absolutely. I usually recommend the medical option in most cases, no matter how far along the pregnancy is. And if you've already made up your mind, then you could take the first pill to stop the development of the fetus right now. However," she paused, reaching back into a shelf behind her and pulled out some papers. "I need to stress the fact that the decision to have an abortion shouldn't be taken lightly. And if you're not completely sure, and would like to discuss the matter with an advisor first, then you can contact a professional at any one of these organizations to get some advice." She handed Francesca three different pamphlets.

"OK, yeah, I'll take those. Thanks. I... I think I just need a bit more time."

"Of course."

"But if I do decide I'd like to come back here, then how would I go about it?"

"We can schedule an appointment for you to come back next week. That'll give you a little bit of time to think and contact an advisor if you wish to. And if you find you don't want to have the abortion, then all you have to do is call and let us know, and we'll cancel the appointment."

"Alright, that sounds good."

"So, would you prefer any particular day?"

"Um..." Francesca paused to think. She knew she had that second business meeting and presentation on the Tuesday, and wanted to make sure and get that over with first. "How about the Wednesday, maybe – would that work?"

"Let's see..." The doctor scrolled down on her computer screen. "Yes, that should be fine. Let's say at 11 o'clock, is that OK?"

"Yeah, sure."

"OK. Good luck with the decision-making in the meantime."

"Thanks for your help." Francesca got to her feet and held her hand out.

The doctor shook it. "You're very welcome. And, remember; don't hesitate to contact us should you have any questions."

"OK, thanks."

"Thank you," Adrian said, finishing off the appointment by shaking the doctor's hand as well.

Francesca hurried out of the doctor's office; flew through the waiting room; down the endlessly long L-shaped corridor, and didn't stop until she was standing outside on the street, desperately drawing the frosty air in through her nostrils — commanding it to freeze the tears that were welling up dead in their tracks.

"So..." Adrian caught up with her. "Is there anything I can do?"

She marched straight over to the nearest bench, and plopped down. Then she pulled out the pamphlets the doctor had given her and leafed violently through all three of them.

"Francesca, I know—"

"It's fine," she snapped. "I'm fine."

"I don't think—"

"God, these things are completely useless — they aren't going to help me." She jumped up, and stuffed the pamphlets back into her bag.

Adrian placed his hand on top of hers.

"This is crap," she said, raising her voice. "I can't think straight; I can't breathe; it's... it's all just crap. I hate my dad so much right now. And I always will. This is all his fault — why does he have to go and ruin my life? All I really want is to truly be free of him once and for all. Is that so much to ask?" She got to her feet, and flung her bag over her shoulder. "No offense, but I'd like to be alone right now," she said, and stormed off in the direction of her dad's house."

*

Once she was back inside the house, she kicked her shoes off, then banged both of her palms up against the wall.

And then, she cried. Hysterically. Allowing the tears to drain out. So many tears; impossible to count. Flowing so uncontrollably. She liked being in control; she had always craved it, gasping for it like air. But now, she knew there just wasn't anything she could do. Her dad was the one in control ...and that scared her to death.

The muscles in her legs gave way, and she sank down toward the floor, her palms sliding against the wall all the way down until she was on her knees. Then she collapsed completely, curling into a ball on the floor.

She lay there for several minutes, allowing herself to wail for as long as she needed to. There was no use trying to stop it; she knew she would never be able to anyway.

Gradually, after about ten minutes, the force of her sobbing calmed, and eventually turned into something resembling silent hiccups, gradually slowing as they rippled through her body.

Finally, she was able to breathe normally; able to think normally. All that was left were her damp eyes and cheeks, still lying on the floor in the middle of the small puddle that had accumulated.

She continued to lie there motionless for awhile, like she was half dead. *This*, she thought, this excruciating pain must be what dying feels like.

Yet, she was not dead. She still needed to continue on, pushing through life, somehow coming up with the right decision to her problem, although she had no idea how to do so.

Then... after a little more time had passed, she sensed a hint of strength starting to grow within, and she managed to push herself into a seated position.

She sighed, tired, wanting nothing more than to go to bed. But she also knew that she had to do something — anything — and that it needed to be done soon, that if she didn't *actively* do something, then time would end up making the decision for her.

Supporting herself with her hands against the wall, she got to her feet. All she could think of was what her mom would have done. If she were here right now, what would she have told Francesca to do?

Then, she thought of how after her mother had passed away, Francesca had placed a small box of Anna's stuff up in the tiny crawl space above her bedroom. Her dad had never known about it, though, and to her knowledge, there was nothing else up there, either. The loft was so tiny, and the ceiling so low, that it probably wouldn't fit more than four or five boxes.

Right after her mom died, she'd managed to salvage a few of Anna's personal belongings before her dad had gotten to them. When she had confided in Adrian that she didn't know where to hide the box from Phillip, it was Adrian who had told her about this tiny loft in the ceiling above Francesca's bedroom. His row house next door had the exact same kind of loft, hidden in the ceiling above Adrian's childhood bedroom. Adrian was also the one who had helped her get it up there.

Francesca wasn't sure what exactly was in the box. All she remembered from the moment right after she'd been told her mother had been in that car crash, was herself scrabbling together whatever little things she could find, and immediately sealing the box shut with packing tape.

As a little girl, she remembered thinking how, as long as that box with her mom's stuff remained sealed shut, then in a way it still belonged to Anna; and somehow, to Francesca that had meant that her mom was still around. That her mom was still alive — she was just sitting up there in the loft above her bedroom, watching over her. Keeping her safe.

Back then, Francesca had also imagined that if she ripped the box open, exploring the contents, then the items would suddenly belong to her, meaning they didn't belong to Anna anymore, and her mom would instantly be gone forever.

She let her eyes travel up along the staircase toward the second floor. She took a deep breath. Now would be the time to finally open the box. Maybe one of her mother's old belongings would be able to provide her with some guidance or, at the very least, some comfort in the shape of a fond memory.

Francesca started climbing the staircase, and upon reaching the landing on the second floor felt herself breathing heavily; working through her emotions related to her childhood vision of her mom sitting up there looking down at her.

Of course, she knew this had just been a foolish little image she'd created in her head as a kid, and that her mother had never really been up there. Yet, to this day she still hadn't told anyone about this mental picture of hers, for fear that they would laugh at her; thereby bursting her bubble, tearing it forever from her imagination.

But now, she, herself, was about to destroy that image that had meant so much to her as a child; the thing that had gotten Francesca through her darkest moments. She was about to rip the box open, removing the very last part of what she had left of her mom.

She continued down the hallway, slowly.

...But then it dawned on Francesca that her mom could still be there, looking down at her, if she really wanted her to be. All she would need to do was replace her old image of the attic with an image of her mom sitting up there looking down at her from heaven instead.

As she took those last few steps and pushed her door open, she suddenly realized that she was OK with the change of image, because now she felt herself being controlled by other emotions. Stronger emotions. Finally, she would find out what was in that box; what she had managed to salvage for another day. A day when she would be needing it the most. Today was that day. Her excitement and nervousness intensified faster than she could bear. What was in that box? Would she be disappointed after all this time?

In the very back of her closet, she found the wooden stick with a hook at the end that she needed in order to access the crawl space.

She reached the stick up and inserted the hook into the little metal ring on the outside of the trapdoor, yanking it toward her.

Bits of dust sailed down onto her face.

She closed her eyes, and coughed, before looking back up into the dark cavity.

Then she pulled the tiny, rickety ladder down, extending it to the floor before starting to climb up.

When she got to the top, she reached into her pocket for her cell phone, and switched on the flashlight.

There it was, the shoe box with her mother's stuff.

She pulled it toward her and made her way back down the ladder.

Placing the box on the floor in front of her, she took a deep breath. This is it, she thought, and used the tip of her key to break the seal created by the packing tape.

Then she gently lifted the lid off, making sure to not let the thick layer of dust slide off the edge and down onto her hardwood floor.

Inside were a diary; some letters; and a small, white porcelain box with a picture of a rose painted on the porcelain lid; along with a few other trinkets.

Francesca reached into the box and tenderly picked up the diary, caressing it in much the same way as she imagined lifting her own baby out of a bassinet, if she were to ever have children someday... either in the near or distant future.

As she ran the tips of her fingers all across the violet binding, she noticed her fingers begin to tingle. The weight of the book in her hands was making her throat turn to gravel, and she knew she couldn't wait any longer. Opening the front cover, she heard the spine of the old book creak, and as she started flipping through it, she immediately recognized her mother's handwriting.

Anna had filled nearly every page and, at some point, Francesca wanted to sit down and quietly read every word, getting to know her mom in a new way, learning her deepest, most inner thoughts. After reading through it all, she realized she would most likely come to see her mother in a different way than before, as one grownup to another.

However, for today she only had time to read through parts of it. And the parts she knew she'd need to look for were those containing any clues as to what had really happened between her parents toward the very end. Anything that might indicate what she could do in order to get her dad to change his mind and come back with Jenny.

It took her several minutes, her eyes quickly scanning the pages as her fingertips leafed through them.

But then... She gasped, realizing she might have found something useful.

It was — in Anna's own, private words, meant for Anna's eyes only — her reasons for leaving Phillip.

Francesca felt her hands shake, and her tears threaten to fall. She pinched her eyes shut, took a deep breath, and looked back down at the page, eventually finding the courage to start reading:

I have tried to understand Phillip; as well as tried to make him see where I'm coming from — how I feel. I really have. But he just won't listen. He doesn't understand how much he is hurting Francesca with his words. He thinks that you can only hurt someone with actions, or physical violence, or by denying them necessities like food. But his weapon is his words, and he doesn't realize that, sometimes, words can shoot someone dead in the heart, even if it might only be on the inside. Indeed, it usually remains unseen to other people. But the person in question — if wounded badly enough — can carry the damage with them for the rest of their life, like a bruise that never seems to heal completely.

Lately I have begun to fear, though, that I might sadly be, at least partially, to blame for his lashings out toward Francesca. I have always known how jealous he can get, and how much attention he requires in order to avoid having his abandonment issues from his childhood resurface. And I am also aware that I do choose to give most of my attention to Francesca rather than Phillip. But she is my child, and I want nothing but the best for her. She is perfect to me, and I have never known such an intense feeling of love and fulfillment as becoming a mother has given me. She deserves only the best; to have the greatest childhood that I can possibly provide her. A childhood a thousand times better than the ones Phillip and I went through. ...even if this might mean my having to leave the man I love in order to give her that childhood. I do still love him. I really do. It's just that he has changed so much; become so destructive.

I have just found out that I am pregnant again, though Phillip doesn't know it yet. This pregnancy makes me feel so incredibly blissful, but at the same time I'm also afraid that it will only make Phillip become even worse, even more jealous over having to share my attention with yet another child.

Yesterday, I consulted with an expert on the field of healing the emotions of children who have grown up in orphanages, and unfortunately, there doesn't seem to be much I can do in order to help Phillip... The man I talked to said that considering Phillip is still like this, at the age of 31, he isn't likely to change at all...

Of course, I have always felt the lack myself ...how could I not have, growing up the way that I did. But still, Phillip and I are different. I am softer, more loving; and sometimes he can be so harsh and unforgiving.

When I asked the expert why he thought I had turned out differently — less damaged, somehow (I feel bad about putting it this way, but I also believe that it is true.) — we started talking about how I was always very close to Laura, who worked at the orphanage, and that I could always come talk to her about my emotions when anything bothered me, and that that might have saved me in a way. I know that if Laura could have, then she would've adopted me. But she was unmarried, and didn't make enough money to be allowed to adopt a child. Still, though, I felt her love for me every day.

The expert also explained that Phillip, like most other orphans, often would have been left completely to himself whenever he was hurting. Having no one to turn to, these children bottle up their emotions, and many times end up exploding in fits of rage later, in an attempt to get the attention that they so sorely crave and need. I have tried to sit down and talk to Phillip about this, but he just won't listen to me anymore. Not the way he used to listen to me when we were growing up.

I'm afraid that if I don't leave Phillip now, then he might end up breaking Francesca as well as our second child beyond repair, and I just cannot allow that to happen. What kind of a mother would I be if I did? I wouldn't be worthy of calling myself a mother.

I've never given up on anything or anyone before and, now that I think about it, that might very well be a big part of the reason for why I so badly wanted to be with Phillip in the first place. I believed I could be there for him, and love him like no one else ever has, or probably ever will, sadly... I thought I could heal him, and that together we'd become stronger. And I do truly believe, with all my heart, that we did become stronger for each other to begin with. But once Francesca was born, our bond gradually weakened, and slowly started becoming more and more destructive...

There is love there for me; really, there is great love there for me from him. ...But, it's just the things around it that are the problem. And those things need to change in order for it to be good love. And that's the point. Now that I'm a mother I cannot have a destructive element within that love, because my children are completely dependent on me, and I can't — I just won't — let them down, like Phillip's and my parents let us down.

And... because the expert I consulted with has made me see that these things are not going to change, I believe that... I might just have to finally give up. I am not a quitter; it goes against my very nature. But maybe, for the first time in my life, I may have to give up and walk away. Maybe, in this case, walking away from this damaging situation is the only right thing to do for me and my children...?

Francesca slowly lifted her eyes from her mother's old diary, her heart hurting, for her mother, for her father, and for the circumstances in which they had ended up finding themselves. So, silently, she sat there, with nothing but her tears to keep her company.

She took a deep breath, trying to digest what she had just read. It was so overwhelming, sitting there with her mother's words literally in her hands. It had made her feel like a little kid again, eavesdropping on her parents. But then again, she hadn't known what else to do. She exhaled and closed the diary. That was enough reading for one day.

She realized that her dad had been right about her mom, in a way, although, it seemed like the situation hadn't been quite as black and white as her dad had portrayed it. More than that, Francesca had a hard time believing that on the night her mom was in that car crash, Anna had actually told Phillip that she didn't love him, and never had; that she was only using him in order to have kids — like the version of the story that Phillip had told Jenny — even if the essence of what Anna had told him, as well as how their relationship had started to change after Francesca was born, might have made him feel like that was what she meant.

And then she thought about her and Adrian's relationship. Would they be able to stay together? What if she did end up having this child; would that only make them stronger? Or, would it in the end weaken them, just like it had done with her parents? And... was there ever any real guarantee that Adrian wouldn't end up leaving her — just like her mom had left her dad?

No, she realized. She would never have any guarantees that the people in her life wouldn't just one day get up and walk out of her life.

But, maybe, she thought... it was still worth pursuing something good, and trusting the people in her life, if at this point in time it felt right. The future was the future, and all she could really take into consideration was the way that things were right now at this very moment. Scary, yes; but maybe also the way it was supposed to be?

She exhaled, deciding to put these feelings aside for the moment.

Peering back into the cardboard box, she saw that small white porcelain box that she remembered having seen sitting on top of her mother's nightstand. It was always there, and Francesca had never been allowed to fiddle with it. When she had asked her mother why not, and what was in there that was so important, Anna had said that it protected an item that was very sacred to her; something that symbolized pure, innocent happiness.

Francesca dried her eyes with her fingertips, and started lifting the white porcelain lid off; finally revealing what her mother had been hiding inside.

It was a ring, a beautiful, Victorian gold ring with a round, opal stone in the center, and a string of tiny diamonds all around the opal, framing it.

She remembered having seen her mother wear this ring when she was a little girl. She held it up to take a closer look, brushed the dust off of it, and slipped it onto her ring finger. It fit perfectly.

Then her eyes fell on the letters at the bottom of the box. Flipping through them, she saw that one of the letters was actually addressed to... Richard.

She gasped. There really must have been more between them than Francesca had initially realized. Turning the letter over, she noticed that it was still sealed. She took a deep breath, and closed her eyes.

She couldn't handle any more waves of emotions right now. She needed some time to process it all; some time to figure out what her next move was going to be. So she stuck the letters in her ballet bag for later, closed the cardboard box back up, and left the house.

*

Francesca stood in the center of the studio, preparing for the adagio exercise; her legs and feet crossed in a tight fifth position, and her arms elongating slightly down and out to either side, like a breath of fresh air.

She listened to the music so intently, not only with her ears but with her entire body. It softened and humbled her, yet at the same time made her stronger as it fused with her body's movements.

She was dancing not only for one; but for now, she was still dancing for two.

Francesca lifted her right foot up off the floor, letting the sole of her ballet shoe wrap around and caress her left ankle, travelling continuously up toward her knee, before extending her leg slowly in an unfolding movement in front of her body, pointing her foot up toward the ceiling as high as it would go.

The ballet teacher observed her for a moment, then started walking toward her. "Good, Francesca. That's beautiful." She held her hand out a couple of inches above the tip of Francesca's extended point shoe-clad foot. "Now, make your foot touch my hand. Come on, you can do it — I know you can."

Francesca's entire body shook, her muscles burned as they begged her to give up; to let her leg plummet to the ground. "I... I can't."

"What you need to do is release and extend the leg from your hip," the teacher continued. "Reach it further out of its socket; don't pull it in."

Francesca's leg felt like it was going to explode, and she was getting a strong urge to slap the woman.

"It's your tension and the fact that you're holding back that's creating your pain. Release; let go — only then will you be able to achieve it. Only then will your leg be free to go where it needs to go."

Francesca panted harder than ever, and was about to tell her teacher to shove it. But then she caught a glance of herself in the mirror.

Her ballet teacher was right; she looked ridiculously tense with her to-mato-red face, and wispy strands of her hair sticking straight out from her head like she was a cactus.

"As long as you keep tensing and holding it in, you'll never be able to release your leg — the two actions are opposites, so it's one or the other."

Francesca focused, and imagined a string of air bubbles appearing in-side her hip socket; creating space to breathe; creating some distance. Her foot reached out farther, way beyond what she thought it was capable of, and the tip of her point shoe touched her teacher's hand.

"Yes, Francesca. Excellent." The teacher nodded, and smiled knowingly. "See, I told you you'd be able to do it, all you needed was to take a different approach; to look at it a bit differently." The teacher walked away, and started correcting the girl standing next to Francesca.

Francesca smiled discreetly, and began repeating the same movement with her leg out to her side. She studied herself in the mirror covering the entire front wall of the studio. Then it dawned on her; her leg wasn't the only part of her that she needed to release.

For as long as she could remember, she'd wanted to be completely free of her dad. Yet, in holding onto all her built-up anger and all her tension, she, herself, was making it impossible to fulfill her own wish. The two ac-tions were, like her teacher had said, opposites — she could only have one or the other. Francesca could choose to hold on to all the pain; or she could choose to let go, creating some distance between the two of them, thereby finally becoming free.

She understood that try as she might, she would never be completely free of him; he was her father and always would be. But what she could do, and what she needed to do, was to let go of her bitterness toward him. She needed to forgive him for all that he had done — not for her dad's sake, but for herself. Just for Francesca.

No matter whether she decided to keep the baby or not, whether she actually managed to get Jenny back somehow or not — no matter if she never saw her dad again in her entire life — she would still never be completely free of him. That was, not until she let go; not until she forgave him. If she never let go then he would still always be a part of her — he would still be in the back of her mind, causing her pain.

Her old experiences and hard feelings relating to the past, she suddenly realized, were equivalent to the term *sunk costs* that she had been taught in her economics class. There was nothing she could do to change them anyway, so she needed to stop figuring them in when accounting for each and every day.

What she could change, however, was her present and her future. And this was the time to do it. Starting with herself and her own voice — not using her ballet to express herself this time — she would be strong enough to admit that her dad was only human, and that he had made some mistakes.

And maybe... that kind of understanding and forgiveness was that one thing he had never had; what he really needed in order to come to his senses and bring Jenny back home.

And with her voice loud and clear; when she finally forgave him — that was when she would finally be free. She was an adult now, and she alone would decide what her life would be like from here on out.

Her dad had his issues; there was no doubt about that. He had been through some rough things in his life. And now, especially after having read her mother's side of the story, Francesca for the first time in her life found herself pitying him.

But then again, what had happened to her dad had not been her fault, and she would not be punished for it any longer. She would be the bigger person and reach out to him one last time. And then it was up to him to decide whether he was willing to change enough for them to continue being part of each other's lives.

Francesca continued lifting her bent knee high up to the side, before fully extending her leg. She held it strong and steady, and this time was able to also let go of the tension that had been holding her back. She felt her leg release and lengthen from her hip joint, freeing it to reach farther and higher than ever before.

"Exactly, Francesca!" her teacher exclaimed. "You've got the right feeling down now."

Chapter Thirty-six

Francesca kept looking nervously around the café; checking to see whether he'd shown up yet. After they'd spoken on the phone last night, she hadn't been able to sleep very well. A couple of the hours originally allocated for sleep had instead been filled with the exercise of repeatedly going over and over in her head what she wanted to tell him, and what she wanted to ask of him.

She had no idea how this encounter would end — all she knew was that, somehow, she needed to tell her father that she'd forgiven him for all that he had done to her. Whether Jenny would ever forgive him or not was something Jenny needed to figure out on her own.

Of course, by no means did she — or would she ever — agree with all the things he'd done, and the way he'd treated them over the years. But she'd realized that, at least these last couple of months, it had, in fact, been *her* desire to be free from her dad that had created most of her pain — that was what had driven Phillip to the extreme act of kidnapping Jenny.

Although she still couldn't, and wouldn't ever blame herself for her dad's behavior, it had occurred to her that hurt people were only likely to end up hurting other people. So, then... maybe, she thought, if a person was shown forgiveness, then that might somehow trigger them to realize that they, themselves, were also capable of forgiving the people who had hurt them in their lives?

Francesca knew her own challenge was finally being able to trust and embrace the fact that she was loved. Adrian loved her so very much; and her mother had done whatever she felt she needed in order to protect her. And so, knowing this, she had dared to explore the vulnerability within herself, recognizing the love she still had for her dad.

Even though she felt nervous, and even a little scared about facing him, she knew she needed to free herself emotionally from her dad once and for all by forgiving him for what he had done. Not only for herself, but after careful consideration, she had decided that the best way for her to show her dad love as well, was through her forgiveness ...attempting to give him — for the first time in many years — what she believed he needed.

Then she would make one last appeal to get him to bring Jenny back home. Hopefully, her effort in reaching out and opening up her heart to him would be enough to make him see that coming back to Oslo was the only right thing for him to do.

Realizing it all depended on the outcome of today's meeting, she felt her throat tighten and her breathing become shallow. They hadn't arranged to meet until noon; however, she'd arrived at the café 15 minutes early, just in case.

She checked her watch.

It was five minutes to twelve.

She started drumming her fingers nervously on the table, and looked back up from her watch.

There he was, strolling in through the dark brown, wooden door.

She gave him a slight wave.

He nodded to acknowledge that he'd seen her, and made his way over to her table through the thick maze of teenagers, and families with young children and their strollers.

She rose slightly from her chair to greet him. "Hi, Richard," she said, then sat back down. "Thanks for meeting with me like this on such short notice."

He pulled a chair out from the small, round table across from where she was sitting. "Well, it sounded urgent on the phone, so... what's going on?"

"Ah... I have a confession to make. This meeting isn't about the business."

"OK..." He eyed her suspiciously. "So, what is it about, then?"

Francesca took a deep breath, and somewhere during her lengthy exhale found the courage to tell him what was going on. "My dad has disappeared, and he's taken my younger sister along with him."

Richard frowned. "I'm sorry, what?"

Francesca lowered her voice, and filled him in on everything, except for her pregnancy. "...And so, that's why I was so desperate to start this business in the first place."

He leaned back in his chair, raising both eyebrows. "Wow..."

Francesca sighed. "Yeah..."

"Alright, and where exactly do I fit into all of this mess?"

"Well... I need you to help me find him."

"Aha." He laughed scornfully. "Francesca, sweetie, sounds like you're forgetting the fact that I hate your dad — I'm not going to do anything to help him."

"But, you wouldn't be helping him — you'd be helping me, and my sister."

"Still, I don't want anything to do with him for the rest of my life, and now it looks like my wish has just come true. Good riddance for Oslo is all I can say."

Francesca crossed her arms in front of her chest. "Then, I'll quit our business if you don't help me."

"You know, that's exactly why we signed that contract binding both of us to the business until at least the end of August next year, remember? You're not going anywhere."

"Please, I'm begging you to help me. Of anyone I know, you're the person with the most connections and acquaintances spread out over the entire country. In fact, you're probably one of the people with the highest number of contacts in Norway all together."

The corners of his mouth lifted into a slight smile. "Well, I mean—"

"I'm sure you'd be able to find out something about his whereabouts if you wanted to. And I believe you understand why I can't involve the police or any other kind of authority?"

"Be that as it may. I'm not going to help you."

Francesca let out a groan. "Please, help me find him. Please. There's so much at stake for me here."

He studied her for a moment, and then said; "Give me one good reason as to why I should help you."

Francesca stared him dead in the eye. She hadn't wanted it to come to this, but he'd left her with no other choice. "You knew my mom, right?"

"Yeah, so?"

"And you loved her — I know you did."

Richard looked away, rubbing his hand over the light stubble on his face. "Your mom was an amazing woman."

"How amazing?"

He sighed. "The most amazing person I have ever met, alright?"

"Yes." Francesca nodded. "I couldn't agree more." She paused, and contemplated the flames of the tea candle in a square, red, glass holder in the center of their table. She wrapped her cold fingers around the glass, and slid it across the tabletop closer to her. "And..." she continued. "Have you ever loved another woman since my mom?"

He stared at her for a couple of seconds.

She noticed the sadness residing in his eyes, tarnishing his pale blue irises to a washed-out gray.

"Life's different when growing up in an orphanage..." He looked down.

"There's not a whole lot of love going around, so when you're lucky enough to find some, you sure do your very best to hold onto it. And that mom of yours..." He smiled. "You know, she definitely was something else. She had this incredible ability to light up a room. And no matter what happened — and, let me tell you, there are quite a few bleak days when growing up in an orphanage — she still always managed to make you feel like you really mattered, you know?"

Francesca swallowed hard, and whispered. "Yeah, I do know."

"And I guess I've just never met anyone else who's ever made me feel that way, and..." His voice trailed away, and he looked back up at Francesca. He cleared his throat. "But it doesn't matter anymore. That was all a long time ago."

"True. And, unfortunately, we both lost her in the end. But, at least I still have several things that used to belong to her." She paused for a couple of seconds, preparing herself for the attack. "However... I can't help but wonder whether you've managed to save anything of sentimental value from the time the two of you shared together?"

"What do you mean?"

"What was your favorite moment with her? Was it, perhaps, that afternoon by the lake on your 18th birthday; the day you moved out of the orphanage? She was only 15 at the time, so she still needed to continue living at the orphanage for another three years, right?"

He slowly sat up straight. "How do you...?"

"I know you wrote her a letter after having spent that afternoon together, declaring your love for her."

His jaw dropped. "She told you about that?"

"No." She shook her head. "I went through some of her old stuff last night, and I found your letter in an envelope, along with a picture of the two of you."

His cheeks turned red. "She really kept it, after all those years?"

"Yeah, she did," Francesca said, studying her business companion. "But she never wrote you back, did she?"

He instantly lost the rosy color in his cheeks, and lowered his voice. "And how exactly would you know whether or not—?"

"Well, you see, she did write you a letter — she just never sent it."

"What?"

"I found her letter to you in a box along with the one you wrote to her."

"And you're telling me the truth right now...?"

"Absolutely."

"And have you read it?"

"Nope." She shook her head. "It's still sealed. The letter's private; and considering it hadn't already been opened, I really didn't want to be the one to do so."

"And where are the letters now?"

"I can't tell you that. That is — not unless you help me find my dad. And, of course, I can only imagine how disappointed my mom would've been if she knew you were refusing to help me."

"Francesca, this issue is between you and your dad, and I'm not getting in the middle of that mess. Now, hand over those letters — they're *mine*, and not yours."

"Not really. You see, you gave my mom that letter, thereby making it hers. When she passed away my sister, my dad and I inherited her stuff — so, technically, the letter is mine. Finders, keepers. The same goes for the letter she never sent you. She kept it for herself, meaning it was still hers, and now I've inherited that as well."

"Francesca..." he muttered through gritted teeth.

"Of course, maybe I should show your letter to my dad? In fact, why haven't I thought of that before? I'm sure if I told him about it then he'd come back home real fast so he could pay you a little visit."

Richard sighed, wearing a dejected look on his face. "Francesca, what's wrong with you? When did you all of a sudden become so vindictive?"

"Ever since my dad took the one person that means the most to me in the entire world away from me. And I know you feel like he did the same to you — now, please help me. I don't have much time. If I don't find him, and he doesn't come back to Oslo, then I'll lose something else incredibly important to me on Wednesday," she said, her eyes beginning to tear up.

He crossed his arms in front of his chest, and leaned back in his chair. "I'm not helping you."

"Alright." She pulled two old, yellowing envelopes out of her bag. "Then you leave me with no other choice than to destroy these."

He sat up straight, and pointed at the envelopes. "Are those...?"

"Yeah, they are. And they're about to go up in flames, disappearing forever." She inched them closer to the tea candle on the café table.

"Have you completely lost it?" he hissed.

"Nope, not yet. And, so far, you haven't lost these letters, either. But if you don't change your mind real fast then we're both about to lose some something significant." She moved the envelopes even closer to the candle flame.

"Hah, you're bluffing. You wouldn't risk starting a fire at a café."

Her gaze on him remained steady. "Try me."

He didn't waver.

"OK." She held the two letters together and dipped one corner of them down past the rim of the glass tea candle holder.

"No — wait!" he cried.

Francesca immediately retracted the letters away from the flame.

The people at the neighboring tables fell quiet, and turned around to stare at Richard.

He quickly looked around at them, gave a fake smile, and uttered; "Sorry about that, guys. I'll keep it down." Then he turned back to Francesca.

"Yes," she said, holding the letters tight to her chest. "You were saying?"

"Jeez, woman — you're absolutely nuts."

She shook her head. "No. I'm just a girl with everything to lose."

"Fine." He held his hands up. "I give up; you win."

"Ah," she exclaimed. "Really?"

"Yeah, really. You just demonstrated how insane you're capable of being — this must really mean a lot to you."

She nodded rapidly.

He motioned with his fingers. "OK, so just hand over those letters and I'll see what I can find out."

"Nah, I don't think so. Help me first, and then I'll give you the letters."

He shrugged. "Then there's no deal."

"You know," she smirked. "Considering we're business partners, we really don't trust each other as much as we should."

"Agreed. But then again, I think our stubbornness and perseverance is what's working for us, and getting us both to where we want in our lives."

"True." She nodded. "OK, so how about this; I give you the letter you wrote to my mom, as well as the picture of the two of you, right now. And as soon as you provide me with information about my dad's whereabouts, then I'll give you the letter she wrote to you as well — how does that sound?"

He contemplated her for a moment. "I guess seeing as you haven't even opened that second letter, I've got no reason to believe you're bluffing and would withhold it from me later," he said, squinting slightly at her as though that was help him read her better. "OK, done." He held his hand out.

She shook it, and handed him his letter with her other hand.

He jerked the letter away from her, and stashed it safely in the inside pocket of his black winter coat. "Oh, and by the way, you said you were losing something else important on Wednesday — what's on Wednesday?"

"Never you mind," she snapped.

He raised his eyebrows. "Alright, then."

"OK, so just please remember; I cannot stress how urgent it is that I receive whatever information you can retrieve as quickly as at all possible."

"Yes, ma'am; you've already made that ridiculously clear. And obviously I'll do my best — however, I can't guarantee exactly how much, and what kind of information I'll be able to find."

"No, I know. Just any information at all will at least get me further along than where I'm at right now."

He watched her, and broke out into a smile.

"What?"

"You know, you really do bear a striking resemblance to your mother. And, to be honest, I noticed it the very first time I saw you when you came to that talk I held at your university."

"Really? Then why didn't you say anything?"

"What was I supposed to say: 'Hi, you remind me of this girl I grew up with?'"

Francesca shrugged. "I don't know..."

"Anyway, I think that's why I kept pushing you, to the point of almost being obnoxious, about why you'd come to my presentation. And your strong personality as well... it's just... it's just incredible how much you remind me of her."

*

Francesca sat at the kitchen table at her dad's house, holding onto her phone with both hands, staring at the screen; hardly blinking — like the Loch Ness Monster might suddenly emerge from the surface and she ran the risk of missing it.

"Ring—"

Her finger slammed down onto the screen of her phone to answer. She held it up to her ear. "Hi, Richard, what do you know; what've you managed to find out?"

"I know he still works as a cab driver, but for a different company. Obviously, he had to leave his old cab behind when he got fired from his job at *Oslo Central Cab Service*, so he's got a new car now, it's a black Mercedes—"

"OK," she interrupted him. "But more importantly — where is he?"

"He's in Trondheim."

"In Trondheim — seriously?"

"Yes, seriously. I'll text you the name of the cab company, as well as the registration number on his license plate."

"That's awesome, thanks! But, how did you manage to get hold of all this information in just one day?"

"Let's just say I've got a lot of useful friends. It makes being a business-man a whole lot easier."

"Alright, well do you know anything about what his shifts are like?"

"No, but I could probably find out."

"Great. And tomorrow's Monday, so also text me whatever you find out about his shift tomorrow."

"Whoa; whoa; tomorrow? Hang on there, Francesca; you can't leave to-morrow. Wednesday's another day."

"Yeah, I've have to go tomorrow. Wednesday's not an option."

"Oh, come on, Wednesday's only three days away from now — how can anything possibly be that urgent?"

"Richard, I don't really want to talk about it, but I assure you that it *definitely* can't wait."

"You know, our next business presentation is on Tuesday, and I swear, if you're not back by then—"

"I'll be back for the meeting, don't worry."

"OK, I'm counting on you."

"I promise I won't let you down."

Richard sighed. "Of course, I should've realized by now that there's no stopping you once you've made up your mind about something."

"Exactly. Now, let me know as soon as possible so I can book my flights."

"I'll see what I can do."

"OK, great. And what about Jenny? Have you managed to find out how she's doing?"

"Not yet. They only got to Trondheim three days ago, so I'm not sure I'll be able to find out where they're staying, but I'll at least give it a shot."

"Thanks, Richard, you're the best. You really are. You don't understand how much this means to me."

"Oh, I think I might have a vague idea."

*

The cabs pulled up to the taxi stand, lining up one after the other like dominoes.

Francesca had positioned herself on the corner just before the actual stand. That way, if her dad showed up, she'd be able to hop into the backseat before he could pull up in line; avoiding the possibility of another passenger snagging a ride with Phillip ahead of her.

She checked each license plate carefully, while at the same time constantly making sure the hood of the oversized, black raincoat she'd borrowed from Margaret was still covering her entire face.

She looked down at her watch.

It was almost three o'clock in the afternoon.

She'd already been standing there for almost two hours, yet, she still hadn't seen any sign of Phillip. She desperately wanted a chance to go see Jenny as well, but her flight back to Oslo was in three hours from now, and she couldn't afford to abandon post in case he suddenly showed up. According to what Richard had told her, he was supposed to be working this exact taxi stand in between the calls he got to go pick up customers elsewhere, and, of course, people hailing him down while he was driving from one place to another.

Suddenly, her stomach tightened at the thought of what would happen if she didn't manage to talk to him at all while she was in Trondheim — then what?

Another cab neared the taxi stand.

Her eyes scanned the license plate.

That wasn't him, either.

"Damn," she muttered, and kicked a small rock with her black rubber boot in the opposite direction from the taxi stand.

It skidded across the asphalt, before dropping down off the edge of the sidewalk.

She looked up.

There, across the street, was another cab parked at the gas station.

She squinted at the license plate.

It was his car.

Her heart knocked hard and fast against her chest. She peered in through the raindrop-splashed back window as best she could.

There was no sign of him inside the car.

She realized he must be inside the gas station. ...but he probably would-n't be for much longer; she needed to hustle her ass over there pronto.

Francesca looked both ways to check whether any cars were coming toward her, then sprinted across the street. She crouched down and hid behind the parked cars, making sure she couldn't be seen from the entrance of the gas station. Finally, she reached the rear of Phillip's car, and snuck around to the back door on the right hand side.

She tried the door handle.

It was locked, of course.

She got down even lower, and squinted at the entrance.

There he was, striding across the lot toward the car.

Francesca was having a hard time breathing. This was it. She'd have to make absolutely sure that he didn't see her, and then when he unlocked the door and got into the driver's seat, she'd hop into the back seat.

He was only about ten steps away from the car now.

She was afraid her heart was beating so loud that he might actually hear it.

He got his car keys out, and unlocked the door.

Francesca heard the automatic lock open right next to her ear.

He turned his back to where she was squatting down, and got into the car.

She jerked the door open, and threw herself into the backseat.

Phillip spun around, his mouth wide open.

She stared him straight in the face. "Hi Dad."

Chapter Thirty-seven

"Francesca?" Phillip panted. "How the hell did you...?"

"That's not important. What really matters is *why* I'm here."

He pointed at the door, and raised his voice. "You need to get out. I'm working — you can't be here."

"I'll pay you — I have my own business now, remember? And as long as I don't do anything wrong, you can't turn away a paying customer."

"Francesca, I'm serious — now, get out."

She shook her head, and tried to steady her trembling hands. "I'm not going anywhere until you hear me out."

He sighed. "You shouldn't have come here. It was just wrong of you to—"

"Dad," Francesca interrupted him. "I forgive you for what you've done," she blurted out.

He stared at her, the tension in his forehead and jawline gradually ebbing away, and instead being replaced by guilt. He looked away. "Why?"

"Because I have to. I need to forgive you once and for all — for both your sake, as well as mine."

"I don't understand..."

"Make no mistake, I do not agree with what you've done over the years, and how you've treated Jenny and me. And there have been times when you've been so wrong you shouldn't have been allowed to have custody of us."

"So why, then, would you all of a sudden decide to forgive me?"

"Because," she continued. "I've been lucky enough to feel and remember the love my mother expressed for me, for however short a period of my life that was. But I can still feel it. And ever since Mom passed away I've tried to provide this same feeling for Jenny."

"Francesca..."

She held her hand up to silence him. "Please, let me finish."

He hesitated for a moment, then gave her a single nod.

She took a deep breath. "Now, I know you unfortunately haven't been able to experience what it's like to have a mother. Or a father. And for this

I'm truly sorry, because everyone deserves to be loved. And that's why I forgive you for not always having been able to show us the love that we've needed. But it's not too late. Jenny and I love you — we really do, and we always have. I hope you realize that."

"I don't need love — I'm just ensuring I get what's rightfully mine."

"Everybody needs love." She reached out and placed a trembling hand on top of her dad's."

Phillip looked down at Francesca's hand, his eyes growing wide. "Where did you get that?"

"Get what?"

"That ring you're wearing — where did you get it?"

"It belonged to Mom."

"Yeah, I know it did — that's the ring I proposed to her with."

Francesca gasped. "What? How is it possible that I never knew that? I mean, I remember seeing her wearing it and all, but still, I just never realized..."

"I don't know... but when your mom passed away I went through all her jewelry looking for it, but I couldn't find it."

"Yeah, well..." Francesca felt a pang of guilt. "I kind of grabbed it right after she died and stored it in a cardboard box right up until a few days ago."

Phillip broke out into a smile. "Really? Well, I'm just glad it didn't disappear. I was afraid she'd gotten rid of it when we... when we split up."

Francesca shook her head. "No, not at all. After we moved out, Mom kept the ring in a small, oval porcelain box with a lid on it, and the box was always sitting right next to her on her bedside table."

He nodded, continuing to smile. "OK, that's just... that's good to know."

Francesca contemplated her father. She couldn't remember the last time she'd seen him smile like that. "And you got married in that meadow, right? ...the one at the top of that ridiculously steep hill that Mom always used to drag us up to?"

"Yeah, we did. The rain was pouring down on our wedding day, and the hill was so incredibly muddy, but that didn't stop your mom from climbing it to get to the top, even though she was wearing her white wedding dress. I remember being so incredibly nervous during the ceremony; literally shaking. But then I looked down and saw how black the bottom part of her dress was from the thick layer of mud covering it, and I couldn't help but start laughing." He chuckled. "Your mom had a very special way of always making everyone around her feel calm and at ease, and when I saw her muddy dress I couldn't for the life of me find those nerves again — even if I had really wanted to. And that's when I knew that I didn't have to be nervous, because there was nothing to be nervous about, really. I would never need to be perfect, because we were not perfect. We were just us. And that was enough."

Francesca felt her own nervous tension slip away.

"And... your mom was no girlie-girl; she was more of a tomboy, in a way. Yet, she still had the prettiest feminine features and a petite frame — just like you. And if she got an idea in her head, then she made sure she managed to see it through. Again — just like you."

"Yeah, I actually went through some of her old stuff the other day, and found a picture of her when she was my age, and I must admit I was able to see the resemblance. Except for the fact that her hair was curly and more golden in color than mine."

"Oh, absolutely, you're the spitting image of her. Apart from her hair, as you said; you've got my fine Nordic straight hair."

She nodded. "You know, Dad, I've actually never heard the story of how you proposed to Mom. Is there... is there any chance you'd be willing to tell me?"

He glanced at his daughter's face, and hesitated. "Oh, I don't know..."

"Please, Dad? I think every girl has the right to know that story about her parents."

"Er..." He checked his watch. "Alright, I'll tell you quickly."

"Thanks!" She beamed.

Phillip cleared his throat. "Well, as you know, your mom was two years younger than me. So, when I moved away from the orphanage at the age of 18, she still had to stay there for another two years. But, she would come over to my apartment as often as she could. And then as soon as she turned 18, she moved right in with me." Phillip paused for a moment, his bushy eyebrows looking heavy. "Of course," he continued. "I already knew I wanted to be with her for the rest of my life — I was nine years old the day I realized she was the one for me."

"Really — only nine years old?"

He smiled weakly. "Yeah."

"What made you so sure?"

Phillip sank further down into the driver's seat. "At the orphanage we had this couple come around, looking to adopt a boy. The rumor being whispered in the dormitory was that they wanted an older boy — which was really rare, as most couples wanted infants — and I had also heard that they'd shown an interest in me. And..." He hesitated, looking away as his face went pink. He cleared his throat. "And, apparently... they had been interested in Richard, as well..." His voice faded away. "So, anyway, I did my very best; combed my hair; practiced my smile in front of the bathroom mirror; and stood up real straight when they came by to make their final decision."

"Yeah..." Francesca leaned forward in between the two front seats, and put her hand on her dad's shoulder. "And then what?"

"Well, for whatever reason, they didn't want me after all. From what I heard, they ended up choosing a different boy — a younger boy from a different orphanage." He sighed. "And that's when I truly realized that I was too old; that I would never end up having any parents."

Francesca felt his pain; imagining it reaching her through where her hand lay on his shoulder.

"So then I started crying, and ran outside. Your mom was also outside, sitting at a picnic table drawing pictures with some of the other girls. She walked over and sat down next to me on the concrete steps leading down from the back door and into the garden. She was only seven at the time, but she took my right hand and drew a heart in my palm with a red marker. Then she put down a P for Phillip, and an A for Anna, and said; 'It's OK, don't cry — we can be a family, if you want to.'"

Francesca felt her heart go mushy. "Dad, that's such a great story."
"Yeah..." he muttered. "So, getting back to the story, your mom and I had been living together for about two years when I decided it was time to propose to her. And I remember being so incredibly nervous about it all, I must've spent at least two or three months obsessing over finding the perfect setting, and the perfect way to propose."

Francesca noticed her dad's forehead tense up, and the lines running across it deepen, and she realized he still felt nervous just talking about it, even after all these years. "Really?" she said. "So how did you finally do it — how did you finally propose?"

"Well, we were out taking a walk through Frogner Park one evening in October, when it suddenly started pouring — just like on our wedding day, actually. So we looked at each other and burst out laughing, before sprinting over to the nearest big tree so we could wait it out, even though we were already soaking wet. We stood with our backs up against the huge tree trunk for a minute or two, watching the rain stream down off the leaves all around us like silver-colored tinsel. And, like I said, I'd been obsessing over finding the perfect time and place for a few months by then, but when I

looked over at your mom, I realized that there would never be a better moment than right then and there. And because I was afraid she might find the
ring if I left it lying around in the apartment, I was always carrying it around
with me anyway. So I got down on one knee in the mud and said: 'Anna —
you're amazing. I will always want you; not only on the perfect days, but
also, and especially, on Monday nights when we're standing soaked underneath a tree in the park, and your hair is flattened to your face, and your
makeup is running all over the place — you will still always be the most
beautiful woman that I know. Will you marry me?'"

"Wow." Francesca dabbed at the corners of her eyes with her fingertips.
"I had no idea you were so romantic. Thanks for telling me the story, Dad."

Phillip shifted around in his seat, and muttered; "Yeah, well you know,
that was a long time ago and all..." He sighed. "And, that's actually why I
started working as a cab driver in the first place; so I could make enough
money to buy that engagement ring, as well as pay for our wedding. Of
course, that was back in the day when you could actually make a living as a
cab driver working eight-hour shifts. Not like now, where you need to work
12 hours a day in order to earn the same amount of money as before."

"OK, so why didn't you start doing something else instead after you'd
gotten married? Why didn't you go back to school and get some kind of a
degree? I mean, I know how much you hate being a cab driver and all."

"Yeah..." He looked away.

"Yeah — what?"

"Well, then you mother got pregnant with you, and I needed to keep
working in order to be able to support the three of us. Your mom hadn't
been working much since she was a student at the time, and we had no sav-
ings, so we couldn't afford for me to go back to school when she was staying
at home taking care of you."

Francesca felt a wave of guilt, even though, of course, it wasn't her fault
that her mom had gotten pregnant.

"So that's why I've been telling you that you need to get your university
degree right away — don't wait until it's too late; don't wait until after you
start having kids."

She felt the now all-too-familiar nausea well up inside her.

They both remained silent for a minute or two.

"But, Dad?"

"Yeah?"

"Um..." She hesitated, knowing her question was regarding a very tender subject for her dad. A few days ago, she had learned her mom's side of

the story, but she still wanted to hear her dad's version for herself, coming directly from him, and not just through Jenny. She was still confused about how it was possible for her parents' seemingly blissful relationship to turn so bitter after they'd had a child — after they'd had *her*. And she needed to hear his side of the story in order to hopefully gain some insight into what her final decision was going to be with Adrian and their unborn child. "So... what really happened between you and mom; how come you ended up getting separated? I mean, you seemed so happy."

Phillip looked down at his hands resting in his lap. He shook his head sadly. "I don't know... I didn't really understand it at the time — and I still don't completely understand — or, maybe I've just never wanted to understand... But, somehow, at some point, she just stopped needing me."

Francesca felt her stomach tighten. "I'm so sorry, Dad."

"Yeah, well, you know that's just the way..." His voice suddenly cracked. He took a deep breath. "So," he said, changing the topic. "When's your flight back — I could take you to the airport if you want?"

Francesca checked her watch. "I should probably be at the airport in about an hour and a half to be on the safe side."

"Alright, so we might as well just head on over, then, and—"

"Wait," she interrupted him. "Please let me see Jenny first."

Phillip sighed. "Francesca, in my entire life I've loved three people...only three. First I lost your mom; and now I've lost you. I cannot afford to lose Jenny as well. I need a second chance to prove myself as a father. I need to prove that all that I've sacrificed — that my entire life — hasn't all been for naught."

"Dad, please take me to see her, I've come all this way. She's my sister; she's my family, too."

"I can't; you know I can't — I'm working."

"And you know that's not a good excuse — I'll even pay you to make up for the time you won't be able to work. Please, just do this one last thing for me."

He stared out the window, and pulled his fingers through his blond, pin-straight hair several times. "I'm not going to take your money. I'll foot the cost."

*

"Francesca!" Jenny exclaimed, and ran full speed toward her sister, nearly knocking her over.

Francesca hugged her sister harder than she'd ever done before, kissing the top of her head over and over. "Hey, Jellybean, how are you? I've missed you so much!"

"I can't believe you're really here — how did you know where to find me?"

"It's a long story, I'll tell you some other time."

Jenny looked up at her sister, her deep blue eyes all red and swollen. "Have you come to save me; have you come to take me with you?"

Francesca took a deep breath, and bent down so her eyes reached Jenny's eye level. "Jellybean, you need to live with Dad for a while now — OK?"

Her face hardened, her resentment sharp as a knife. "What? You lied to me?" She took a couple steps away from Francesca. "You promised me I'd live with you in the end."

Francesca moved in closer so she could wrap her arms around her sister.

"No!" Jenny shouted, and backed away. "Do you know that he's keeping me captive in here — that he's not letting me go anywhere outside of this apartment?"

Francesca immediately got flashbacks to when she was fifteen years old, and Phillip had held her captive in their house for three days, so she couldn't go to her ballet audition. He had stayed at home from work in order to stop her from doing the one thing she wanted — the one thing that mattered more to her than anything else in the world. The rage she had felt back then surged through her again, threatening to destroy her from the inside. She turned around, and stared at her dad standing by the entrance door. "Is that true?"

"It's only temporary, just until I get her into school and all."

"She's not even going to school?" she hissed. "What about her old school, don't you realize that they're going to start calling you if she doesn't show up soon?"

"Of course, I already notified her old school that we've moved. And I've made some calls. There's a school right around the corner that will have a spot opening up for her next week. I mean, she doesn't even know anyone here yet, and I want her to be safe."

Francesca's eyes burned. "What's wrong with you?"

"Seeing as you've been trying to take her away from me, I had no choice but to move."

"That," Francesca spat. "Is the biggest and most destructive lie anyone can ever tell themselves — you always have a choice. Come back to Oslo with Jenny."

Phillip checked his watch. "You know, we really need to get going so you can catch that flight of yours."

She turned back to Jenny. "I'll be back for you, J-love — that's a promise."

"Stop... stop making... promises that... that you can't keep." Jenny sobbed.

Francesca kissed Jenny on the cheek and wiped away her tears. "Trust me; I won't let anything get in the way of us being together."

"Francesca, we've got to go," Phillip repeated.

She started marching toward her father, not blinking once. When she was right in front of him she muttered through gritted teeth: "You better start seriously thinking about what you're doing and come up with a bit of love real fast."

Neither of them spoke a single word during the 25 minute long drive to the airport.

Then, as Phillip pulled into the taxi stand by the departing terminal, he said: "Not being a parent yet, you wouldn't understand."

"Oh, I'm a mother, alright. And I have been ever since the day Mom died. That's when I stepped up and accepted the role as Jenny's mom."

He looked at Francesca in his rearview mirror.

Francesca noticed his gaze, and stared back at her father's face through the mirror.

They sat there for a few seconds, maintaining eye contact with each other; neither one of them blinking.

Then Phillip broke the silence. "I really do love you and Jenny. You know that, right?"

"Yes." She nodded, still staring at her father in the mirror. "I know you love us. And you know what? I used to think that love was all you needed; that that could fix every relationship in the world. But today you've just proven me wrong. Love *isn't* enough. So, yes, I do know that you love us. And so does Jenny, deep down. But that doesn't give you the right to neglect the fact that you also need to treat us with respect, and common decency. You don't get to hide behind a simple statement of love." She got out of the car, slamming the door behind her. She stormed over to the airport entrance, her heart about to break, and her tears threatening to spill.

*

Adrian met Francesca as she arrived at the Oslo airport, and tried to catch her evasive glance. "Hey, you OK?"

She looked as if her head were almost too heavy for neck to support and her eyes were as swollen as if she'd recently suffered a major allergy attack. "Not really," she said, her voice lifeless. "Could you... could you just hold me for a sec?"

"Of course; come here." He wrapped his arms around her.

Life at the busy airport carried on all around where they stood in the middle of the floor.

"So, how's Jenny doing?"

"Not great, but at least after Wednesday I'll be able to focus the majority of my energy on the business and getting her back again. And if I can find some of those dirt cheap train tickets I'll need to go up there and visit her."

"Right..." Adrian kissed her on the cheek.

"Can we go back home now? I'm exhausted."

Adrian eyed her; saw how she was about to break, and again, felt a strong loathing for Phillip flare up inside him. What kind of a father was he? Didn't he care about his kids at all? And who the hell did he think he was, pushing his daughter — the woman Adrian loved — to such extremes that she felt she needed to have an abortion, even though, clearly, she didn't want to go through with it.

Phillip was the worst parent Adrian had ever known, which meant that he should be the *last* person in the world with the power to indirectly control whether or not Francesca and Adrian became parents at this point in time.

Not only was Phillip leaving Francesca with no other choice than to have an abortion, but as long as he continued to act like a complete idiot, then Francesca would always have to keep fighting for Jenny — meaning she would never choose to prioritize Adrian and their relationship. She would never be able to completely trust him and finally give in to the thought of the two of them — or maybe even three of them, if he was able to turn this situation around in time — being together. "Absolutely, let's go," Adrian told her. "Just er... let me stop off at the men's room first. Do you have to go?"

"Nah, I'm pretty sure I've already cried every single drop of liquid out of my body." She smiled weakly.

"Alright," he escorted her over to the nearest bench. "You just wait right here, and I'll be back in a sec."

"OK," she whispered. "Oh, and could you maybe get me a bottle of water as well?"

"Yeah, 'course."

Adrian hurried over in the direction of the restrooms. He glanced back over his shoulder a couple of times, and when he saw that Francesca was staring aimlessly down at the floor rather than at him, he slipped in behind a vending machine.

He pulled his phone out, and scrolled down to Phillip's phone number, having copied it off of Francesca's phone a few days ago, just in case.

He stared down at the screen, wanting to call Phillip and give him a piece of his mind. But he realized Phillip might very well be with Jenny, and he also knew Francesca really didn't want her sister knowing about her pregnancy and possible abortion. Besides, he thought, if he called Phillip, he probably wouldn't manage to stay calm, and might end up saying stuff he'd regret; things that could end up only making the situation worse for Francesca.

More than that, he knew Phillip despised him and his meddling, so as soon as Phillip realized who it was calling him, he'd probably just hang up anyway.

Like any good lawyer, Adrian weighed the pros and cons, and decided that texting him would probably be the best strategy. That way, he wouldn't have to tell Phillip who he was until the very end of the text, at which point, he would already have read through his message.

And again, like any good lawyer, he knew that in order for them to win this case, he needed to make Phillip see that their side was the only right one, so Phillip would end up ruling in their favor.

He started texting: *Phillip, Francesca is pregnant and planning on having an abortion on Wednesday. What she really wants is to keep the baby, but because you have taken Jenny away from Oslo, Francesca is willing to do anything to make sure she gets to have Jenny in her life again — even if that means terminating her own pregnancy. She doesn't know I'm texting you, but I can promise you one thing; If you let her go through with this, then you will never have what you want. The girls will be gone, and they will never trust you ever again. You need to make this right before it's too late. You need to come back to Oslo with Jenny. Show the girls that you're the bigger man. Only then will they trust and respect you again. Please, before it's too late. Adrian.*

Chapter Thirty-eight

As Phillip's shift ended, he went back to the taxi central in order to switch back to his private car.

He pulled out of the parking lot, and headed in the direction of Jenny's and his new apartment. With no more passengers to shuttle around, he suddenly became aware of the fact that he'd been left with nothing more than his churning thoughts to keep him company.

The rain was really coming down now, dropping onto his windshield like miniature water balloons.

He set the windshield wipers at maximum speed.

Then he tried to mentally wipe away every single one of his gnawing thoughts as well, all the while realizing that that was a battle he was rapidly losing.

How could Francesca have forgiven him for the past, just like that? He'd caused her so much pain through the years, yet she'd been able to look past it; to rise above it. Francesca was the strongest person he knew, and he had no idea how she'd turned out so well, considering the kind of father he'd been.

And then — even though he concentrated all the effort he could muster on blocking out these particular thoughts — he could no longer ignore the fact that he was finding himself wondering whether he'd ever be able to forgive the people who had caused him such intense pain. Would he ever be able to let go of his own resentment?

The streetlights flooded his path from either side as he sped down the road; seeming to highlight his shame; making sure he had nowhere to hide this time.

After a short time he reached their street. He pulled into their driveway and turned the engine off. Then he sat in his car for a moment, dreading having to face his youngest daughter; having to explain to her, yet again, how what he was doing really was for the best.

He took a deep breath, before unlocking and pushing the front door to their apartment open. "Jenny, I'm home," he called out.

There was nothing but complete silence.

"Jenny?" he repeated.

Still nothing.

His heart started racing. Had she run away? Had she tried to follow Francesca back to Oslo?

All the lights were switched off, making it impossible to see anything clearly.

He banged the front door shut, and started heading over to the nearest light switch in the large, combined kitchen and living room area. On his way over, he stubbed his little toe on something lying on the floor. "Aw, crap..." he moaned, and clutched his throbbing toe. He reached over and hit the lights.

The room instantly lit up.

Phillip blinked a couple of times as his eyes adjusted to the light, then looked down.

Jenny's backpack was lying on the floor in front of him; the object he had stubbed his toe on.

He lifted his gaze, and let it circle the room.

There, in a tattered, mustard-colored wingback chair in the far corner sat Jenny. She was hunched over, hugging her knees to her chest with the soles of her feet placed on the seat of the chair.

Phillip felt relief roll over him. Then came a serving of guilt at the sight of what his actions were doing to his daughter. "There you are, Jenny. Why are you sitting in the dark? And why didn't you answer me when I called out your name?"

"I'm not talking to you," she shrieked.

"Then what do you call what you just did?"

Jenny opened her mouth, then closed it again.

"Listen, I'm sorry, but—"

"Please let me go," she whispered, getting to her feet.

He glanced at her face.

Her eyes were bloodshot.

"It's not that easy."

"Please," she sobbed.

He sighed, and shook his head tiredly.

"Ding, ding."

Phillip jumped, and put his hand up against the back pocket of his jeans. He pulled out his phone, and peered at the screen.

The text message was from a number he didn't know.

It might be from someone at his new work, he thought. He hesitated for a moment, but then decided to open it. His eyes ran down the text before he could stop them, as though they were a car with faulty brakes, speeding out of control. His jaw dropped.

"What is it?" Jenny asked.

He looked at her. "Nothing," he snapped.

"I know something's wrong by the look—"

"I said, it's nothing — OK?" he bellowed.

Her face as well as her body contracted.

"Now, go to your room." He pointed toward a door that stood ajar at the other end of the living room.

Even though her body was shaking, she continued to stare at him. "You have to let me go back to Oslo and live with Francesca."

"Only bad parents give their kids away," he spat.

She swallowed hard; then shook her head. "Sometimes the good parents are the ones who realize that giving away their kids is the only right thing to do." She turned her back on him, and shuffled off toward her bedroom.

Phillip watched her until she'd slipped through the doorway of her room, shutting the door behind her. Then he walked over to the mustard-colored wingback chair and collapsed into it. He reread the text message. And then again. And then once more.

He closed his eyes.

The words were still there, as though they had been inscribed on the inside of his eyelids. At the same time, Jenny's words pounded in his ears.

It was time. He would have to fly down to Oslo tomorrow night after his shift, and he'd stay the night at one of the airport hotels. From having taken numerous passengers there throughout the years, he knew exactly which hotel had the cheapest rate, one that he'd be able to afford. Then, first thing the following morning, he would go talk to her, before catching a flight back to Trondheim in time for his next shift.

*

This time it was Phillip's turn to be nervous. He had no idea what she'd say, or how she'd react. She might not even be at home. The only thing he knew was that he needed some answers, and that he needed them fast.

He took a deep breath, and knocked three times on the large, white entrance door.

There were muffled footsteps coming from inside the house. Then the lock was twisted, giving off the sound of a single click as the door was unlocked.

Phillip was breathing heavily now, realizing she might not even be willing to talk to him.

A woman with partly blond but mostly gray hair cut to just below her jaw line, appearing to be in her mid fifties came into view. She wore a puzzled look on her face. "May I help you?" she asked, her voice soft and warm.

Phillip nodded slowly. "Yes, I believe so. That is, if you are Mrs. Ramsland?"

She looked wary. "Yes... I am. What's this regarding?"

"Well, my name is Phillip Hansen, and I believe you are my birthmother."

The woman's face went white. She gasped, and one hand covered her mouth, while the other clutched the door handle, supporting the weight of her full figure. "Phillip...? I can't believe it... I mean... is that... is it really you?"

He nodded once more, and mumbled; "Yeah."

She seemed to be holding her breath. "Can I... Could I just — would it be possible for me to give you a hug?" She held her arms out.

Phillip took a step back. "Ah... I don't really feel comfortable with that, so..."

She quickly dropped her arms down by her sides, and nodded. "Of course, I understand."

An awkward silence fell between them.

"But," she started, breaking the stillness. "All those years ago I was told by the County Governor's office that you'd asked to find out who I was; that you wanted to meet me. That was the happiest day of my life, and I willingly agreed to meet you, but then you never showed up at that café we were supposed to meet at. And then..." Her eyes filled with tears. "Then I never heard from you again. That must've been..." She seemed to be counting.

"24 years ago, yes," Phillip said, and looked down at his feet. "I was 18 at the time."

"I... I just never thought that... that I'd ever see you again," she sobbed.

"Yeah..." Phillip shifted uncomfortably. "I was intending to go through with our meeting all those years ago, but then on my way over to the café I realized I never wanted you to be a part of my life — that I couldn't ever forgive you for what you'd done."

She went silent, while tears trickled down her round cheeks.

"However," Phillip continued, "some things in my life have changed recently, and I'd like talk to you for a moment, if you've got a few minutes to spare?"

She nodded rapidly, wiping away her tears with the tips of her fingers. "Yes, of course." She opened the door wide. "Please, come in."

"Yeah, thanks." Phillip crossed the threshold, and peered around the narrow entrance hall.

The off-white walls were covered with framed pictures — pictures of kids taken at all ages.

"Please," she gestured. "Come with me into the living room."

He followed her.

The entire house looked neat. And it smelled almost too clean, like whoever had cleaned the house hadn't diluted the lemon-scented cleaning solution with enough water.

He studied his birthmother as she moved about in her house, imagining what her life was like. His mother; the woman whom he knew nothing about — except for the fact that she hadn't wanted to keep him those 42 years ago.

Her hair was blond, fine, and straight as a rod — just like his. But her face was rounder in the middle, an oblong oval shape, completely different from Phillip's square-as-a-block face.

"Can I get you anything? Coffee; tea; or maybe a glass of water?"

"No, I'm good, thanks Mrs. Ramsland."

"Please, call me Philippa."

Even though he already knew her name, the sound of it as it came out of her mouth still made him wince. "Alright..." He hesitated. "Philippa."

She plopped down on the left hand side of the fluffy, beige, three-seater sofa.

Phillip sat down on the other side, leaving as much space between them as possible.

Her eyes zoomed in on him; then they darted away. Then again, she stared at him; then she looked away.

Phillip felt his familiar anxiety toward socializing surround him like thick smoke. "So... um... do you have any kids, or...? I mean, I saw pictures out in the hall, so I just figured..."

She gave a slight smile, almost seeming embarrassed. "I do have kids, yes. A girl and two boys."

"Oh." Phillip nodded, and looked down.

"How about you — any kids?"

"Yeah, I've got two girls."

"Really?" she cried out. "So, technically that means that I have two granddaughters that I didn't know about, then. Oh, how exciting—"

"Why'd you do it?" Phillip cut her off mid-speech. He twisted his torso sharply so it was facing her. "I mean, clearly, you're not opposed to having kids or anything."

She blinked a few times, and whispered; "Nothing in my life has caused me more sorrow than having to let you go."

"That didn't answer my question."

"I was only 15 years old when you were born. Obviously, I was still in school, and I had no money to support us, and—"

"That's not a good enough excuse — you could've tried harder, if you'd really wanted to."

She looked at him, her eyes glazed so thickly in tears that drops sloshed out over the rims of her eyelids. Yet, she still managed to keep her voice steady. "Oh, I wanted nothing more than to keep you — there's no doubt about that."

"So then why didn't you?"

"My parents took you away from me."

"What do you mean?"

"They forced me to give you up."

"But how..."

"Things were different back then. If I'd kept you they would've kicked me out of the house, meaning we'd have no place to go."

"Oh, please," Phillip spat, sending her a disgusted look. "Why can't you just admit that you didn't care enough to really fight for me?"

"Why do you think I gave you the masculine version of my own name?" she asked, her voice trembling.

"I don't know — why did you?"

"Because I loved you so much. I gave you that name to prove you were a part of me — both then and now."

He shook his head resignedly. "Well, then you've failed at your attempt — we've never been a part of each other's lives." He got to his feet. "I came here looking for some answers, but it's clear that you don't have any good ones. So I guess I'll just go then."

She reached out and touched his arm. "Wait."

Phillip's initial reaction was to shake her hand away, but instead he took a deep breath, waiting for her to elaborate.

She didn't speak.

He wriggled with annoyance, his patience running low. "What?"

"Please let me explain in detail what happened."

He sighed. "It's too late for that." He started walking past her toward the entrance hall.

"Well, then at least let me show you something that might make you understand," she called at his back.

He hesitated, turned, and glanced at her face.

Her warm, hazel-colored eyes seemed to glow, somehow strangely providing an effect similar to that of toasty campfire logs on a cold winter's night.

He felt the warmth go through him, unable to explain what was happening; nor to tear his eyes away.

"I'd like to show you something we've kept for you through all these years," she repeated.

"What do you mean by *we*?"

"Your dad and I, of course. As soon as we were old enough we got married, and have remained so until this very day."

He felt like he'd gotten the wind knocked out of him. "I thought... I mean, I had no idea the two of you'd actually married. The County Government's office didn't provide me with any information about him, so I kind of assumed that he was just some random..." His voice trailed away.

"Your dad is the love of my life, and I have never wanted to be without him," she said, unable to conceal the love in her eyes. "So, if you'll just let me show you this one thing then I think you'll understand."

Phillip realized he was afraid he might not like whatever it was; thinking it might just be better — easier on his heart — to leave things the way they were. "I don't know about this..."

She rose from the couch, and walked over so that she was standing right in front of him. She contemplated him for a couple of seconds, and then smiled — the softest, most gentle smile he'd ever seen. "Come, follow me." She turned, and started walking back out toward the entrance hall.

He sighed, checking his watch. "You know, I really don't have time for this — I've got a plane to catch."

She stopped walking. "I'm pretty sure you're going to want to see this," she said confidently.

"Can't you just *tell* me what it is?"

She peered over her shoulder at him, winked and said; "Now, Phillip, don't be so impatient; you'll see in a moment."

The way she'd spoken to him — like all had suddenly been forgiven and forgotten — really bothered him. "I'm not a child," he snapped. "And just because you gave birth to me doesn't give you the right to all of a sudden act like my mom after all these years."

She took a deep breath. "You've got every right to be upset — livid, even. However... I think the easiest way for you to understand how loved you've always been, is by first taking a look at what I'd like to show you."

He flinched at her words. "Don't you dare talk to me about love."

"But, I do love you, Phillip," she whispered.

"That's bullshit — you can't love someone you don't even know."

"You don't think so?"

"Hah," he snorted. "I know so for a fact."

"Then why did you at age 18 decide you wanted to find out who I was, after not knowing me for all those years — what was it that made you want to meet me?"

"Because..." He paused. "Because I just did — alright? It's normal to want to have parents, and they're supposed to love..." he stopped himself.

"See? It's an instinct; a knowing that there's love there — even if you can't physically see it, you just know."

"I'm leaving now." Phillip marched past her and out of the living room.

"You've got siblings as well, you know," she called as he walked away. "Siblings that would love to meet you."

He stopped mid-step, and turned. "They know about me?"

"Of course they know. As soon as they were old enough to understand we told them about their older brother."

"Fine, then," he huffed, rolling his eyes. "Quickly show me this amazing thing that you're referring to."

"Thank you." She led the way out across the entrance hall before making a left toward a long hallway, stopping at the first of three closed doors in a row. She pushed the door open, crossed the room, and pulled out the top drawer of a large oak dresser. From the drawer, she extracted a big, light blue covered book. Holding up the front cover for him to see, she said; "This is your baby book."

Chapter Thirty-nine

Phillip's jaw dropped. "What the...?" He stared at the book for a moment, then read the name on the front cover out loud; "Phillip."

"That's right," she said, smiling carefully. "Feel free to look inside, if you want."

"I... I don't understand..." he mumbled, though noticed that his hands were already starting to open the book.

"See," she said, pointing at the very front page. "Here's a picture of the two of us not long after you were born."

Phillip stared at the picture of the young mother and chubby baby boy.

"And then," she continued, flipping over to the next page. "Here's one of your tiny baby socks that I glued onto the page. And..." She turned another page. "There's a picture of you and your dad."

"I think... I've just gotta sit down for a sec here." He hurried over to the bed, and reached it just before his legs gave way, dropping him onto the beige bedspread.

Philippa followed, and sat down next to him on the king-sized bed. "I apologize for springing all this on you; I realize it must be very overwhelming."

He rubbed his temples forcefully. "Yeah... So why, exactly, do you have this book here for me...? I mean, why... Yeah — just... *why*?" He looked over at his birthmother. "I really don't understand what's going on here."

"Well..." she said, taking a deep breath. "You see, I was somewhere between four and five months along when I realized I must be pregnant. And when I told my parents, they became absolutely... enraged, I guess is the best way to describe it. So they took me straight to an adoption agency, where I was presented with an adoption contract."

Phillip looked at her, while simultaneously blinking over and over again in an attempt to relieve his burning eyes.

"And at the time," she continued, "I was 15 years old, scared and confused, and so they managed to convince me that signing the contract was the only right thing for someone in my situation to do." Again, her eyes filled with tears. "And so... regretfully, I did, before I was able to fully think it through."

His mother's tears were starting to make him feel really uncomfortable, and he looked away from her as she wept. "OK, so then what happened?" he said, urging her to continue.

"Tim — your father — and I talked about it back and forth a lot. And, about a month before you were born, we realized that we'd — well, I'd — made a horrible mistake. We told our parents we were going to keep the baby after all, which, of course, they wouldn't accept. So we took Tim's dad's car and ran away."

"Wow..." Phillip looked down at his fingers, and noticed that they had decided to busy themselves with nervously pulling at some loose threads from the bedspread.

"But, obviously, seeing as we'd stolen your grandpa's car, we were easy to track down and stop."

"And how old was Tim at the time?"

"He was 15 — same as me."

"OK, so what happened after you got caught."

"Well, we were too young to become legally married, and were therefore kept as far away from each other as possible until we'd both turned 18, when our parents could no longer keep us apart. I mean, during those three years we managed to smuggle each other some letters by way of our friends, and we also managed to meet up every once in a while. But other than that, we had no form of contact."

"Wow, I'm sorry..."

She sighed. "Yeah, it was a pretty bad situation, that's for sure. However, we've been together ever since and, although every relationship requires a great deal of work, we can both say that we're extremely lucky and happy to still be together."

"So... have you and Tim ever forgiven your parents for what they did?"

"All four of them have actually apologized several times over the years, and I'd have to say that yes, I've forgiven them for keeping your dad and I apart, as they truly thought at the time that what we had was nothing more than puppy-love. And I actually believe that they were only trying to do what they thought was best at the time."

Phillip nodded. "OK."

"However," she continued. "I've never quite forgiven them for taking you away from me, because I don't think anyone deserves to go through the agony of having their own child taken away from them against their will."

Phillip sat up straight. "I couldn't agree more. You see, I've got this situation with my youngest daughter where..." He stopped himself.

She leaned forward toward him a bit. "What about your youngest?"

He shook his head. "Never mind, this isn't the time."

"OK, I understand. Maybe you'll tell me at some point later — that is, if you feel like sharing."

"Yeah, maybe."

A silence fell between them.

"But... uh..." Phillip started. "Would you mind sharing what happened to me after I was born?"

"Of course. You deserve to know." She pulled her legs up off the floor and folded them into a cross-legged position on the bed, before turning her body to completely face her son. "In those days, if you'd already signed an adoption contract, the practice at the hospital was to place a sheet over the woman's face while she was giving birth."

"What — why?"

"The theory behind it was that if the mother never saw her own baby, then it would be a lot easier for her to part with it."

"God, that's... barbaric."

"Yes, and no. I think for the women who truly believed that giving up their baby would enable them to provide their child with a better life, then not having seen it first might've made it easier. Some women didn't even want to know the sex of their baby. But... for me, it was different."

"So, I'm confused... If you're saying that you never got to see me after I was born, then how do you have these pictures of us in my baby book?"

"Oh, I got to spend a lot more time with you than either of my parents was ever aware of. You see, you were placed in an orphanage right away, and one day I managed to tell my story to one of the women working there. She felt so sorry for me that she gave me permission to come nurse you once a day, as long as no one ever found out about it. I wanted to make sure you got a strong and healthy start in life. Therefore, I was also the one to give you your name. And I prayed every night that no one would adopt you, so that the very day your father and I were legally married, we could come back for you and the three of us would finally be reunited."

"But, then I was adopted."

Philippa swallowed hard. "Yes, one day when you were seven months old you were adopted. And once the paperwork was finalized, I was denied all contact with you, as well as any information about the family who had adopted you. So, I had no idea whether you were even still in Oslo, or if they'd changed your name, or anything..." She sniffled. "And so... I could only hope that you'd ended up in a good home, with parents who loved you every bit as much as your dad and I did." She paused for a moment, pulling herself together. "Therefore," she continued, "this book started out as a baby book, more for our own sake than yours, really. A way for us to feel like we could still be a part of your life when you were a baby ...even though we couldn't be with you all the time. But then, once you were adopted, the book instead became a scrap book that we hoped we'd be able to give you one day. And if you look through it, then you'll find pictures and tiny items from various special occasions and family events, all glued onto the pages. We wanted for you to one day see the book and realize that we've always thought of you; that we've always remembered you. And when we finally saw you again, we wanted to share some of our family memories with you, to help you feel like you're a part of us." She smiled warmly.

Phillip's heart ached like someone was prying it open with a crowbar, and he turned slightly away from her so she wouldn't see the pain on his face.

"So, how was your childhood? Were your new parents good to you?"

He spun his head back around to look at her so quickly that he heard one of the vertebrae in his neck crack. "You never knew, did you?"

"Knew what?"

"When I was two and a half I was returned to a different orphanage, though of course I'd already been given their family name, Hansen, and—"

She gasped. "What?"

"Yeah... Back then, according to law, there was a five year cancellation period, if you will. And it gave the adoptive parents the right to return an adopted child if the child was considered to be too unruly, or had any kind of illness, or they just didn't feel like they were able to take care of it any-more... And, kids who'd been returned to an orphanage were almost deemed unadoptable after that... like they were damaged goods." He sighed. "But luckily, in 1986, they repealed the law giving adoptive parents the right to do so, as it was determined that the interest of the child should come before all else."

"Oh my God — I think I'm going to be sick." Philippa covered her mouth.

"Hey now, it's OK." He patted her awkwardly on the back. "You never knew; it's not your fault."

She looked him in the eye. "I'm so sorry, Phillip. I can't imagine what you must've gone through."

He looked at her for a moment, then down at the floor. "It's OK," he whispered. "I'm OK."

They sat there for a moment, neither one of them saying a word.

"I uh..." Phillip broke the silence. "I'm really sorry, but I've got to get going so I can make it to the airport on time."

Philippa sat up straight, dabbing her fingertips underneath her eyes and across her cheeks. "Of course, I understand. But, if you don't mind, then I've got a favor to ask of you. I mean, I know I'm in no position to do so, but..." Her voice faded away.

He smiled softly at her. "Yeah, maybe — depending on what the favor is, obviously."

She choked out a laugh. "Well, it's really a favor for your dad. You see, he's a cab driver, and—"

Phillip's eyes grew wide. "I'm sorry; did you just say that my father's a cabdriver...?"

"Yes, that's right."

"I'm a cab driver," he whispered.

She gasped. "Really?"

He nodded slowly.

Philippa placed both of her palms in front of her heart, and smiled. "The reason your dad decided to become a cab driver in the first place, was because he had this theory that everyone needs to take a cab every once in awhile, and he was convinced that one day you'd get into his cab; he'd realize who you were; and we'd all finally be reunited."

This time it was Phillip's turn to shed a tear, and he didn't even attempt to be strong and hide it. "That's crazy."

"It certainly is," she half giggled. "And your dad's a real talkative guy, too, always wanting to make conversation with his passengers about who they are, what makes them tick, and where they're from and all... And you know what? He's never given up hope that he might one day run into you."

"Wow..." Phillip shook his head. "That's just — wow."

"But, of course, the irony here is that the person who's probably the least likely to call a cab is in fact—"

"Another cab driver," he finished her sentence.

She nodded. "Exactly. And so, that's the favor I wanted to ask of you — for us to call your dad up and let him take you to the airport. That is, if you think you feel up to it after all the other emotional things you've already been through this past hour?"

"Yes. Yes — of course. I'd say it's about time." He managed a slight chuckle.

Her hands covered her mouth, and her entire face started to quiver, "I just... I just cannot believe that this day has finally come," she whispered. Then she shook her head, causing her tears to spill out. "Your dad is going to be so proud." She took a deep breath. "And so incredibly happy."

Phillip looked down, half uncomfortable; half afraid he'd start crying as well if he continued looking at her. "Well... do you want to come along for the ride to the airport?"

"Oh, I would love to, but I think your dad deserves to have this moment with you all by himself. Just exactly the way he intended for it to happen when he decided to become a cab driver in the first place. Because... I always blamed myself," she said, sniffling. "I always blamed myself for signing those adoption papers. I was the one who took you away from us. It was my fault that your dad didn't get to watch you grow up. And today, the two of you are finally going to be reunited, after 42 years. So, it's your dad's turn to have a little moment alone with you. After all, I got to spend a small amount of time with you while nursing you, right after you were born."

"Hey," he said, putting his hand on her shoulder. "It wasn't your fault. You said so yourself — your parents would have denied you any contact with me anyway." He sighed. "You know, sometimes parents don't always know what's best for their kids. Sometimes they just take away—" he started, but then the text message from Adrian suddenly flashed before his eyes, and he choked. No matter how much he'd tried to dismiss his thoughts; ever since he'd read that text, deep down he knew what he was doing to Francesca was wrong. That in a way, he was doing the same thing to his daughter that his grandparents had done to his parents. Denying a parent their very own child. All of a sudden, he was having a hard time breathing. He closed his eyes, and started slowly counting to ten.

But... he also knew it was wrong of Francesca to ask him to give up Jenny — *his* own child. How was that any different than what he was doing to her? He cleared his throat. "It's getting late; we should make the call to book that cab ride with Tim."

*

Phillip stood waiting outside the building of the used-to-be-white-but-now-turned-a-sallow-yellow shopping mall, located six blocks away from his parents' house.

He checked his watch. Then cracked his knuckles. Then gently rubbed his stomach in an attempt to still the tornado spinning out of control in there, making him feel like he might be sick. Then he checked his watch again.

There, in the distance — coming around the corner and pulling into the mall's parking lot — was a white Mercedes cab.

Phillip squinted at the car. Was that him? It must be. Hiding his hands behind his back, he clenched his fists as tight as he could, and then released, shaking his fingers down toward the ground. "Oh, God..." he muttered to himself. "This is it."

Slowly, the cab moved closer and closer to where Phillip stood in front of the mall's entrance.

Phillip gave a wave in the driver's direction to get his attention.

The cab pulled up in front of him, and the driver rolled down the window on the passenger side. "Are you a Mr. Hansen?" he asked.

Phillip swallowed, then nodded. "Yes, that's me."

"Great — hop in," Tim said, and smiled; revealing a set of perfectly straight, white teeth, before rolling the window back up.

Phillip opened the rear door, and slid in.

There it was, clipped right onto one of the air vents located above the radio — a laminated ID card with the driver's name: *Tim Ramsland*.

Phillip stared at it, transfixed.

"Alright," Tim said, twisting his torso around toward Phillip. "You're going to the airport — correct?"

"Correct," he confirmed.

"So, where are you flying off to, then?"

"I'm headed back to Trondheim. I just moved there, but I've been down here in Oslo for a quick er... family visit."

"That's nice. I'd say there's nothing better than family — am I right."

Phillip smiled. "You couldn't be more right."

"So whereabouts does your family live — close by, I'm assuming, seeing as you had me pick you up here?"

"Yeah, not too many blocks from here."

"No kidding. I actually live just down over there a short way myself."

"Is that a fact?"

"Yep, true story." Tim smiled.

"It's a nice area, I really like it."

"Yeah, I mean, I personally love it here, myself. Well, anyway," Tim said, turning back to face the windshield and buckling his seatbelt. "We'd better hit the road."

Phillip studied the reflection of his father's face in the rearview mirror.

His eyes looked tired; liked they'd experienced a lot — yet, at the same time they were the kindest eyes Phillip ever remembered seeing. He also had deep lines on either side of his mouth, right where creases formed when he smiled. But despite his slightly wrinkled face, he was broad-shouldered — a characteristic that immediately offset any initial impression of him seeming old or weak.

As Tim rolled out of the parking lot and onto the road, his glance darted back and forth; alternating between looking at the road and Phillip in his rearview mirror. After a little while, he started frowning, and began letting his eyes linger on his passenger; his glances becoming longer and longer each time. "So uh..." He paused, shaking his head a couple of times. "What's your first name, then, Mr. Hansen," he finally asked.

Phillip took a deep breath, and was unable to prevent his lower lip from quivering ever so slightly as he answered his father. "Phillip," he said, and smiled. "My name is Phillip."

Tim gasped, and his eyes on his son in the rearview mirror intensified with realization. He quickly swerved off the road and onto the shoulder, stopping the car. His hands shook as he slowly turned around to face his son. "Oh, my God — it's you, isn't it?"

Phillip nodded rapidly. "Yeah, it's me."

Tim covered his mouth, and blinked several times. "How'd you...? Does your mom know?"

"Philippa is the family I was referring to having just visited."

"I can't believe... I don't know..." His breathing increased in speed, to the point of almost hyperventilating. "After 42 years..." His eyes glistened, and he pinched his own arm. "I cannot believe it's you..." He stared at his son, looking like he was mentally saving the image in order to store this moment in his long-term memory forever. "Could I just maybe... give you a hug or something?"

Phillip smiled. Even though he hardly knew anything about his dad, one thing he had just learned was that his parents hadn't ever *not* wanted him, like Phillip had spent his entire life believing. So somehow, hugging this stranger now didn't seem all that strange after all. "Of course," he said. "Though, it might be easier if we got out of the car first."

"Yes. Yes, it would." Tim quickly unbuckled his seatbelt and leapt out of the car.

Phillip followed, and met his father in front of the hood of the car.

Tim studied his son, interlacing his fingers tightly and nearly bouncing up and down. "God... look at you — you're just... exactly how I imagined you would be."

Phillip chuckled. "Really?"

"Oh yes, you look just like me. Except you've got your mom's hair; and her slightly pointy nose as well ...though, if you ever tell her I referred to it as pointy, I'll deny it to my last breath."

"Hah." Phillip held his right hand up. "Well, I promise you, your nose-depiction is safe with me."

"Oh good." He chuckled. "And, I think we're pretty much the exact same height."

"Yeah, we seem to be. As well as the same kind of build — I've got your broad shoulders."

"True; and, you're welcome." Tim winked.

Phillip laughed. "Yeah, thanks."

They stood there, awkwardly looking at each other for a moment.

"So... um..." Tim took a couple of steps toward Phillip, and held his arms out. "What about that father-son hug I was promised?"

Phillip took another step closer to Tim, accepting the hug.

"Phew." Tim sniffled as he let go of his son, blinking a few times. "OK, so what made you decide to come and find us after all this time, and how? I mean, tell me everything."

"I will on our way to the airport. But first, how about we pick up Philippa and bring her along for the ride?"

"Absolutely," Tim agreed, and headed back around to the driver's seat. "I know your mother won't want to miss a moment of time spent with you if she can help it."

*

They arrived at the airport, and Tim pulled up into the drop-off zone right out front.

Philippa shed a few silent tears. "So... I guess this is goodbye, then?"

"Yeah... But, I mean, just for now, though. I'll try to get back down to visit you guys, and to finally meet my three siblings at some point."

"Oh, yes — you've got to!" Tim said, taking his wife's hand in his.

"And bring our granddaughters with you the next time," Philippa added.

Phillip looked down into his lap. "Well, at least my youngest will be easier to bring, but uh..." He paused. "I've come to realize that no matter how hard we want them to be, things aren't always within our control, so... I think it's time for me to let go of the old grudge I've held toward you guys."

He looked first his mother, and then his father in the eye.

Philippa sniffled, and held her arms out. "I think we need another hug before you go."

Phillip leaned forward in between the two front seats, and the three of them sat there for a moment with their arms around each other.

Again, Phillip could see Adrian's text message before his eyes, and no matter how many times he blinked, it still remained. He let go of his parents, leaned back, and said, "So, Tim; I already asked Philippa, but I'd really like to hear your answer as well, if you wouldn't mind." He took a deep breath. "And, my question is... have you ever forgiven your parents for taking me away from you?"

"To be perfectly honest," he started, the grave shake of his head already giving him away. "No, I've never quite forgiven them for what they did. Of course, I realize they were only doing what they thought was best at the time, and never meant to hurt your mother and I, but... when it comes to children, then I firmly believe no one has the right to decide to take them away from you."

"And," Phillip continued, "what if I had never come to see you? What if we had never been reunited?" He looked from one parent to the other.

"You know," his mother started. "It's a sad, sad thing having to spend the rest of your life feeling like someone that important is missing; having been wrongfully taken from you. Knowing that you can never have them back. And to be honest, today has been the very best day of my entire life. So, to answer your question, if you had never come to see us, then we would've carried on just like before, but like I said, I would've felt less whole than I do today. And speaking from experience, I think that the not knowing is the absolute worst part. Knowing what has happened to someone, and then hopefully being able to take part in your loved one's life is always so much better."

"OK. Thank you for your honest answers," he said, strangely realizing he was sitting in his dad's car, agreeing with his parents that he hadn't even met just a few hours ago. "Alright," he sighed, glancing out the window at the airport. "Well now I've really gotta run."

Philippa nodded. "Of course. And..." She hesitated for a second. "We love you."

Phillip felt a warm sensation spread in his chest, and found that he wasn't strong enough to fight it off; nor did he even want to. Though, for him to actually use the word *love* himself was more than he was able to bring himself to do, at least at this point. After all, they'd felt love for him his entire life; when Phillip had known nothing but resentment for them in return, until today. But maybe, someday, he would be able to say it. He smiled, and reached for the door handle.

"We'll see you again soon, then?" Tim called out of the open car door on the passenger's side.

"See you soon," Phillip confirmed. He shut the door, and started heading over to the entrance.

His eyes felt swollen, and his body completely drained. Though, more than that, Phillip knew that after Francesca had gone through with that abortion, then — like Adrian had said — Francesca would never completely forgive him. It also dawned on him that, once it had been done, it could never again be undone. Francesca would never have a moment where she would be reunited with her child.

Chapter Forty

Francesca stepped lightly; precisely, all across the meadow. Her steps were those of careful consideration, and, like always, she was in perfect control of the situation.

She inhaled, and exhaled. Three times. Three was her lucky number. Then she reached her arms out to either side — just once. One time was enough. She only needed one beginning, as long as she got it right. After that, there was no going back. Only forward; onward.

She shifted her weight from one leg to the other, before letting her feet melt down onto the soil of the meadow, placing them on a line as straight as a ray of light. Rolling through her feet as seamlessly as if they were liquid poured out of a jug and into ballerina feet-shaped molds placed one after another on a tightrope.

Behind her, someone let out a cry.

She felt it rush through her, like wind rippling through a sweater left hanging out on a clothesline in a storm; and immediately, her torso spun around, seeking the source of the cry.

...But there was no one there.

She noticed that her shoulders were tense and raised, and she exhaled deeply, letting her gaze drop down to her feet, still in place on the perfect line on the grassy meadow floor. After allowing another short moment to pass, she found the strength to continue drawing up the rest of her line; reminding herself that the sooner she finished, the better.

She had nearly completed the first row. Her footprints like seeds planted deep into the ground, laying the foundation for a wall. A wall that could withstand anything; protect her from everything. And she knew that, soon, she would be safe.

Turning abruptly at a ninety degree angle, she started drawing up the second line. Setting up the invisible barrier that she'd need in order to carry on.

Then she felt something hit her in the chest; almost knocking her over.

She glanced all around, frantically. Then stopped abruptly as her eyes landed on her dad.

She darted behind the first wall she had created, uprooting the soles of her feet from the second wall she'd started to build.

Phillip continued to stare at her through the invisible barrier.

Invisible, yes, Francesca knew. Though, it was still there. He could stare at it for as long as he wanted to, but that didn't mean he'd be able to take it down. Francesca was the only one who could do so. One side of her was now blocked off; one side of her was completely numb to the pain he was capable of causing her.

She took a deep breath, turned around, and with her first completed wall shielding her back, she picked up the pace to finish the second wall of her square box.

Then, out of nowhere, a flash of her mother's dead body hit her like a lightning bolt. She blinked over and over again, though several tiny particles remained, obscuring her vision forever. What she had once seen could never be unseen again. She panted hard; her heart being pushed to its limit, and she knew that if she were to stop now, the pain would cause her heart to explode, and she would cease to exist. What would happen to Jenny if Francesca, too, were gone?

Through her burning eyes and welling nausea, she picked up her feet, forcing herself to complete and block off another side.

She jumped inside her v-shaped shelter, and noticed how she felt calmer already; the pace of her breathing beginning to slow back down to normal.

Then she started feeling strange — different — as though, somehow, she'd left something behind on the outside. Something important, though she didn't know exactly what it was. As she searched inside herself, she realized her heart had gone numb; she could not feel her previous emotions anymore, at least not in the same way as she could before.

From where she sat huddled in her corner, Francesca gazed at her surroundings. Two of her walls, as well as the ceiling, were still missing. She pushed the weight of her body over onto the soles of her feet, and walked over to the open side of the first wall she had built. She felt exposed; vulnerable. It was terrifying to think that when she turned her back to the outside in order to set up her third wall, anything could happen, and she might not be able to stop it in time.

Suddenly, a large hook attached to a bungee cord appeared in her hand. She swung it around above her head, her glance darting back over her shoulder a couple of times. Then she tossed the hook as far as she could.

It latched onto the very edge of her second wall sticking out.

Francesca had originally intended to build a square safety box, though she now realized there was no time. A triangular one would have to do. She leapt up into the air, and began flinging herself over to the other side.

As she dangled across the abyss, in some strange kind of slow motion, she felt Jenny; Adrian; and a teeny tiny baby dart at her repeatedly like flies, attempting to get in before it was too late; before she had sealed the gates forever. But all three of them missed, every single time. "No, come on in!" she urged them in sheer panic. "You can do it! Hurry!" she yelled.

But no matter how hard they tried, none of them managed to get in.

She watched herself nearing the edge of her second wall; reaching the end.

"No!" She sobbed as she crashed into her destination, closing off the last opening. "Please," she begged them. "Please, find a way to get in!" She banged on the invisible walls, but they were unable to hear her. They couldn't see that her pain would eventually cripple her; killing her only on the inside, where she lived. Soon, she wouldn't feel a thing — not even her love for them. Now, she was completely blocked off. Before long, nothing would matter anymore.

With a jolt, Francesca sat up in bed, her body shivering. She clutched at her heart. It felt sick; badly bruised and beating irregularly.

Then she felt her stomach turn, and managed to throw herself into Adrian's bathroom just in time.

A couple minutes later, she was able to draw a deep breath, her spine resting up against the cold, white tiles on the bathroom wall. She planted the soles of her feet on the floor, pulling her knees to her chest and resting her arms on top of her knees. She stayed there for several minutes, maybe even as many as ten; her head hanging heavily on her arms.

Eventually, she found the strength to push herself back onto her feet, her hands grabbing the edge of the sink, pulling her body to the upright position. She brushed her teeth, trying very hard to not look at her exhausted reflection in the mirror staring back at her.

She sighed, and began making her way toward Adrian's spare bedroom down the hall. She pushed the door open, and gazed out into the dark at the small, narrow bed. Again, she shivered, imagining the bed being cold and lonely.

"No," she said out loud, shaking her head. She needed Adrian; she wouldn't sleep in a separate room. They belonged in the same room.

She shut the door, and wandered back down through the apartment. Entering his bedroom, she contemplated him lying there asleep, and felt her heart go warm. She smiled. Her heart was still capable of feeling. She loved him. And he loved her. They deserved to be together; they were supposed to be together. Slipping underneath the duvet, she slowly inched her body toward his, curling up in his arms, feeling his heart beat steadily against her back.

*

As Francesca dressed that morning, she studied her body in the mirror behind the sink in Adrian's bathroom. Was she starting to show yet, she wondered? She turned and looked at her profile.

No, of course not — she was only about seven weeks pregnant.

And she would never show. At least, not with this baby. Maybe — most likely — she'd have kids later on when she was older. And maybe — hopefully — it would still be with Adrian.

She sighed. It was for the best, though; this was not the right time. She'd been telling herself this over and over; repeating it like a mantra ever since she'd left Trondheim two days ago. And with any luck, by the time she reached the hospital for her appointment at 11 o'clock, she would actually believe it.

Francesca opened the bathroom door, and headed into the kitchen.

Adrian sat at the small, square, white kitchen table that had been shoved into the one corner, leaving only two of the four sides exposed.

She walked over to him.

He looked up from his tablet on which he was catching up on some news. "Good morning, beautiful."

She slipped her legs in between his body and the table, before sitting down sideways on his lap, putting her arms around his neck. "Hey, handsome."

He kissed her on the cheek.

She rested her head on his shoulder, and whispered the words she'd felt so uncomfortable saying to anyone other than Jenny; training herself until it came more naturally to her; "I love you."

"Love you, too."

She closed her eyes for a moment; then reopened them. "So, is it 11 o'clock yet?"

He checked his watch. "Yes — well, in just three and a half short hours from now it will be."

She sighed. "Right..."

"Do you wanna go for a walk or something? You know, just to take your mind off of everything."

"Yeah, some fresh air sounds good."

*

The air was cold; it was crisp; and it made Francesca feel alert, and stronger, somehow, than she'd felt before.

"You know," Adrian said, and glanced over at his girlfriend. "You don't have to go through with this, there's still—"

"Adrian..." She interrupted him.

"I'm just saying, your dad might still—"

She halted, the look in her eyes daring him to finish his sentence.

He sighed. "Yeah, alright."

They continued walking in silence; the only sound coming from their shoes squishing down on the soggy leaves covering the sidewalk.

"Ring, ring."

"Now what?" Francesca pulled the mitten off her right hand, and reached down into the front pocket of her gray woolen coat.

"Ring, ring."

"Who is it?" Adrian asked, immediately leaning over to see her phone.

Francesca looked down at the screen; then up at Adrian. "It's Jenny."

"But, I thought your dad took that phone away from her?"

"Yeah, me too." She answered the call. "J-love, is that you?"

"Francesca?" Jenny's little voice said into the receiver.

"Yes, sweetie, it's me. Are you OK?"

"I'm OK."

"Good — it's nice to hear your voice. Did Dad give you your phone back?"

"Nah, I found it hidden in a drawer. But guess what; Dad's disappeared again."

Francesca sighed, and rubbed her forehead. "OK, so when was the last time you saw him?"

"Yesterday morning before he left for work. And I'd just really had it this time — so last night I caught the night train from Trondheim, and I'm at the Oslo Central Station right now."

Francesca couldn't believe her own ears. "You what?"

"I'd already found some of Dad's money stashed away. And so when he didn't come home last night when he was supposed to, I bought a ticket for the night train, and here I am," Jenny said proudly.

"What?" Francesca said again, this time raising her voice to a near shriek. "Have you lost your mind — do you have any idea how dangerous it is for you to travel at night by yourself like that?"

"The question is, big sis," Jenny said, keeping her cool. "When and where should we meet up?"

Jenny had never been afraid of talking back to, or challenging her older sister, and Francesca knew it all too well. Those kinds of fears were reserved entirely for their dad.

Francesca pulled the phone away from her mouth, and put her hand over the transmitter. "Ah, shit. Shit; shit; shit." She panicked. Under no circumstance could Jenny find out about the abortion; she couldn't live with her sister possibly blaming herself for something that wasn't her fault.

Adrian looked alarmed. "What's going on?" he asked.

"I'll fill you in as soon as I hang up," she muttered to him, then held the phone back up in front of her mouth. "No, no, no, Jelly bean. I've got something... eh... really important scheduled for today and the next couple of days, and so I won't be able to see you until Saturday. But just hang in there, and go back to Trondheim and—"

"Ah, hell no!" Jenny bellowed.

"Watch your language, young lady."

"Francesca, let's face it: if this ain't a *hell no moment*, then I don't know what is."

Francesca rolled her eyes. "Whatever. But you still really need to go back home, alright? Just trust me on this one."

"For your information, Oslo is my home — not stupid Trondheim. And there's just no way I'm going back there. Why do you think I waited to call you until after I got to Oslo? I knew you'd only say no if I asked you about it first."

"Yeah, and for good reason."

"So anyway," Jenny continued, completely ignoring her sister. "I guess I'll see ya soon, then. Should I just come over to Adrian's apartment, or where do you wanna meet up?"

"Jenny, I'll call you back in a minute." She hung up, and turned to face Adrian. "OK, so Jenny — that annoyingly stubborn child — is at Oslo Central Station and refuses to go back to Trondheim."

"Yeah, I kinda got that... But then, where's your dad?"

She sighed. "Who the hell knows, Jenny just said he never came back home last night."

"Hmm..." Adrian bit his lower lip. "So, what do you wanna do?"

She rubbed her temples, and drew a few deep breaths. "Alright, here's the plan: you go get Jenny and take her to your apartment. Then the two of you hang out, and make sure you keep her occupied until I've fully completed my uh... process of... well, you know what. I'll go stay at my dad's old house, and then on Saturday I'll be ready to see her. Oh, and please, please, please say yes and help me."

"What? No way, I'm not letting you go through this whole thing by yourself."

Francesca looked away, and blinked twice the average number of times. "It's OK."

"No, it's not OK."

She looked back up at his face. "Yeah, you're right. But sometimes shit happens."

"You know what the doctor said; you're not supposed to be by yourself after you've taken that pill on Friday. This just isn't—"

"Adrian, please help me, I don't see any other way... And I'll get Margaret to come stay with me."

He sighed, and kicked a sodden clump of leaves on the ground in front of him off to the side. "Fine," he muttered. "But I'll have you know that I'm not happy about it."

"No, of course not — who said anything about being happy in the midst of all this crap?"

"Call Jenny back, and tell her I'll come pick her up at the train station," he moaned.

"Thank you; thank you; thank you. You're the best."

"Yeah, yeah, whatever."

She pulled his body close to hers. "Hey, I mean it. You really are the best, I don't know what I'd do without you."

He ran his fingers through her hair. "Yeah, I know, I'm awesome."

"So smug..." She gave him an extra squeeze, and took a deep breath, then hesitated for a moment before saying; "Love you."

"Love you."

She let go of him. "OK, well I've gotta call Jenny."

"Yeah, I'll start heading on over to the train station."

She kissed him on the lips. "Thanks. And hey, I'll see you guys on Saturday."

His face drooped down like the face of a pug puppy.

Francesca suddenly felt her stomach tighten, and fought to hold back her tears.

He took a step away from her. "See you Saturday. And make sure you get Margaret to stay with you until then," he said, his face unyielding .

She gave him a single nod. "I promise."

*

Adrian turned and started walking briskly away from Francesca. He slipped his phone out of his pocket. Even though he'd texted Phillip two days ago, he still hadn't heard back from him. ...Not that he really expected Phillip to text him back, if he was being completely honest with himself. It was just that he so desperately wanted Phillip to grow a pair and stop acting like the biggest idiot in the world.

In Adrian's mind, the fact that Francesca had chosen to go ahead with this abortion told him, in a way, that she'd decided to not trust Adrian completely, and that she still didn't really believe that the two of them would end up together.

Of course, he also knew Francesca was doing this for Jenny. But what Francesca didn't seem to completely realize — or maybe she just didn't want to admit it to herself — was that even though she had that abortion, and ended up getting Jenny for now, certain things would still never change. Phillip would still continue to look for ways to split the two girls up, so he could get Jenny back.

Meaning, Francesca would probably never be able to completely give in to Adrian and the thought of the two of them together. ...And, unfortunately, as a result of that, Adrian would most likely have to end up leaving her in the end — making what Adrian knew was Francesca's biggest fear finally come true.

He really hated the thought of it, and, as much as he never wanted that to happen — sooner or later, he'd have to face the fact that he was only human, and he couldn't keep subjecting himself to this kind of pain and rejection, if he knew that their relationship wasn't ever going to lead anywhere.

But, he knew he at least needed to give it one more shot. He took a deep breath, and dialed Phillip's number.

The phone rang once; twice; and a third time. Then, finally, there was a voice on the other end of the line. "Hello."

"Phillip? This is Adrian."

"I know," he said coldly.

"Listen, I know you don't like me, but Francesca is having that abortion in an hour and a half, and if you don't at least talk to her about it first, then I know you'll both regret it," he blurted out as fast as he could to prevent Phillip from cutting him off.

There was complete silence on the other end of the line.

"Please," Adrian begged. "You need to look past the fact that I'm the one asking you, but please, just do this one last thing for your daughter."

Phillip still didn't say anything.

Adrian was aching to yell at him; to tell him what a horrible father he was. But from his studies he knew that when attempting to sway the other party, it was crucial that he, too, shut up at this point. Continuing to babble on would only take Phillip's focus away from making a decision. He also knew it was very important that he not get impatient and hang up, and so he stood there silently on the sidewalk, with the phone up against his ear, waiting for Phillip to give his final ruling.

Eventually, Phillip decided to speak. "When and where is her appointment?"

*

Francesca walked in through the front door of the hospital. The stupid, ugly hospital, which, at the moment, she hated more than anything she'd ever remembered hating before.

Just like last time, she wandered down the endlessly long, L-shaped corridor, following the arrows on the walls directing her to the women's clinic.

Finally, she reached the waiting room. She discretely peered around at the other women sitting on the navy-blue upholstered chairs, and counted them in her head.

Altogether there were eleven. Ten, plus herself. She saw that some of the women had brought someone along with them.

Were any of the other women there to have an abortion as well, she wondered?

There was no way of knowing for sure. Their reasons for coming to the women's clinic could be many and varied.

Realizing that she didn't know what others were there for was somewhat comforting, for it meant that they, in turn, couldn't possibly know for sure why she was there, either.

One after another, women exited the doors of the six different doctors' offices. And one after another, new women were called in to replace them.

Slowly, Francesca started cracking her knuckles one at a time, and when she'd finished cracking them all, she began biting her nails instead, tearing them off with more force than she had intended.

"Ring, ring."

She jumped, and felt a small piece of her one nail get involuntarily sucked into her throat, bringing on a coughing fit.

"Ring, ring."

"Excuse me, Miss," one of the receptionists said, looking over at Francesca. "All cell phones must be either switched off or put on silent mode within the clinic."

Francesca immediately muted her phone, and looked at the screen.

It was Adrian.

She looked back up at the receptionist, and smiled apologetically. "Yes, of course. Sorry about that," she said, and crept out the door and back down the corridor a ways.

If recent events were any indicator, she'd learned that these unexpected calls never seemed to bring her any good news. However, Adrian might be experiencing issues with Jenny, in which case she would need to be informed about what was going on.

"Adrian, what's up? I'm about to go in and see my doctor any minute now."

"Yeah, I know," he said, sounding out of breath. "Sorry for calling you..."

"What's going on? Is everything OK with Jenny?"

"Yeah, she's fine. I just wanted to let you know that I'm on my way over to the hospital — don't do anything until I get there, OK?"

"What? Then where's Jenny?" Francesca felt her heart rate rising. "You're not bringing her with you, are you?"

"No, no, Margaret's watching her. I managed to drop Jenny off with her, and I'm on my way over to you now," he panted. "So don't start anything without me — can you promise me that?"

Francesca checked her watch.

It was two minutes to eleven.

"OK, but please hurry. If they call my name before you get here, then I'll need to go in. But I'll notify the receptionists that you're on your way so that one of them can let you in."

"Yeah, great," he heaved. "I'll be there in about 15 minutes."

"Alright, see you soon." She hung up, and hurried back into the waiting room, once again plopping down into one of the chairs.

A moment later, the same doctor she'd talked to the last time appeared from her office. "Francesca Hansen?" she called.

Francesca got to her feet. "Yes, that's me."

"Good." The doctor smiled, and gestured toward her office. "Please, come with me."

She nodded, and swerved a quick detour over to the window in the receptionists' glass cubicle. "Excuse me?"

The nearest receptionist looked up from her computer. "Yes."

Francesca lowered her voice to a mere whisper. "My boyfriend — the father of the baby — is on his way over and will be here shortly. His name is Adrian. When he gets here, could you please show him into that office?" She pointed at the half-opened door behind her doctor.

"Sure."

"Great, thanks for your help." Francesca smiled at the receptionist, before turning and entering her doctor's office.

The doctor closed the door behind them, and took the chair on her side of the desk. "So, Francesca, how are you feeling?"

"I'm alright," she lied.

"That's good to hear. And I assume you have reached a decision, is that correct?"

"Yes." She nodded. "I've thought about it a lot, and decided that the right thing for me to do at this point in time is to have the abortion."

"OK," the doctor said, and started typing away on her keyboard. "So, as I mentioned the last time, the procedure is for you to take one pill today while you're here in my office in order to stop the development of the fetus, and then in two days you'll come back to complete the procedure. Do you have any questions?"

"No, I don't think so. It all seems pretty clear to me."

"OK, good." She continued to type for about another minute. Her printer on the shelf behind her produced a single sheet of paper. "Now," the doctor said, pulling a several-page document off the shelf below her printer, and handing it to Francesca. "What I need you to do is to read through this information right here, and make sure you fully understand it all. And then, after that." She paused, reaching back over and grabbing the sheet of paper lying in the printer's paper tray. "You'll need to sign this form, stating that you understand and agree with the procedure of the abortion."

Francesca nodded once more.

"I'll leave you to yourself for about 15 minutes so you can have a chance to look it all over in peace and quiet, and then I'll be back in to check on you and answer any questions you might have. Is that alright?"

"Yeah, that's fine, thanks."

"Great, see you in a little while, then." The doctor rose from her seat; crossed the floor; and exited through the door, shutting it behind her.

Francesca took a deep breath, and stacked the papers on top of each other right in front of her on the desk. She rested her elbows on either side of the gathered papers, and let her chin and jaw drop into her hands. Then she started reading slowly, making sure she wasn't missing any important details.

Several minutes later, when she had finished reading, she reached for the blue ink pen the doctor had given her. Then she wrote down today's date and signed her name at the bottom of the form stating that she understood the process of, and agreed to, the termination of her pregnancy.

There was a soft knock on the door.

Francesca sat up straight, relieved that Adrian had been able to make it after all. She twisted her torso in the direction of the door, and called; "Come in."

The door opened, and Phillip entered. "Hi, Francesca."

She instantly felt extremely light headed, and realized she wasn't breathing properly. "Dad," she said, gasping for air. "What are you doing here?"

Chapter Forty-one

Phillip shut the door to the doctor's office behind him, and took a couple of steps toward Francesca.

"You can't be here," she said, raising her voice.

He lifted his hands up into the air, and started speaking, calmly; "Now, Francesca—"

"Why are you here?" she asked again, cutting him off. "And I don't have Jenny — as you can clearly see — if that's why you've come."

He frowned. "Why would I come here for your sister when she's back at our apartment in Trondheim?"

"Hah," she scoffed. "Jenny is definitely not in Trondheim, that's for sure."

His face went white. "Why — where is she?"

"She's in Oslo."

"How did she...?"

"You know, if you'd started coming home to her when you were supposed to, then she wouldn't have felt the need to hop on the night train to Oslo."

"Well, seeing as she's not with you, then who is she with — is she OK?" he said, his voice going up an octave.

"She's fine. But I'm not telling you where she is until you answer some of my questions. Now, how did you even know I was here — have you been following me or something?"

"Adrian told me what you're about to do."

She felt her face begin to burn. "He what?"

"Right after you got back from Trondheim on Monday night — when he picked you up at the airport and you told him about your final decision — he sent me a text message."

She was livid. "I don't believe you — he'd never do that to me, so you can just stop your lying right now. He'll be here any minute, and when he gets here then I'll ask him, right in front of you," she said, crossing her arms in front of her chest.

"He's not coming."

"Of course he is," she spat. "I just talked to him."

"Yeah, well, he only told you he was coming because, obviously, you'd never agree to let me in here."

Her eyes grew wide with disbelief. "He lied to me? How could he possibly betray me like this..." she said, her voice growing faint.

"More like he's trying to help you, I'd say." Phillip looked away. "He's a good guy, that Adrian of yours. And as a dad, I'm glad you've got such a great man in your life."

She got to her feet. "You still didn't tell me why you're here — now, what do you want?"

"The question is; what do you want?"

"What?" she said.

"Do you want that baby?"

She sighed, pinching her eyes shut as hard as she could in an attempt to strangle some of her mounting tension; wanting to avoid lashing out on him. "Dad," she said, taking a deep breath. "I'm kinda in the middle of something here — as you already seem to know, apparently. So can you please just get to the point, and tell me why you've come?" she repeated.

"I wasn't going to... at first."

She felt her patience shedding quickly. "Then why did you?"

"No one deserves to have their child taken away from them, and so I'm not going to do that to you. It is not — nor will it ever be — within my right to do so.

"OK... so, what're you saying...?"

"A very wise young woman — in fact, she's the strongest and smartest young woman I know — once told me that it's what happens at the very end that matters. That that's what you remember the most; what stays in your mind, and what you base your future decisions on. So..." He paused. "That's what I'm trying to do — to just do the right thing in the end so that... maybe... you'll remember it, and one day appreciate how I'm trying to become a better father."

Francesca didn't trust him. What was he trying to achieve, coming all the way down from Trondheim to see her at the hospital like this? "I'm not giving up on getting Jenny — no matter what."

"No." He sighed. "I've finally realized how far you and Jenny are willing to go in order to be together — you would even give up your own child in order to have your sister come live with you. Therefore..." He pursed his lips together for a few seconds, as though he were struggling to hold onto something. Then he suddenly let go, spewing out his words rapidly; "Jenny can live with you if she wants."

Francesca's jaw dropped. Her exhausted mind must be playing tricks on her. She blinked a couple of times, then flared her eyes open. "What did you just say?"

"I'm letting Jenny move in with you," he repeated.

Francesca peered at him. "And how do I know that you'll *actually* allow her to come live with me? How do I know that you're not just pretending; that you won't end up taking Jenny back at some point when it's too late for me to have an abortion?"

He shook his head tiredly. "Unfortunately, you don't know for sure ...because I haven't proven it to you yet. But the way I see it is that I've reached a point where I don't have a choice anymore. You and your sister don't want to spend a single moment with me, so I've actually already lost both of you. Therefore, I can either let Jenny come live with you, and hope that at some point in the future you guys will want to spend a little bit of time with me. Or I can hold onto Jenny as tightly as I possibly can, only resulting in both of you resenting me... You already forgave me once for what I did in the past, but I think that if I force you to abort your baby, then you'll probably never forgive me again. And... that's just not a risk I can afford to take"

There was another quick knock on the door, before it opened, and the doctor entered. "So, Francesca, have you had a chance to—" She noticed Phillip, and immediately stopped talking. Then she looked over at Francesca. "I'm sorry, I wasn't aware that you had company..."

"Yeah," Francesca said, motioning toward Phillip. "This is my dad."

The doctor gave Phillip a short nod, though the perplexed look on her face remained. "Hello."

"Hi," Phillip replied.

"Um," Francesca started, and turned toward the doctor. "Would you mind just giving us a few more minutes?"

"Is... is everything alright, or...?"

"Yes, everything's fine, thanks. I'm just going to need maybe another ten more minutes. Would that be OK?"

"Certainly. I'll be back again soon, then," the doctor said; frowning as she turned away from them.

"Great. Thanks." Francesca smiled at the woman, and watched as she closed the door behind her.

Then Francesca turned back to Phillip. "If Jenny comes to live with me, it needs to be on our terms — not yours."

"OK, meaning...?"

"If I have this baby then I'll be breaking our deal about me completing my university degree on time. I'd need to postpone my education for a year in order to stay at home with the baby."

He nodded slowly. "Yes, I realize that."

"And you still wouldn't demand that Jenny move back in with you?"

"You know, a lot of things have changed just these past few weeks since we made that deal. And we both know that I set those criteria based on the fact that I was completely sure you'd fail to fulfill them... However... you've proven that you were somehow able to achieve this mission impossible after all. You were even willing to give up your own unborn child, so I think you deserve to have that deal of ours removed now. And... despite my behavior — especially my recent behavior — I really do want Jenny to be happy. Clearly, Jenny is happier living with you than with me, so no, I won't force Jenny to move back in with me, regardless of you having to take a break before completing your university degree."

Francesca's gaze latched onto Phillip's, searching for possible lies; waiting for him to flicker. "You promise?"

"I absolutely promise. However, we'll need to look at the financial aspect of it. A baby is not cheap to raise, nor is an eleven year old."

The exact same thought had been lodged firmly at the top of Francesca's chest as well, slightly blocking her airways. "No, I know... But I have my business that I'll hopefully be making a decent living off of—"

"No." Phillip held out his hand to silence her. "That won't do. Providing for Jenny is my responsibility. I am, after all, her father, so I'll pay for what she needs ...even if she's living with you," he said, sinking down slightly; his shoulders rounding forwards.

Francesca looked at him, the tension in her jaw loosening, and her eyes moistening.

"Nevertheless," he added, his face hopeful. "I will leave Jenny's room exactly the way it is, should she decide she'd like to come over and visit me sometime. And, of course, the same goes for you. All good parents make sure they have a special place for their kids, just in case they return back home one day..." he mumbled, seemingly more to himself than to her.

Carefully, secretly, Francesca studied her dad's face; searching for his reason for giving up what he had fought so hard to keep. His facial expression wasn't revealing anything, though.

He was devastated. There was no doubt about it. Even the lines on his face seemed to have deepened, instantly making him look a bit older.

Francesca hesitated for a moment, then reached out and touched his arm. "Thanks, Dad," she said, forcing herself to smile through her tears.

He glanced at her honest face, and gave her a sad smile in return.

"But," Francesca continued. "There's also another issue that we need to discuss."

"Like what?"

"Well..." She paused for a moment. But then the reality of where she was — and the fact that she didn't have any time to waste in getting the details sorted out before having to make her final decision — hit her hard, and she knew she just needed to say it. "If the Child Welfare Authorities find out that Jenny's living with me instead of with you, then we could all be in trouble. So, we might actually need to keep her officially registered as living at your place, just in case."

He shrugged. "Yeah, sure, that's fine."

She gazed up at him. "But, Dad..." She began, still wary of him having suddenly changed his mind so drastically; and even more worried that he might end up taking Jenny back at some point after it was too late for her to have an abortion. "We're the only family you've got, how could you possibly...?"

"Yeah, well, that's not exactly true..."

"What do you mean?"

"I actually took your advice, and went to see my parents this morning."

She gasped. "Your parents — really? Both of them?"

"Yeah, it was time." He smiled. "Turns out I've got two parents, and actually... three siblings as well — can you believe it?"

"Wow, that's amazing!"

He nodded. "It's a long story; I'll tell you about it later. ...But apparently, you were right." His bottom lip quivered. "They never wanted to give me up."

Francesca watched him shed the first tears he had ever cried in front of her. When she was growing up, she'd assumed that he was incapable of crying; that somehow, he'd been dealt double the amount of anger, instead.

Francesca was hardly ever angry. She was a crier. Phillip was a yeller. As a kid, she'd come to the conclusion that they must've somehow gone through a swap in relation to the way that they expressed their emotions.

She took a deep breath, and as her lungs filled with air; her eyes welled up with tears. "So that means that you've finally gotten what you wanted all those years growing up, then — you finally have parents now, even if it didn't happen until you became an adult?"

"Yes, I'm an extremely lucky guy," Phillip admitted, though after having uttered the words, frowned as though he, as well, was attempting to work out just exactly what was happening to him.

She felt her body begin to prickle; almost like a tinge of resentment was pumping through her. She'd offered her love to him so many times while growing up; begging for him to take it. Praying that it was enough — that *she* was enough — but he'd always rejected her; brushed her off. She'd thought long and hard, and tried many different approaches, but she'd still failed to make him truly happy for any great period of time. It seemed that her dad had needed something, or someone, more. And so... eventually... she had closed herself off.

Out of nowhere, she felt a shot of pain zap through her chest, and her hand automatically flew up, compressing the area. She swallowed, then exhaled slowly.

Suddenly, she remembered the dream she'd had last night, and plump tears began to form in her eyes. In her dream, she'd been boxed in; she had shut herself down in order to avoid the pain.

Then she realized that after her mother had passed away, and Francesca had reached out to her dad, having failed to make him show love for her she had come to believe that she just wasn't worthy of love.

And then Francesca thought about what she'd wanted more than anything for the past ten years; her wish to one day finally be completely free of Phillip.

...But then it struck that if she were to never see her dad ever again, then that would essentially make her an orphan — just like both her parents had been when they were growing up. And she suddenly realized that that was in fact the exact opposite of what she truly wanted and needed. She had already lost her mom; there was nothing she could do about that. But she hadn't lost her dad — not yet.

Then she thought about her unborn child, and how if they stayed completely away from Phillip, then this child, as well as any other children she might have in the future, would never get to know their grandfather ...just like Francesca and Jenny had never known their grandparents ...and that just felt so excruciatingly wrong.

True, after her mother had passed away, she hadn't believed she was worthy of love, or belonging to a functional family. And for the most part, she had blamed her dad for that. But... she also knew that he had suffered from the same feeling of lack and abandonment growing up that she did — and that it had been even worse for him.

She sighed, and closed her eyes. Allowing herself a moment to think, she imagined that she was back up at the meadow; blocking out the sight of

Phillip standing there right in front of her.

She didn't believe he was evil. And she didn't think that the things he'd done had been in an attempt to truly hurt Jenny and herself. It was more like he'd been confused; like there were certain things in the world that he had misunderstood.

More than that, they had both hurt themselves, and each other, by refusing to acknowledge that they *were* enough, and that they were loved. Those lies had been such a waste.

Anna had loved them both more than anything else. Despite her having left Phillip toward the end, lack of love for him had not been her reason for doing so; and Adrian cared for Francesca so openly and honestly that it made her blush just thinking about it.

As for Phillip, he now knew that his parents had never not wanted him. Even though Francesca didn't know the details yet, the look on her dad's face when he'd told her that his parents had truly wanted to keep him after all, showed her that he'd finally realized that he was loved, too.

So... maybe... they could now finally find the courage to love themselves, and each other, as well? If she were brave enough to reach out to him one last time, showing him that she really cared — would he do the same with her? If she showed him love; would he then show her love in return?

"Dad," she whispered. "I want Mom back."

"I want your mom back, too."

"And... and I want you — I want a dad," she continued. "A real dad who loves me; and listens to me; and treats me with respect."

Phillip took a couple of steps toward her. "Well, unfortunately, I can't bring your mom back to you ...at least, not in the way that you want me to. But what I can do is to tell you every great story I know about her — and trust me, there are a lot of good ones."

She let out a sound somewhere between a sob and a laugh. "Yeah, I'd like that."

"But more importantly; what I need to do is to give you a real dad — if you'll have me? I mean, I know you're all grown up now, but that seems to have become the family tradition — to have a shitty childhood, and to only gain your parents once you're a grownup."

She chuckled. "Yeah, we can definitely give it a shot and see what happens."

"OK." He smiled, nodding eagerly. "That's more than what I deserve, and more than I'd ever hoped for — so I'll definitely take it. Hopefully, I'll be able to show you that, with time, things can indeed be different."

"OK."

He hesitated for a couple of seconds, then took a few more steps toward her, wrapping his arms around her in an embrace.

Francesca stood there, allowing herself to feel vulnerable for a moment; realizing how nice it was to finally have a parent to lean on; to not always have to be so incredibly strong. She ran the tips of her fingers underneath her eyes. "Thanks for coming down here, Dad. And for stopping me from doing something that would've been a horrible mistake."

"Well, really, you need to thank yourself."

"What to do you mean?"

"If you hadn't come all the way up to Trondheim to tell me that you'd forgiven me; then I never would have gone to seek out my mother, which resulted in me forgiving my parents as well. So — thank you. And I'm pretty sure that, if you hadn't come to see me in Trondheim, I never would've come over here to stop you from having the abortion, or be willing to let Jenny live with you."

Francesca broke away from Phillip, and grabbed the form she had just signed from where it lay on top of the doctor's desk. She ripped it into little pieces, and let them flutter down into the garbage can like snowflakes.

*

Francesca unlocked the entrance door to Adrian's apartment building, and started climbing the stairs. Phillip followed close behind. They reached the second floor, and continued down the hallway to Adrian's door.

"OK," she said, turning toward him. "So I'll just head in first, and then I'll let you know when we're ready for you."

Phillip nodded. "Yeah, I'll be here."

"Great," she said, taking a deep breath, before twisting her key around in the lock and pushing the door open. "Hello?" she called out into the apartment.

"Francesca!" Jenny exclaimed. She scampered over, and flung herself around her sister.

"Hey, Jellybean!" Francesca said, hugging her tightly. "It's so good to see you."

"But," Jenny started, "what are you doing here? Adrian said you weren't coming back until Saturday; that you were off doing something important. Though..." She crossed her arms in front of her chest and scowled at him. "He wouldn't tell me what you were doing — no matter how hard I tried to get him to confess."

"Um, yeah... well there's been a slight — or rather, a substantial — change of plans. I'll tell you about it in a minute," she said, and let go of Jenny, studying her. She noticed her nerves flare up in anticipation of how her sister was going to react to her news. She cleared her throat, sweeping away the remaining bits of emotional turmoil left over from this morning. Taking a deep breath and looking back up from her sister, she told herself; *It's going to be OK; she's going to be OK.*

Adrian wandered over toward them.

Francesca felt butterflies start to dance around in her stomach. She smiled bashfully at him. "Hey, you."

He positioned himself right in front of her; her favorite dimples creasing his face. "Hi."

She wrapped her arms around him, and they hugged in silence for several seconds. Then she rose up onto her toes. "Thank you!" she whispered in his ear. She didn't know what else to say. Though she tried with all her being, she was unable to come up with anything remotely close to measuring up to his actions.

He combed his hand through her hair, and opened his mouth; then closed it again. Apparently, he didn't know what to say, either.

Francesca took Adrian's hand, and interlaced her fingers with his, before turning back to her sister. "J-love," she said, and bent down slightly so she reached her sister's eye level. "I've got a couple of surprises for you."

"Really?" Jenny grinned. "Like what?"

"Well, first of all..." She walked over to the door, her footsteps echoing in time with her pounding heart. Exhaling slowly, she opened the door.

Phillip stepped into the apartment.

Jenny gasped. "What's *he* doing here?"

"It's OK," Francesca said, and produced a smile for her sister that quivered at the corners against her will. "The reason Dad didn't come back home to you in Trondheim last night, is because he's been down here in Oslo. And we've agreed that, from now on, you'll be living with Adrian and me."

Jenny's jaw dropped. "Dad's actually agreed to that? Francesca, are you sure he's not just trying to—"

"Yes," Francesca interrupted her. "I'm absolutely sure. Come sit on the couch with me, and I'll tell you everything."

Jenny looked wary, scrutinizing Phillip for a moment. Then she sighed, and reluctantly plopped down next to her sister on the couch.

"OK, so here goes..." Francesca started filling her in on the entire story. First Phillip's news; then, her own news.

A little while later, Jenny put her hands out to either side, and burst out; "Whoa! Whoa! Whoa! Hang on there for a sec... So, you're telling me I'm gonna be an aunt?!"

Francesca nodded, and noticed that her hands were trembling slightly. "Yeah, sweetie, that's right. So... how do you feel about that?"

"That is... soooo awesome — it's the coolest news ever!" She grinned. "That means I'm not the baby anymore." She got to her feet, and started dancing around Adrian's living room.

Francesca laughed. She had been dreading telling Jenny about her baby, but now she realized she might even have found a very valuable babysitter.

*

"I cannot believe you're going to be a mom!" Emily repeated for probably the tenth time.

"And, we're going to be aunts!" Margaret squealed.

"Yeah." Francesca smiled at her three best friends. "Me either... it's still pretty surreal."

"So, have you thought of any names yet?" Tina asked.

"No, I only just decided yesterday that I was going to keep the baby."

"Well, someone's getting a baby shower — that's for sure," Margaret said.

"Thanks, girls! But before we start worrying about names or showers, I just need to speak to Richard about the business. And I want everything to come from me, so just let me do the talking, OK?"

The girls nodded.

"OK, good." Francesca checked her watch. "He's supposed to be here any minute, and I can't *wait* to just get it all over with."

"How do you think he'll react?" Tina asked.

Francesca shrugged. "I really have no clue... I mean, I'm guessing he won't be thrilled, but beyond that I just really don't know. Hopefully he won't be too pissed, either."

"Pissed about what?" Richard said, showing up from around the corner behind them.

Francesca spun around, her heart thumping. "Ah, hey, Richard — you scared me there."

"Sorry, but you scared me, too. So, that's always a good start to a meeting when you overhear your partners talking about something sounding an awful lot like bad news."

"Well, I a..."

"Relax, I'm just pulling your leg. I don't even know what you were talking about." He unlocked the door to his office, and held it open for the four girls. "Now, shall we get started?"

Francesca nodded, and led the way. She drew up a chair, and sat down at the meeting room table.

The others followed her, grabbing chairs of their own.

Richard got his notebook out, and clicked the button at the top of his blue ink pen. "Alright, so on the agenda for today—"

"Richard," Francesca interrupted him, and then took a deep breath. "I'm just going to come out and say it: I'm pregnant."

He looked her up and down a couple of times. "...So, this means I'm up-to-date on the bad news you guys were discussing out in the hall, I presume?"

"I prefer to think of it as exciting news, but yeah, this is the news we were talking about."

"So, when's the baby due?"

"Mid-July."

His face remained expressionless as he sat there staring at her for a moment. "Well, congratulations, then," he finally said.

Francesca smiled. "Yeah, thanks. And I know I'm bound to the contract until September 1st and all, but—"

"You know," he said, cutting her off. "I'm sure the majority of the franchisees will be away on vacation for most of July and August anyway, so I can guarantee you we won't be holding any presentations at that time."

She nodded. "Alright, then. So I guess the timing was as good as any."

"I guess you could say that. But then again, that also means that we've got to increase our sales for the previous months in order to make up for the slow summer months if you'd still like to achieve that goal of yours."

"Yes, well things have changed a bit. My sister is moving in with me, but my dad is still going to be the one to support her and pay for all her needs."

"Really?" he said, scratching his head, making his wavy, brown hair flutter around. "Huh. I guess that's kind of what your mom was talking about, then."

"What do you mean?"

"In her letter — the one she wrote to me but then never sent."

"Yeah... what about it?"

"She explained how Phillip really was a good guy." He rolled his eyes. "I don't know, I always hated him and probably always will. I mean, he did after all steal the girl I loved from me, as well as scare away a couple that might have adopted med," he spat.

"Yeah, I'm really sorry about those incidents..." Francesca grimaced.

"I just can't imagine him ever doing anything nice for anyone. That is, unless it was only in order to get him something he wanted in return."

"Yeah..." she mumbled. "However," she continued, wanting to get back to the point. "Even though my dad will be supporting my sister, I still need to make as much money as I possibly can before the baby comes, so that I'll be entitled to a decent amount of maternity pay next year."

Richard nodded. "Yeah, of course. But there's also the possibility for someone who's self-employed to work a certain amount while they're on maternity leave, in order to compensate for the fact that they might not have anyone around to keep their business up-and-running while they're off."

"Are you sure? I mean, how would that work out legally?"

"Yeah, I'm sure. I was in a similar situation a couple of years back with another woman I worked with. If you end up working part-time while you're on leave, then what the government does is they stretch your original maternity pay out so you get less money per month, but for an increased number of months instead."

"OK, sounds like an option I might want to look into."

"Yeah, I mean, the market potential for the grocery bag racks is definitely there, and we could even get into the larger carousel racks later — that is, if you should come to find you need some extra money. Of course, I won't pressure you to work while you're on leave. But even when you start studying later on, we could still hold a few presentations every once in awhile as a job on the side, in case there's a need for it. It would make for a pretty decently paying part-time job."

"You would help me with that? I thought you said it would be more trouble than it was worth for you if we only did it on a small scale every once in awhile like that?"

He shrugged. "Yeah, well, you may be your dad's daughter, but you're also Anna's daughter, and that means I don't want you getting screwed over. And besides," he added. "You're a pretty cool kid, so you know..." he said, and seemed lost in thought for a moment. Then he looked back at Francesca. "In that letter, your mom also told me how much she cared about me, though, in the end she'd felt it was right of her to choose Phillip instead.

She said the two of them were supposed to be together; that they needed each other more. And she also wrote that she knew I was stronger and more independent; that she knew I would be OK on my own. Which, makes me wonder why she never ended up sending that letter in the end..." he muttered, seeming to have drifted off into his own little world again for a few seconds. "I think maybe some things would've been better — easier — had I read her letter back then. The worst part, I guess, was just not knowing for sure why she had chosen someone else over me. And it wasn't exactly the easiest time for me — or for anyone, for that matter — transitioning from the orphanage to something unknown, without a safety net; with no family," he said, melancholia tingeing his voice. His gray eyes looked tired and lonely; like they needed another pair of eyes to notice them.

Francesca watched him, and felt her heart ache; knowing he was all alone. She wanted to walk over and give him a big hug, though sensed that that would be somewhat inappropriate. However, his words also made her appreciate how grateful she was for the fact that she'd probably never again feel like she was all alone. "So..." she started, reaching her hand out to pat him on the arm a couple of times, realizing that might be a somewhat strange and awkward thing to do, but hoping it helped. If only a tiny little bit. "So, what do you think about what my mom had to say? Do you think she was right about you?"

Richard cleared his throat. "Well, in a way I see her point, and where she was coming from. I think that, at least at the time, I was stronger and more independent than Phillip. But then again, I wouldn't have minded having your mom in my life. I think everyone should've had an Anna in their lives — especially while growing up. She was always there for me throughout my childhood when I needed someone; she made me believe in myself when no one else would; like I could do anything I wanted as long as I remained confident, and worked hard to achieve it. I actually attribute a great deal of my business success to having had her support me and believe in me when we were kids."

Francesca smiled. "Really?"

He nodded. "Yeah. And so now it seems appropriate for me to return the favor to her daughter, and to be there for you at a point when you're in need of some extra help," he said casually, like it meant nothing.

To Francesca, though, it meant everything.

Chapter Forty-two

The cool, late September air chilled Francesca's face, and the smell of moist dirt on the ground below their shoes seeped into her nose, refreshing her.

She pushed the pram up the steep hill, navigating around the trees. She felt her breathing grow heavier and heavier the farther up she climbed, and realized it might not have been the smartest decision she'd ever made to take her baby and the rest of her family on this outing a mere two and a half months after she had given birth. However, today was her birthday, and the one year mark of when all of last year's craziness had begun. She intended to make her 20th birthday symbolize something else — a new beginning, and the letting go of the old.

Adrian watched her, grinning to himself. "So, uh... are ya' sure ya' don't need any help?"

Francesca shook her head. "Nah," she panted. "It's gotta be me. Just like the way my mom did it."

"Alright. That's your call."

"Damn right it's my call." She winked at him.

Jenny sighed, dragging her feet. "Are we there yet?"

"Jellybean, aren't you excited? The last time you were up here was eleven years ago, when Mom was the one pushing *you* up in your stroller. Now, suck it up — I don't hear Lucia complaining."

"'Course not — she doesn't have to walk all the way up this hill."

Francesca ignored her sister; their destination was too beautiful and too important to her for anyone to be allowed to spoil it.

She paused for a brief moment, and turned to look back down the hill.

Phillip, Philippa and Tim waved at her, while doing the sensible thing and moving at a much slower pace.

She waved back at them, before turning and continuing upward.

There was only a short little way left to go; they would reach the meadow at the top of the hill in about 30 seconds.

Francesca peeked down at Lucia, asleep in her pram. She felt a warm, tingling sensation spread through her entire body, and she couldn't understand how she'd possibly created something so beautiful.

She glanced over at her boyfriend. But then again, she thought, she had created Lucia with Adrian, and he was the most amazing person she'd ever met, not to mention — at least in her eyes — the most attractive man she knew ...so maybe it wasn't so strange that Lucia had turned out this perfect, after all.

Jenny skipped the last few steps up to the top. "Yesss," she sang, and threw herself down onto the soft, dewy grass. "We're finally heeeere!"

Following right behind, Francesca rubbed the back of her hand across her glistening face and allowed a few seconds to pass as she could caught her breath. "Alrighty, let's get this picnic blanket rolled out." She grabbed the red and blue plaid blanket out from the underneath storage compartment of the pram, and handed it to Adrian.

He shook it out, and laid the huge blanked down on the ground, before pulling at the four corners to smooth it out.

Eventually, Phillip, Philippa and Tim reached the top of the hill as well, joining the others in the meadow — Francesca's own personal paradise.

"Ah," Phillip said, looking around. "I haven't been up here in so many years. The last time must've been probably close to 15 years ago, with your mom." He smiled, then added; "It sure is beautiful, though."

Francesca gazed around at the light morning mist hovering above the ground in the distance, while the sun shone through the mist from behind a large oak tree, creating bursts of pure, bright energy. She listened to the silence for a moment, and sighed happily. "Yeah, there's just no place quite like it."

She was so lucky; she had it all. Well... at least almost. There were two things she still didn't have, nor would she ever have them. Lately she'd come to accept that, and she realized that she'd still done pretty well.

Lucia stirred in her pram, and started letting out soft cries.

Francesca bent down and picked her up. "Hi, sweetie. It's OK," she whispered, and held Lucia up against her chest while rocking her body slowly from side to side.

"Hey," Phillip said. "Do you need any help over there?"

"Yeah, sure. Do you want to hold her for a minute?"

His eyes smiled. "I'd love to."

She gently placed Lucia into Phillip's arms. "There you go."

"So," he started. "I wanted to thank you again for giving me another chance, and for letting me spend some quality time with you and Jenny."

"Well, you see, a wise man once told me that no one deserves to have their children forcefully taken away from them, so you know, it seemed like the right thing to do," she said, smiling.

"Wise words, indeed."

Francesca gazed at her dad and Lucia for a moment, then realized this was as good a time as any to carry out what she had come up here to do. "Hey Dad, do you mind just watching her for a few minutes?"

"Yeah, sure. We'll be over here by the picnic blanket with the others."

"Great, thanks."

Phillip held Lucia tenderly, kissing the top of her head. "Hey, pretty baby," he cooed, and started heading over toward the blanket.

Francesca turned and walked a ways in the opposite direction of where her family sat.

Yes, she thought once more, there were two things that she would never again have in her life. She knelt down on the soft grass and pulled out a small wooden box from her coat pocket. Inside the walnut wood box was a picture that she had placed in there the previous night.

It was her favorite picture, and she would leave it here, buried in the ground inside this box. Although, this was only a copy of the photo. The original was still at home, framed and sitting on her bedside table. And in the evenings, when she looked at her picture just before she went to bed, it would remind her of the one buried right here in her favorite spot in the entire world.

She pulled a garden spade out of her other coat pocket, and started digging a hole.

When she was satisfied with the depth of the hole, she wiped her hands first on the dewy grass, and then on some tissue paper she had brought from home. Then she opened the lid of the rich brown wooden box, and gently lifted the photo out; holding it with the same tender, loving care that she held Lucia.

It was a picture of her and her mom, from the very first time they had gone to see the ballet when Francesca was only six years old. She was wearing a purple long-sleeved top, and a long, fluffy purple skirt with several layers of tulle material, resembling the longer old-fashioned tutu. Across her face, was the biggest, happiest smile as she looked up at her mother in admiration. Anna was holding Francesca's hand firmly as she looked down at her daughter, smiling as well.

True, Francesca would never have her mom back. And true, she would never become a proper ballerina.

She took a deep breath, and felt a single, fat tear crawl down her cheek.

But then maybe, she stopped to think... Maybe the two things she would be missing in her life were really only one thing? Maybe they were, in fact, one and the same?

Francesca had so desperately wanted to become a ballet dancer after she had lost her mother; thinking that that was the only way she'd still be able to stay connected to her mom.

But then she realized, she would always be connected to Anna. Anna was, after all, Francesca's mother. Just like Lucia would always be connected to Francesca. And just like Phillip would always be connected to Philippa. The memories that Francesca had been lucky enough to share with Anna would always be there; they would always be with her.

She wiped her tears with her fingertips. Then she gazed over at her family sitting on the picnic blanket in the distance.

She heard them chatting, and she heard them laughing.

Her future would be challenging, though. She knew it would. Francesca would be a young mother raising her child, as well as her younger sister. At least for now, Jenny would continue to live with Francesca, Adrian and Lucia. And a year from now, Francesca would go back to school for another two to four years in order to get her university degree, before starting to build a career.

It would be tough. But, she had done tough before, and she had gotten through it. She had pushed to the top of the hill; refusing to give up — just like her mother had taught her. And she'd succeeded, too.

Even though she knew her future would be challenging, she still knew she would be able to do it. But more than that, she wasn't doing it by herself — she had her family on her side this time.

She looked back over at Phillip holding Lucia.

It would be hard work, yes. But she also knew it would be so worth it.

She placed the picture back in its box, and laid the box into the hole she'd dug in the ground. Then she covered it up with dirt. Sitting there for a moment, she studied the slight pile of dirt in front of her.

Francesca would always have the memories of her mom and the ballet — they weren't going anywhere. And for the first time in her life, she felt confident that her dad wasn't going anywhere, either.

GET A FREE NOVELLA

Building a relationship with my readers is the very best thing about writing.

I occasionally send newsletters with details on new releases, special offers and other bits of news relating to my writing. And if you sign up to the mailing list, I'll send you my novella *Family Beginnings* for free. A story about a defining moment in Phillip and Anna's lives, and the beginning of them building their family.

This novella is exclusive to my mailing list – you can't get it anywhere else.

If interested, please use this link subscribepage.io/ENQ6JW to sign up to my newsletter & receive my novella for free.

Like the chance to read my stuff before it hits Amazon? Read on...

I am in the process of setting up a team that I lovingly refer to as *Nova's Ninjas.*

It is critically important to get reviews on new books as soon as they launch. You probably weigh reviews highly when making a decision whether to try a new author or rely on an old favorite – I know that I do. Apart from helping to persuade people to give a new writer a shot, reviews help drive early sales which, in turn, means that Amazon takes notice and starts to market on my behalf. And no-one markets books better than Amazon.

In order to make that happen I have a small team of Advance Readers. It's pretty simple and is, I hope, good fun. It involves them being sent an eBook copy of whatever book I've just finished and then, when it is published, firing up a quick and honest review. Simple as that.

Some members of the team have picked up errors that I've been able to correct and others have suggested changes to the plot that I have incorporated. I always value your feedback greatly.

I try and keep the team relatively compact. There are some vacancies at the moment and if you would like to get involved, please let me know by sending an e-mail to nova@novafornell.com

Best wishes,
Nova

Enjoy this book? You can make a big difference

Reviews are the most powerful tools in my arsenal when it comes to getting attention for my books. Much as I'd like to, I don't have the financial muscle of a New York publisher. I can't take out full page ads in the newspaper or put posters on the subway.

(Not yet, anyway).

But I do have something much more powerful and effective than that, and it's something that those publishers would kill to get their hands on.

A committed and loyal bunch of readers.

Honest reviews of my books help bring them to the attention of other readers.

If you've enjoyed this book I would be very grateful if you could spend just five minutes leaving a review (it can be as short as you like) on the book's Amazon page.

Thank you very much.

ABOUT THE AUTHOR

Nova Fornell passionately danced ballet from the age of four until twenty-one, when injuries forced her to stop. In the pursuit of a new career where it would be easier for her to get a job than in the ballet world, she went back to the university to get a Bachelor's degree in Economics and Business Administration. The lack of opportunity to express herself creatively in the business world prompted her to find a new creative passion, which turned out to be writing fiction in her spare time. Now she is hooked on writing and hopes to write several more novels in the future.

She makes her online home at www.novafornell.com. You can connect with Nova on Facebook at www.facebook.com/NovaFornell and Instagram at www.instagram.com/novafornell/

www.ingramcontent.com/pod-product-compliance
Lightning Source LLC
Chambersburg PA
CBHW032002060426
42446CB00041B/1005